THE EVERYTHING FRENCH PRACTICE BOOK

Dear Reader,

Learning a new language is always an adventure. For me, it has always been a way to discover other people, cultures, and literatures. When you get acquainted with a new language, learning new concepts and vocabulary is fun—but also challenging. In order to truly grasp a language, you need to repeat the exercises over and over. Practice is key.

Unless you can spend an extended period of time in a French-speaking country, practice is the only way to improve your French language skills. The best way to practice is by using books and audio materials and watching films.

This book and its audio CD are aimed at lovers of the French language who are already learning it but need some extra practice to fine-tune their knowledge. As you go along, you'll make progress and enjoy all the nuances of the language. Before you know it, words and idiomatic expressions will come to you instinctively.

Bonne chance!

Annie Heminway

Hemmah@aol.com

Welcome to the EVERYTHING® Series!

These handy, accessible books give you all you need to tackle a difficult project, gain a new hobby, comprehend a fascinating topic, prepare for an exam, or even brush up on something you learned back in school but have since forgotten.

You can choose to read an *Everything*® book from cover to cover or just pick out the information you want from our four useful boxes: e-questions, e-facts, e-alerts, and e-ssentials. We give you everything you need to know on the subject, but throw in a lot of fun stuff along the way, too.

We now have more than 400 *Everything*® books in print, spanning such wide-ranging categories as weddings, pregnancy, cooking, music instruction, foreign language, crafts, pets, New Age, and so much more. When you're done reading them all, you can finally say you know *Everything*®!

PUBLISHER Karen Cooper

DIRECTOR OF ACQUISITIONS AND INNOVATION Paula Munier

MANAGING EDITOR, EVERYTHING SERIES Lisa Laing

COPY CHIEF Casey Ebert

ACQUISITIONS EDITOR Lisa Laing

ASSOCIATE DEVELOPMENT EDITOR Elizabeth Kassab

EDITORIAL ASSISTANT Hillary Thompson

Visit the entire Everything® series at *www.everything.com*

THE
EVERYTHING®
FRENCH PRACTICE
BOOK
with CD

Practical techniques to improve your
French speaking and writing skills

Annie Heminway

Avon, Massachusetts

To all my students..

An Everything® Series Book.
Everything® and everything.com® are registered trademarks of F+W Media, Inc.

Published by Adams Media, a division of F+W Media, Inc.
57 Littlefield Street, Avon, MA 02322 U.S.A.
www.adamsmedia.com

ISBN 10: 1-59869-777-3
ISBN 13: 978-1-59869-777-3

Printed in the United States of America.

J   I   H   G   F

Library of Congress Cataloging-in-Publication Data
is available from the publisher.

This publication is designed to provide accurate and authoritative information with regard to the subject matter covered. It is sold with the understanding that the publisher is not engaged in rendering legal, accounting, or other professional advice. If legal advice or other expert assistance is required, the services of a competent professional person should be sought.

—From a *Declaration of Principles* jointly adopted by a Committee of the American Bar Association and a Committee of Publishers and Associations

Many of the designations used by manufacturers and sellers to distinguish their products are claimed as trademarks. Where those designations appear in this book and Adams Media was aware of a trademark claim, the designations have been printed with initial capital letters.

This book is available at quantity discounts for bulk purchases.
For information, please call 1-800-289-0963.

Contents

Acknowledgments

I thank my family, who are always supportive during my book writing ventures.

Lots of credit goes to my editor, Lisa Laing, for all her efforts and encouragements.

Many thanks to the staff of Adams Media, especially to the copyeditors of this book.

And finally thank you to Domingue Clement for lending his voice for the recording of the CD.

Top Ten Reasons to Learn French

1. You will be understood in fifty-five countries across five continents and by more than 200 million people.

2. Because French is the third most common language on the Internet, you can connect with pen pals, visit foreign websites, and find student exchange opportunities.

3. You'll have a head start on learning other Romance languages like Spanish, Italian, Portuguese, and Romanian.

4. Learning a second language helps you develop critical, creative thinking, and problem-solving skills.

5. French provides the base for more than half the modern English vocabulary, so learning it can help you improve your performance on standardized tests.

6. You'll be more competitive in the international job market in disciplines like business, medicine, aviation, law, transportation technologies, global/international distribution, and luxury goods.

7. You'll discover a new appreciation for other cultures in French-speaking countries such as France, Belgium, Monaco, Cambodia, Madagascar, Burundi, Gabon, Zaire, Niger, Morocco, Burkina Faso, Algeria, Djibouti, Canada, Haiti, and many others.

8. You'll open the doors to learning about French art, music, fashion, food, architecture, and literature.

9. French is an official working language of the UN, NATO, UNESCO, the International Olympic Committee, the European Union, and the International Red Cross.

10. You'll be able to order anything you like from your favorite French restaurant.

Introduction

▶ DO YOU REMEMBER HOW you learned to speak English? Since you began learning from earliest childhood, chances are you do not. Learning to talk was something you did by repeating what was said to you and then practicing it until you were able to speak on your own. This process took some time—and because we continue to learn new words and expressions all our lives, you're probably not done yet.

When we study another language, the learning experience is very different. There is much more information competing for our brain-processing time. We have a lot more on our minds, and we often cannot give language study our full attention. Some of us are also hesitant and self-conscious about making mistakes or sounding foolish.

Learning another language is not easy, but it can be made easier through practice. Practice raises our level of comfort when we speak, read, or write, and it ultimately leads to fluency. That is where this book comes in. The exercises in this book are designed to help you practice French grammar: parts of speech, verb conjugations, idiomatic expressions. The book is divided into parts, each one covering a particular topic or topics. It is not necessary to begin with Part 1—if a particular aspect of French grammar is giving you trouble, go to that part first. Once you have conquered that topic, move on to another until you have reviewed them all.

In addition to written exercises, there are also exercises that work in conjunction with an audio CD. When you do an audio exercise, repeat it several times. It is through repetition that you will improve your speaking ability and your listening comprehension—remember, this is how you learned as a child. It worked then, and it will work now.

However you approach it, try to make it fun. Once you have worked on the exercises, try to find ways to incorporate what you have learned whenever you speak, read, or write in French. Read a French book, listen to some French songs, go to a French film, order dinner from a French menu—and do it all with the confidence and comfort that come from practice and repetition.

Bonne chance!

Part 1

Articles and Nouns

Articles and nouns are key to forming proper sentences. Even if you have a fairly good grasp of the French language, take advantage of this review to figure out the masculine and the feminine so you can stay out of trouble.

Masculine or Feminine?

In French, nouns have a gender—either masculine or feminine. The ending of a noun indicates, for the most part, the gender of noun. However, you cannot solely rely on this, as there are quite a few exceptions.

Nouns ending in *-age*, *-eau*, *-ment*, tend to be masculine.

le fromage	cheese
le plateau	tray
le bâtiment	building

Nouns ending in *-t*, *-al*, *-ail*, *-eil*, *-isme* also tend to be masculine.

l'achat	purchase	*le journal*	newspaper
le travail	work	*le soleil*	sun
le romantisme	romanticism		

Nouns ending in *-ure*, *-ence*, *-ance*, *-sion*, *-tion*, *-té*, *-ouille*, *-eille*, *-ie*, *-ette*, *-eur* tend to be feminine. However, nouns that end in *eur* and refer to professions and machines are masculine.

la nature	nature	*la connaissance*	knowledge
la patience	patience	*la télévision*	television
l'exposition	exhibition	*la nationalité*	nationality
la grenouille	frog	*la veille*	the day before
la pâtisserie	pastry shop	*la fourchette*	fork
la hauteur	height		

Exercise 1-1: Masculine or Feminine?

Identify each noun either as masculine or feminine.

1. *sentiment* ....

2. *différence* ....

3. *garage* ....

4. *merveille* ....

5. *tendance* ....   8. *sommeil* ....

6. *citrouille* ....   9. *objet* ....

7. *chaleur* ....   10. *idéalisme* ....

Exercise 1-2: Indefinitely Yours

Place the right indefinite article before the noun.

1. .... *lampe*   5. .... *avion*

2. .... *bureau*   6. .... *bicyclettes*

3. .... *amis*   7. .... *exposition*

4. .... *bouteille*   8. .... *parapluie*

Exercise 1-3: Do I Hear Un or Une?

TRACK 1

Listen to the audio track as you read each sentence below. Repeat each sentence aloud.

1. *J'ai un chien et un chat.*
2. *Avez-vous un dictionaire?*
3. *Il y a des stylos sure la table.*
4. *Un oiseau est sur la branche.*
5. *J'ai acheté un journal et des magazines.*
6. *Est-ce que vous avez une voiture?*
7. *C'est une belle ville.*
8. *Elle a des amis à Paris.*
9. *Patrick cherche un appartement.*
10. *Je connais un bon restaurant dans ce quartier*

Definite Articles

A definite article refers to a specific example of a noun. All nouns in French have a gender. While English has only one definite article—the—French uses *le* for masculine singular nouns, *la* for feminine singular nouns, and *les* for both masculine and feminine plural nouns.

le	masculine/singular	le pont	the bridge
la	feminine/singular	la plage	the beach
les	masculine/plural	les documents	the documents
les	feminine/plural	les fleurs	the flowers

Le and la become l' in front of nouns starting with a vowel or a mute h.

Exercise 1-4: Definitely Yours

Place the right definite article before each noun.

1. .... gâteau
2. .... tableau
3. .... jardin
4. .... vie
5. .... château

6. .... enfants
7. .... route
8. .... régions
9. .... village
10. .... leçons

Exercise 1-5: Where Is the Noun?

In each sentence, identify the noun or nouns by underlining them.

1. Le train arrive en gare.
2. Ils dînent toujours sur la terrasse.
3. Pourquoi acheter tant de fromages?
4. Elle a déjà contacté trois agences.
5. Qui a fini ses devoirs pour demain?
6. Les tableaux sont exposés dans la grande salle.
7. Être ou ne pas être? C'est la question.
8. Il a choisi un ordinateur et une imprimante.
9. Ce château a été construit au dix-septième siècle.
10. Où sont mes gants et mon écharpe?

Exercise 1-6: Let's Figure Out the Gender

TRACK 2

Listen to the audio track and repeat. Then listen again and write down each sentence. Check your spelling in the answer key.

1. ....
2. ....
3. ....
4. ....
5. ....
6. ....
7. ....
8. ....
9. ....
10. ....

Nouns with Masculine and Feminine Forms

Some nouns that refer to people have various feminine forms. Some can be changed from masculine to feminine by adding an *e* to the masculine form.

l'ami	*l'amie*	friend
l'avocat	*l'avocate*	lawyer

Nouns with certain endings form the feminine in other ways.

-eur / -euse	*le danseur*	*la danseuse*	dancer
-teur / -trice	*le rédacteur*	*la rédactrice*	editor

-(i)er / -(i)ère	le conseiller	la conseillère	adviser
-ien / -ienne	le technicien	la technicienne	technician

Exercise 1-7: What's Your Job?

Change the profession from masculine to feminine.

1. *Ce musicien est italien.*

   ....

2. *Le cabinet de leur avocat est fermé en août.*

   ....

3. *Cet acteur est vietnamien.*

   ....

4. *Son coiffeur est en vacances.*

   ....

5. *Le directeur est à Paris.*

   ....

6. *Le conseiller est en réunion.*

   ....

7. *L'informaticien était en retard.*

   ....

8. *Mon rédacteur a trouvé un nouvel emploi.*

   ....

Nouns and Family

Let's get acquainted with the family members.

le père	father	la mère	mother
le mari	husband	la femme	wife

le fils	son	*la fille*	daughter
le frère	brother	*la soeur*	sister
le grand-père	grandfather	*la grand-mère*	grandmother
l'oncle	uncle	*la tante*	aunt
le neveu	nephew	*la nièce*	niece
le cousin	cousin (male)	*la cousine*	cousin (female)
le beau-frère	brother-in-law	*la belle-soeur*	sister-in-law
le gendre	son-in-law	*la belle-fille*	daughter-in-law
le beau-père	father-in-law/stepfather		
la belle-mère	mother-in-law/stepmother		
l'arrière-grand-père	great-grandfather		
l'arrière-grand-mère	great-grandmother		

Exercise 1-8: C'est Qui?

Answer the following questions relating to family matters.

1. *Le mari de ma fille, c'est mon . . .* ....

2. *Le père de mon père, c'est mon . . .* ....

3. *La femme de mon frère, c'est ma . . .* ....

4. *La femme de mon oncle, c'est ma . . .* ....

5. *Les enfants de ma tante, ce sont mes . . .* ....

6. *Le fils de ma soeur, c'est mon . . .* ....

7. *La grand-mère de ma mère, c'est mon . . .* ....

8. *Le deuxième mari de ma mère, c'est mon . . .* ....

The Traps of Gender

Some nouns take on different meanings in the masculine and feminine.

le livre	book	*la livre*	pound
le manche	handle	*la manche* *la Manche*	sleeve The English Channel
le moule	mold/form	*la moule*	mussel
le page	page (boy)	*la page*	page (of a book)
le poêle	stove	*la poêle*	frying pan
le poste	job, television set	*la poste*	post office

Exercise 1-9: Mix and Match

Make an appropriate sentence by matching the phrase in the right-hand column with the phrase in the left-hand column.

1. *La page*
2. *Le tour*
3. *La poêle*
4. *Ce poste*
5. *La Tour*

a. *Eiffel est illuminée.*
b. *est pleine d'huile.*
c. *est vacant.*
d. *quinze a disparu.*
e. *de la ville en vélo est fantastique.*

Plural Nouns

Changing most French singular nouns to plural nouns is quite simple—and quite similar to English. Most nouns require you to add an *s* to the end. As always there are exceptions, and keep in mind that proper names remain unchanged in French. If you are inviting Monsieur et Madame Audiard to dinner, you are inviting les Audiard, with no *s*.

As a rule, an s is added to a noun to make it plural.

un vase	vase	*des vases*	vases

If a noun begins with a vowel or a mute *h*, a liaison with a z sound is required.

une habitude	habit	*des habitudes*	habits

Nouns ending in -*s*, -*x*, or -*z* do not change in the plural.

un repas	meal	*des repas*	meals

Nouns ending in -*eu*, -*eau* usually take an *x* in the plural.

un tableau	painting	*des tableaux*	paintings

Nouns ending in -al usually change to -*aux*.

un journal	newspaper	*des journaux*	newspapers

Exercise 1-10: More Than One

Put the following nouns in the plural form.

1. *le cheval* ....

2. *la voix* ....

3. *le neveu* ....

4. *la tasse* ....

5. *le manteau* ....

6. *la fourchette* ....

7. *l'homme* ....

8. *la montagne* ....

Geographical Nouns

Like all nouns, countries, continents, states, provinces, and regions are either masculine or feminine. As a rule, geographical nouns ending with *e* or *ie* tend to be feminine. Others tend to be masculine. Let's look at a few examples.

Feminine:

la France	France	*l'Afrique*	Africa
la Grèce	Greece	*l'Argentine*	Argentina
la Bretagne	Brittany	*la Caroline du Sud*	South Carolina

Masculine:

le Canada	Canada	*le Japon*	Japan
le Danemark	Denmark	*le Guatemala*	Guatemala
le Languedoc	Languedoc	*le Nevada*	Nevada

Of course, there are a few exceptions. Some countries and states ending in *e* are masculine:

le Mexique	Mexico	*le Cambodge*	Cambodia
le Maine	Maine		

The countries that are plural, whether masculine or feminine, are preceded by *les*.

les États-Unis	United States	*les Pays-Bas*	Netherlands
les Philippines	the Philippines	*les Seychelles*	the Seychelles Islands

Exercise 1-11: Going to a Masculine or Feminine Country?

Write *le, la,* or *les* in front of the geographical nouns.

1. .... Belgique
2. .... Portugal
3. .... Chine
4. .... Californie
5. .... Venezuela
6. .... Turquie
7. .... Sénégal
8. .... États-Unis
9. .... Provence
10. .... Norvège

Exercise 1-12: Let's Travel the World!

TRACK 3

Listen to the audio track and repeat. Then listen again and write down each sentence.

1. ....

2. ....

3. ....

4. ....

5. ....

6. ....

7. ....

8. ....

9. ....

10. ....

Cognates and False Cognates

English and French have many cognates. Some are exactly the same, while others have slight spelling variations or are pronounced differently. Being aware of them will help your understanding.

Adjectives	Nouns	Verbs
futile	l'admiration	organiser
fervent	la conscience	respecter
banal	la culture	transformer
intelligent	l'affection	manipuler

Many French words starting with an *é* are very close to English when you change the *é* to an *s*.

épice	spice	état	state

False cognates are words that look similar in English and French but are in fact quite different. They are also known as *faux-amis*.

actuellement	currently	*achever*	to finish, to complete
attendre	to wait (for)	*décevoir*	to disappoint

Exercise 1-13: *Can You Guess?*

Translate the following words.

1. *une éponge* ....

2. *un étudiant* ....

3. *un étranger* ....

4. *une étoffe* ....

Exercise 1-14: *What Does It Really Mean?*

Translate the following sentences into English.

1. *Montréal a beaucoup de librairies.*

....

2. *Je vais attendre dix minutes, maximum.*

....

3. *Nous avons passé une bonne journée avec la famille.*

....

4. *Actuellement, elle est en Chine.*

....

5. *Tes amis sont sympathiques.*

....

6. *Son patron est très gentil.*

....

7. *Ils ont cinq semaines de vacances par an.*

....

8. *Elle a perdu le match. Elle est vraiment déçue.*

....

Synonyms and Homonyms

Synonyms are words or expressions with similar meanings. They are useful to learn so you can express yourself in different ways and show off how well you have mastered the language.

chose	thing	*objet*	object
punition	punishment	*châtiment*	punishment
peinture	painting	*tableau*	painting
enfin	finally	*finalement*	finally

Homonyms are words with the same pronunciation (and sometimes spelling) as another word, but they bear a different meaning. Getting your ear accustomed to different sounds is key to understanding.

mètre	meter	*maître*	master				
mère	mother	*mer*	sea	*maire*	mayor		
cent	hundred	*cent*	cent	*sang*	blood	*sans*	without
vin	wine	*vingt*	twenty	*vain*	vain		

Exercise 1-15: Let's Find the Clue to the Puzzle!

TRACK 4

Listen to the audio track and repeat. Then listen again and write down each sentence.

1. ....

2. ....

3. ....

4. ....

5. ....

6. ....

7. ....

8. ....

9. ....

10. ....

Prefixes

Another way of approaching nouns is to study the prefix, the element at the beginning of a word that helps decipher the meaning of a word.

a-, an-	without	*atypique*	atypical
ab-	away from	*abstraire*	to abstract
anti-	before, against	*antitabac*	anti-smoking
auto-	self	*autodéfense*	self-defense
contre-	against, opposite	*contre-culture*	counter-culture
dé-	remove	*défaire*	undo
ex-	former	*ex-mari*	former husband
hyper-	excessive, intensive	*hyperactif*	hyperactive
in-, im-, il-, ir-	negative	*inoubliable*	unforgettable
poly-	many	*polyglotte*	polyglot, someone who speaks multiple languages
pré-	before	*prédire*	to predict
re-, ré-	again, back	*recommencer*	to start again
sub-, sous-	under	*sous-estimer*	underestimate
sur-	over, above	*surcharger*	overload
trans-	beyond	*transculturel*	cross-cultural
vi-, vice-	substitution	*vice-président*	vice-president

Exercise 1-16: Matching Game

Match the sentences in the right-hand column with the corresponding sentences in the left-hand column.

1. *Il réécrit la lettre.*
2. *L'ex-directeur est en Asie.*
3. *Il débouche la bouteille.*
4. *Le message est transmis.*
5. *C'est incroyable.*

a. *Un nouveau gère l'entreprise.*
b. *Il a envoyé le courriel.*
c. *On a du mal à y croire.*
d. *Il a écrit la lettre de nouveau.*
e. *Il enlève le bouchon.*

Suffixes

A suffix is an element added to the end of a word to modify its meaning. Here are a few examples.

-âtre	pejorative	*blanchâtre*	whitish, off-white
-able	relative to possibility	*discutable*	arguable
-cratie	relative to power	*aristocratie*	aristocracy
-ette	diminutive	*maisonnette*	small house
-logie	relative to science	*anthropologie*	anthropology
-mane	relative to obsession	*toxicomane*	drug addict
-philie	relative to love	*bibliophile*	book lover
-phobe	relative to fear	*claustrophobe*	claustrophobic
-vore	that feeds itself on something	*carnivore*	meat eater

Exercise 1-17: What Makes Sense?

Match the sentences in the right-hand column with the corresponding sentences in the left-hand column.

1. *Elle est mythomane.*
2. *Elle est mélomane.*

a. *Elle adore la musique.*
b. *Elle n'aime pas l'espace fermé.*

3. *Elle est claustrophobe.*   c. *Elle aime tout ce qui est français.*
4. *Elle est francophile.*   d. *Elle ne peut pas le boire.*
5. *C'est imbuvable.*   e. *Elle ne dit pas la vérité.*

Exercise 1-18: Let's Recap!

Let's see if you have your genders together. Place the proper indefinite article before the noun.

1. .... *priorité*   3. .... *actualités*

2. .... *maisonnette*   4. .... *quartiernationalité*

5. .... *chapeau*   8. .... *restaurant*

6. .... *librairie*   9. .... *amies*

7. .... *nationalité*   10. .... *agence*

Exercise 1-19: Eavesdropping

TRACK 5

Élodie is sitting at the terrace of a café. The woman at the table next to her is talking on her cell phone. Élodie picks up some fragments of conversation. Listen to the audio track and repeat. Then listen again and write what you hear.

1. ....

2. ....

3. ....

4. ....

5. ....

6. ....

7. ....

8. ....

9. ....

10. ....

Part 2

Pronouns

Pronouns are simply words that are used to substitute for a noun or a noun equivalent. This sounds simple enough, yet it is often the way people use pronouns in a given language that identifies them as fluent speakers or struggling beginners. In French, there are many types of pronouns, and each has a specific role to play. In this part, we will take a look at five different categories: subject pronouns, direct object pronouns, indirect object pronouns, disjunctive pronouns, and relative pronouns. It is a lot of grammatical ground to cover, but each category has its own functions and its own rules, making them pretty straightforward after all.

Subject Pronouns

Using pronouns enables us to avoid being repetitive and makes communication more efficient. Subject pronouns are the most familiar because these are the pronouns we use when we conjugate verbs. Let's review them:

je	I
tu	you (singular familiar)
il	he, it (masculine)
elle	she, it (feminine)
on	one, we, they
nous	we
vous	you (singular formal and all plurals)
ils	they (masculine or mixed masculine and feminine)
elles	they (feminine)

The third person pronouns, both singular and plural, apply to people, animals, or things.

Now let's see how this pronoun is used. Take a look at the following examples:

Marianne est actrice.	**Marianne is an actress.**
Elle est actrice.	**She is an actress.**
Les deux frères sont très gentils.	**The two brothers are very nice.**
Ils sont très gentils.	**They are very nice.**
L'océan est très pollué.	**The ocean is very polluted.**
Il est très pollué.	**It is very polluted.**

Both *tu* and *vous* are used to say *you*. When speaking with friends, family members, children, and animals, use the familiar form *tu*. If you are addressing a stranger, someone you don't know well, or when you want to show respect or to maintain a certain degree of distance, use *vous*. Nowadays, the trend is toward familiarity. It all depends on the setting and the crowd.

The Pronoun On

The pronoun *on* is extremely versatile. It has several different meanings. It may mean *one*, *we*, or *they* depending on how it is used.

On can be used to replace an indefinite person.

On ne sait jamais.	**One never knows.**
On ne peut pas plaire à tout le monde.	**One cannot please everybody.**

On can also mean *people in general*, when speaking about habits or customs.

En Angleterre, on boit du thé.	**In England, one drinks tea.**
Au Japon, on mange du sushi.	**In Japan, one eats sushi.**

On can be used to mean *we*, replacing *nous* in informal conversation.

On va au théâtre ce soir?	**Shall we go to the theater this evening?**
Sylvie et moi, on passe toujours nos vacances ensemble.	**Sylvie and I, we always spend our vacation together.**

On can replace the pronoun *tu*, also in informal conversation.

Ah, on s'amuse ici!	**So, you are having fun here!**
Alors, on se promène au lieu de faire ses devoirs!	**So, you are taking a walk instead of doing your homework!**

On can also replace a passive voice in English.

Ici, on parle français.	**French is spoken here.**
On n'a pas encore reçu de réponse.	**An answer has not yet been received.**

Exercise 2-1: Is It You?

Replace the noun in parentheses with the appropriate subject pronoun.

1. (*Sa femme*) .... *est avocate.*

2. (*Mon frère et moi*) .... *habitons à Montréal.*

3. (*Nos parents*) .... *habitent à Miami.*

4. (*Le professeur*) .... *enseigne le français et l'espagnol.*

5. (*Ma soeur et ses amies*) .... *vont au cinéma ce soir.*

Exercise 2-2: On

Translate the following sentences using the pronoun *on*.

1. One would like to succeed in life.

....

2. Shall we go to the beach today?

....

3. German is spoken here.

....

4. In France, one drinks good wine.

....

5. My brother and I, we always eat at this restaurant.

....

6. So, you are staying home tonight?

....

7. One never knows.

....

8. We are going to be late!

....

9. Euros are not accepted here.

....

10. In Paris, one takes the subway.

....

Direct Object Pronouns

Another type of pronoun is the direct object pronoun, or *l'objet direct*.

In English we use seven direct object pronouns: me, you, him, her, it, us, them. In French, there are eight since two forms for the direct object pronoun *you* are used: the informal singular *te* and the formal or plural *vous*. In English, we distinguish between a direct object pronoun that replaces a person (*him* or *her*) or a thing (*it*); in French *le, la,* and *les* can replace both people and things.

Let's review the direct object pronouns.

me	me
te	you (familiar)
le	him or it (masculine)
la	her or it (feminine)
nous	us
vous	you (plural or formal)
les	them (masculine and feminine)

A direct object immediately follows the verb without a preposition. A direct object pronoun replaces the direct object noun. In French, the direct object pronoun must agree in gender and number with the noun it replaces. Unlike in English, the French direct object precedes the verb. In a sentence with auxiliary or compound verbs, the direct object pronoun precedes the verb to which it directly refers. The direct object pronoun can replace a noun preceded by a definite article or a possessive or demonstrative adjective.

Le professeur enseigne les langues étrangères.	**The professor teaches foreign languages.**
Le professeur les enseigne.	**The professor teaches them.**
Nous prenons la décision.	**We make the decision.**
Nous la prenons.	**We make it.**
Il t'appelle.	**He is calling you.**
Elles vous remercient.	**They thank you.**
Nous t'invitons.	**We are inviting you.**

In a negative sentence, the direct object pronoun comes immediately before the conjugated verb.

Nous n'aimons pas le film.	**We do not like the film.**
Nous ne l'aimons pas.	**We do not like it.**
Elles n'acceptent pas l'explication.	**They do not accept the explanation.**
Elles ne l'acceptent pas.	**They do not accept it.**

When using inversion in the interrogative form, the direct object pronoun comes immediately before the verb.

Connaissez-vous cet écrivain?	**Do you know this author?**
Le connaissez-vous?	**Do you know him?**
Emmenez-vous les enfants à l'école?	**Are you taking the children to school?**
Les emmenez-vous à l'école?	**Are you taking them to school?**

When an infinitive has a direct object, the direct object pronoun immediately precedes the infinitive.

Pouvez-vous appeler le médecin?	**Can you call the doctor?**
Pouvez-vous l'appeler?	**Can you call him?**
Tu dois finir ce projet.	**You must finish this project.**
Tu dois le finir.	**You must finish it.**
Je viens de lire son dernier roman.	**I just read his last novel.**
Je viens de le lire.	**I have just read it.**

In the past tense the direct object pronoun is placed before the auxiliary verb. The past participle must agree in number and gender with the direct object placed before the verb.

Le chanteur a chanté la chanson.	**The singer sang the song.**
Le chanteur l'a chantée.	**The singer sang it.**
Le professeur a corrigé les examens.	**The teacher corrected the exams.**
Le professeur les a corrigés.	**The teacher corrected them.**

In the positive imperative, the direct object pronoun follows the verb. In the negative imperative, the direct object pronoun remains before the verb. The verb and the pronoun are connected by a hyphen in the positive imperative.

Appelez le médecin!	**Call the doctor!**
Appelez-le!	**Call him!**
Achetez ces chaussures!	**Buy these shoes!**
Achetez-les!	**Buy them!**
Apportez les documents!	**Bring the documents!**
Ne les apportez pas!	**Don't bring them!**

Exercise 2-3: Oral Practice

TRACK 6

Listen to the following questions and write an affirmative or negative answer below. Say your answer aloud.

1. *Vous invitez votre voisin à dîner? (negative)*

....

2. *Comprends-tu les directions? (negative)*

3. *Tu fais livrer le paquet? (affirmative)*

....

4. *Vous les appelez ce soir? (affirmative)*

....

5. *Il cherche toujours ses clés? (affirmative)*

....

6. *Vous les connaissez? (affirmative)*

....

7. *Elle les invite souvent? (affirmative)*

....

8. *Vous les lisez en français? (negative)*

....

9. *Tu la prépares avec de la sauce? (affirmative)*

....

10. *Elle l'écrit à la main? (negative)*

....

Exercise 2-4: You Know the Answer—You Know It!

Rewrite each sentence, replacing the words in parentheses with a direct object pronoun.

1. *Elle a acheté (les tulipes jaunes).*

....

2. *Nous consultons (l'avocat).*

....

3. *Les spectateurs ont applaudi (les acteurs).*

....

4. *J'ai oublié (mon sac).*

....

5. *Il ignore (la raison).*

....

6. *Elle vend (son appartement).*

....

7. *Il accepte (vos explications).*

....

8. *Nous lisons (tous les journaux français).*

....

9. *Elle a trouvé (la maison) sans difficulté.*

....

10. *Tu comprends (la question)?*

....

Exercise 2-5: Here It Is!

Translate the following sentences using the *vous* form and inversion when necessary.

1. She knows me.

....

2. The journalist calls them.

....

3. You invite her.

....

4. We see him.

....

5. She understands us.

....

6. Bring them!

....

7. He is going to sell it.

....

8. Do not buy it!

....

9. I must see it.

....

10. Does he know her?

....

Indirect Object Pronouns

Our next form of pronoun is the indirect object pronoun, *l'objet indirect.*

In English, six indirect object pronouns are used: me, you, him, her, us, them. As with subject and direct object pronouns, in French a distinction is made between the informal you (*te*) and the formal or plural you (*vous*). However, French indirect object pronouns do not distinguish gender; *lui* and *leur* replace both masculine and feminine nouns. French indirect object pronouns replace only animate (people, animals) indirect objects. Inanimate ideas and things are replaced with the pronoun *y.*

Let's look at the indirect object pronouns.

me	me
te	you (familiar)
lui	him, her
nous	us
vous	you (formal or plural)
leur	them (masculine and feminine)

The object is called indirect because it is preceded by a preposition, usually *à.* It is placed in front of the conjugated verb and in front of *avoir* in the compound tenses. The indirect object pronoun, unlike the direct object pronoun, does not agree in gender and number with the past participle. The pronouns *me* and *te* become *m'* and *t'* before words that begin with a vowel or a mute *h*. Note that there is a difference between *leur*, the indirect object pronoun, and *leur(s)*, the possessive adjective.

Let's see how this type of pronoun is used.

Nous parlons au journaliste.	**We are speaking to the journalist.**
Nous lui parlons.	**We are speaking to him.**
Elle écrit à ses parents.	**She writes to her parents.**
Elle leur écrit.	**She writes to them.**
J'explique la situation aux clients.	**I explain the situation to the clients.**
Je leur explique la situation.	**I explain the situation to them.**

In the interrogative or negative, the indirect object pronoun comes immediately before the verb.

Leur avez-vous parlé de ce film?	**Did you talk to them about this film?**
M'as-tu envoyé un message?	**Did you send me a message?**
Vous donne-t-il de bons conseils?	**Does he give you good advice?**
Il ne vous envoie jamais rien.	**He never sends you anything.**
Vous ne m'avez pas dit la vérité.	**You did not tell me the truth.**
Je te prêterai ma voiture.	**I will lend you my car.**

In the positive imperative, the indirect object pronoun follows the verb. Remember to add a hyphen. In the negative imperative, the indirect object pronoun remains before the verb.

Appelez-moi demain matin!	**Call me tomorrow morning!**
Envoyez-lui l'argent!	**Send him the money!**
Ne leur donnez rien!	**Don't give them anything!**
Ne me téléphonez pas si tard!	**Don't call me so late!**

Exercise 2-6: Take the Indirect Route

Rewrite each sentence, replacing the words in parentheses with the appropriate indirect object pronoun.

1. *Le grand-père a lu un conte (aux petits-enfants).*

....

2. *Elle a fait un cadeau (à sa mère).*

....

3. *Je ferai parvenir le paquet (à mon fils) dès que possible.*

....

4. *Il enverra des fleurs (à sa fiancée).*

....

5. *Ce restaurant appartient (à son patron).*

....

6. *Est-ce que vous avez parlé (au médecin)?*

....

7. *Racontez l'histoire (à Louise) ce soir.*

....

8. *Ne dites rien (à vos parents)!*

....

9. *Elle annoncera sa décision (à ses collègues) la semaine prochaine.*

....

10. *Je donnerai le scénario (au rédacteur) demain matin.*

....

Exercise 2-7: I Am Talking to You!

Translate the following sentences using the *vous* form the inversion when necessary.

1. Bring her a cup of coffee!

....

2. Do not call me before 10:00 A.M.!

....

3. Send us your news!

....

4. I will tell him a story.

....

5. They will give you an answer next week.

....

6. He did not return the keys to me.

....

7. This house belongs to them.

....

8. You do not talk to me.

....

9. She told us a lie.

....

10. We'll lend you our apartment for the weekend.

....

The Pronoun Y

Y is an indirect object pronoun that precedes the verb. It typically replaces an inanimate object. The object is preceded by a preposition, usually *à*.

Il s'habitue à ce temps froid.	**He is getting used to this cold weather.**
Il s'y habitue.	**He is getting used to it.**
Vous pensez à l'avenir.	**You are thinking about the future.**
Vous y pensez.	**You are thinking about it.**
Tu t'intéresses à ce film?	**Are you interested in this film?**
Tu t'y intéresses?	**Are you interested in it?**

In the past tense the indirect object pronoun *y* is placed before the auxiliary verb. Note that the past participle does not agree in gender and number with the indirect object.

J'ai réfléchi à ce problème.	**I thought about this problem.**
J'y ai réfléchi.	**I thought about it.**
Elle a répondu à nos questions.	**She answered our questions.**
Elle y a répondu.	**She answered them.**
Nous n'avons pas goûté à ce plat.	**We did not taste this dish.**
Nous n'y avons pas goûté.	**We did not taste it.**

Exercise 2-8: Y Now?

Rewrite each sentence, replacing the words in parentheses with the indirect object pronoun *y*.

1. *Nous nous habituons (à tout).*

....

2. *Ils devraient prêter attention (à ce que vous dites).*

....

3. *Elle s'intéresse (à son oeuvre).*

....

4. *Je m'abonne (à ce magazine).*

....

5. *Il tient (à ses livres).*

....

6. *Nous ne croyons pas (à cette théorie).*

....

7. *Tu ne penses jamais (aux conséquences de tes actes).*

....

8. *Ils n'obéissent pas (aux règles).*

....

9. *Je réfléchirai (à l'emploi que vous me proposez).*

....

10. *Pourquoi n'a-t-elle jamais répondu (à ma question)?*

....

The Pronoun En

En is an object pronoun that precedes the verb. It usually replaces an inanimate object that is preceded by the preposition *de*. The pronoun *en* immediately precedes the verb, except in the positive imperative, where it follows the verb.

Nous avons besoin d'une maison plus grande.	**We need a larger house.**
Nous en avons besoin.	**We need it.**
Elle s'occupera de tous les détails.	**She'll take care of all the details.**
Elle s'en occupera.	**She'll take care of it.**
Je ne me souviens pas de cette histoire.	**I do not remember this story.**
Je ne m'en souviens pas.	**I do not remember it.**

In the past tense the pronoun *en* is placed before the auxiliary verb. Note that the past participle does not agree in gender and number with *en*.

Elle a parlé de son projet à son patron.	**She spoke to her boss about her project.**
Elle en a parlé à son patron.	**She spoke to her boss about it.**
Il s'est occupé de cette affaire difficile.	**He took care of this difficult business.**
Il s'en est occupé.	**He took care of it.**
Je me suis débarrassé de tous ces objets inutiles.	**I got rid of all these useless objects.**
Je m'en suis débarrassé.	**I got rid of them.**

Exercise 2-9: En Use

Rewrite each sentence, replacing the words in parentheses with the pronoun *en*.

1. *Il a parlé (de tous vos problèmes).*

   ....

2. *J'ai envie (d'aller au cinéma ce soir).*

   ....

3. *Vous avez besoin (d'une maison plus grande).*

   ....

4. *Elle s'est approchée (de la porte) très lentement.*

   ....

5. *Nous nous chargerons (de tout ce qui facilitera votre travail).*

   ....

6. *Tu te sers (de cet ordinateur)?*

   ....

7. *Il a peur (des nouvelles idées).*

   ....

8. *Je ne me souviens pas (de son histoire).*

   ....

9. *Nous nous sommes occupés (des réservations).*

   ....

10. *Elle ne pourra jamais se débarrasser (de ses poupées).*

    ....

Exercise 2-10: Perfect Match

Make an appropriate sentence by matching the phrase in the right-hand column with the phrase in the left-hand column.

1. *Elle a peur*
2. *Il s'intéresse*
3. *Il se sert*
4. *Je ne me souviens pas*
5. *Vous vous abonnez*

a. *d'un appareil numérique.*
b. *à un magazine mensuel.*
c. *du nom de votre livre.*
d. *à ce nouveau film.*
e. *des insectes.*

Pronoun Order

You have now reviewed several kinds of pronouns—subject, direct object, and indirect object—and in each case you have become familiar with the placement of each type of pronoun in a sentence or phrase. But what happens when more than one type of pronoun is used? When a direct and indirect object pronoun appear in the same sentence, the indirect object pronoun (*me, te, nous, vous*) always comes first unless the direct and indirect object pronouns are in the third person, in which case the direct object pronoun (*le, la, les*) comes first.

Il te donne l'argent.	**He gives you the money.**
Il te le donne.	**He gives it to you.**
Je vous envoie l'invitation.	**I am sending you the invitation.**
Je vous l'envoie.	**I am sending it to you.**
Vous nous montrez les documents.	**You show us the documents.**
Vous nous les montrez.	**You show them to us.**

If the direct and indirect object pronouns in the third person are combined, the direct object pronoun comes first.

direct object	indirect object
le	
la	*+ lui, leur*
les	

J'envoie le texte au rédacteur.	**I send the text to the editor.**
Je le lui envoie.	**I send it to him.**

Il tend l'ordonnance au pharmacien.	He hands the prescription to the pharmacist.
Il la lui tend.	He hands it to him.
Nous montrons la maison à nos invités.	We show the house to our guests.
Nous la leur montrons.	We show it to them.

In the past tense, the direct object pronoun is placed before the auxiliary verb. The past participle must agree in number and gender with the direct object placed before the verb.

J'ai écrit ces articles.	I wrote these articles.
Je les ai écrits.	I wrote them.
Elle a fait ces tartes délicieuses.	She made these delicious pies.
Elle les a faites.	She made them.

When *en* is combined with an indirect object pronoun it is always in second position. The past participle does not agree in number and gender with *en*.

Nous leur avons donné des explications.	We gave them some explanations.
Nous leur en avons donné.	We gave them some.
Elle nous a prêté des romans français.	She lent us some French novels.
Elle nous en a prêté.	She lent us some.

Exercise 2-11: Say It Loud, Say It Clear

Listen to the following questions and write an affirmative or negative answer below. Say your answer aloud.

TRACK 7

1. .... (affirmative)

2. .... (affirmative)

3. .... (negative)

4. .... (affirmative)

5. .... (affirmative)

6. .... (affirmative)

Exercise 2-12: Multiple Pronouns

Rewrite each sentence, replacing the words in parentheses with the appropriate pronouns. Pay careful attention to the order in which you place them.

1. *Ne parlez pas (de ce projet à Marc)!*

   ....

2. *J'ai emprunté (des livres à ma soeur).*

   ....

3. *Vous devriez envoyer (ces documents à votre comptable).*

   ....

4. *Patrick a raconté (sa vie à son ami).*

   ....

5. *Le compositeur a envoyé (sa nouvelle symphonie au chef d'orchestre).*

   ....

6. *Le professeur a donné (l'examen aux étudiants).*

   ....

7. *Elle a demandé (la signature à l'écrivain).*

   ....

8. *Ils vendront (leur appartement à leurs enfants).*

   ....

9. *Le médecin (a prescrit ce traitement au malade).*

   ....

10. *Nous recommandons (ce restaurant à tous nos amis).*

    ....

Exercise 2-13: In Your Own Words

Translate the following sentences, using the *tu* form if necessary.

1. We are thinking about it.

   ....

2. You need it.

   ....

3. I took care of it.

4. They gave it to you.

5. We sent it to them.

6. We gave them some.

7. We spoke about it.

8. You are not interested in it.

9. They borrowed some from us.

10. She never uses it.

Disjunctive Pronouns

Disjunctive pronouns, which are also known as stressed or tonic pronouns, are yet another type of pronoun with multiple uses. First, let's review the pronouns.

moi	me	*nous*	us
toi	you	*vous*	you
lui	him	*eux*	them
elle	her	*elles*	them (feminine)

Used for Emphasis

Disjunctive pronouns are often used when you want to add extra emphasis to a thought. Take a look at the following examples.

Moi, je trouve ce film horrible!   **Personally, I think this film is awful.**

Lui, il se perd tout le temps!	**He gets lost all the time!**
Toi, tu es toujours en retard!	**You are always late!**

Used for Opinion

Disjunctive pronouns can also be used to solicit an opinion.

Moi, je suis contre! Et vous, qu'est-ce que vous en pensez?	**I am against it. And you, what do you think?**
Eux, ils ne sortent jamais en semaine! Et toi?	**They never go out during the week! What about you?**

Used After Most Prepositions

A disjunctive pronoun will often be used after a preposition. For example:

Il cuisine pour eux.	**He cooks for them.**
Nous dînons bien chez vous!	**We dine well at your house!**
Je ne vais jamais au cinéma avec elle.	**I never go to the movies with her.**

Used as One-Word Responses

Disjunctive pronouns are also used as answers when there isn't a verb present. See the following examples.

Qui a soif?	**Who is thirsty?**
Moi!	**I am!**
Qui est le patron ici?	**Who is the boss here?**
Lui!	**He is!**
Je déteste l'hiver.	**I hate the winter.**
Moi aussi.	**So do I.**
Elle n'aime pas lire.	**She does not like to read.**
Lui non plus.	**Neither does he.**

Used with Another Subject

Disjunctive pronouns can be used in conjunction with another subject. The following examples illustrate how this is done.

Elle et sa belle-soeur, elles ne s'entendent pas très bien.	**She and her sister-in-law do not get along very well.**

Joséphine et moi, nous allons faire des courses ensemble.	**Josephine and I are going shopping together.**

Used to Indicate Possession

Disjunctive pronouns are also used to indicate possession, as in the following examples.

À qui est cet iPod?	**Whose iPod is it?**
C'est à lui.	**It's his.**
Ce portefeuille n'est pas à moi.	**This wallet is not mine.**

Used to Stress Identification

Disjunctive pronouns used after *c'est/ce sont* stress identification. In English, we would do so using intonation. The following examples show how it is executed in French.

C'est toi qui vas payer.	**You are the one who is going to pay.**
Ce sont eux qui ne viennent pas.	**They are the ones who are not coming.**
Ce n'est pas moi qui décide.	**I am not the one who decides.**

Used to Make Comparisons

Disjunctive pronouns can be used to make comparisons. For example:

Le frère d'André est plus beau que lui.	**André's brother is more handsome than he is.**
Évidemment, elle est beaucoup plus efficace que toi.	**Of course, she is much efficient than you are.**
Sylvie cuisine mieux que moi.	**Sylvie cooks better than I do.**

Used to Reinforce a Pronoun

Disjunctive pronouns can be used with *même (self)* to reinforce the pronoun.

Je vais conduire la voiture moi-même.	**I am going to drive the car myself.**
Elle est venue me voir elle-même!	**She came to see me herself.**
Avez-vous pris les photos vous-même?	**Did you take the photos yourself?**

Used to Express Only or Neither

Disjunctive pronouns are also used with *ne . . . que* (*only*) and *ni . . . ni* (*neither . . . nor*). For example:

Il ne voit que vous.   **He only sees you.**
Ils n'ont invité ni toi ni moi.   **They have invited neither you nor me.**

Exercise 2-14: Oral Practice

TRACK 8

Listen to the following questions and write an answer below. Say your answer aloud.

1. ....

2. ....

3. ....

4. ....

5. ....

6. ....

7. ....

8. ....

Exercise 2-15: Say It Yourself!

Translate the following sentences using a disjunctive pronoun and the *tu* form if necessary.

1. He is thinking about her.

....

2. I hate winter!

....

3. You can't make this decision without me.

....

4. She is taller than you are.

....

5. We do it ourselves!

....

6. He works for them.

....

7. You said it yourself.

....

8. She will go to France with us.

....

9. I am not afraid of him.

....

10. Whose car is this?

....

Relative Pronouns

It is essential to know how to connect ideas in the same sentence. One way to link ideas back to persons and things is by using yet another type of pronoun, the relative pronoun (*le pronom relatif*). Relative pronouns relate two sentences, making one dependent on the other. The dependent sentence is called the subordinate clause. Choosing the correct relative pronoun depends on the pronoun's function in the sentence (subject, direct object, or object of a preposition).

The Relative Pronoun Qui

Let's begin our review with the relative pronoun *qui* used as a subject. *Qui* may refer to people or things and may mean *who, whom, which, what,* or *that.* Look at the following examples:

Il remercie son ami qui lui a prêté de l'argent quand il en avait besoin.	**He thanks his friend who lent him money when he needed it.**
L'acteur qui a joué dans cette pièce est un débutant.	**The actor who acted in this play is a newcomer.**
Nous avons vu le tableau qui est le sujet de votre article.	**We saw the painting that is the subject of your article.**

The *i* of *qui* is never dropped in front of a vowel sound.

L'auteur de ce roman est inconnu—
je ne sais pas qui il est.
Elles ne me disent pas avec qui
elles sortent le week-end.

The author of this novel is unknown—
I do not know who he is.
They do not tell me whom they go
out with on weekends.

The verb following *qui* agrees with the noun or pronoun that *qui* replaces.

C'est moi qui ai dit la vérité.
C'est vous qui avez gagné le prix.
C'est toi qui es arrivé tôt.
C'est nous qui sommes heureux.

It is I who told the truth.
It's you who won the prize.
It's you who arrived early.
It's we who are happy.

Exercise 2-16: Oral Practice

TRACK 9

Listen to the audio track and repeat. Then listen again and write down each sentence.

1. ....

2. ....

3. ....

4. ....

5. ....

6. ....

7. ....

8. ....

9. ....

10. ....

The Relative Pronoun Que

Now let's take a look at another relative pronoun, *que*. When the clause introduced by a relative pronoun already has a subject, the relative pronoun is the object of the verb of the clause it introduces. In this case, the relative pronoun *que* (*whom, which, that*) is used. *Que* may also refer to people and things.

C'est le chocolat que tout le monde aime goûter.	It is the chocolate that everyone loves to taste.
Voici un danseur que je n'ai jamais vu.	Here's a dancer whom I have never seen.
Nous n'avons pas encore vu le film que vous avez suggeré.	We have not yet seen the film that you suggested.
Voici les chaussures que j'adore.	Here are the shoes that I love.

Note that the *e* of *que* is dropped before a vowel.

C'est le livre qu'elle a écrit.	It is the book she wrote.
Les robes qu'elle achète sont faites sur mesure.	The dresses she buys are custom-made.

In the past tense, if the direct object is placed before the verb, the past participle agrees in gender and number with the object.

Les tableaux que nous avons vus étaient remarquables.	The paintings we saw were remarkable.
Les directions qu'il m'a données étaient faciles à suivre.	The directions he gave me were easy to follow.

In French, the relative clause is often inserted into the main clause. For example:

Le livre que j'ai lu le mois dernier était un cadeau de ma grand-mère.	The book I read last month was a gift from my grandmother.
Elle a oublié le nom du parfum que son mari aimait tant.	She forgot the name of the perfume that her husband liked so much.

Exercise 2-17: Who Is Who? What Is What?

Complete the sentences with *qui* or *que*.

1. *Il aime la chanson* .... *elle chante.*

2. *Nous irons dans les endroits* .... *vous avez suggérés.*

3. *Je ne sais pas* .... *elle est.*

4. *Tu aimes la musique* .... *il a choisi.*

5. *La maison* .... *est en face est à lui.*

6. *Je ne connais pas le suspect* .... *la police a arrêté.*

7. *J'ai envoyé le paquet* .... *vous m'avez donné.*

8. *Il a lu l'article* .... *le critique a écrit.*

9. *C'est la robe* .... *j'ai achetée pour mon anniversaire.*

10. *Il a retrouvé le portefeuille* .... *il avait égaré.*

Relative Pronouns Preceded by Prepositions

When verbs are followed by prepositions, the relative pronouns *qui, quoi, lequel, laquelle, lesquels,* and *lesquelles* are used. The preposition is placed before the relative pronoun. *Qui* is only used to refer to people, and *lequel, laquelle, lesquels, lesquelles* refers to things. *Lequel, laquelle, lesquels, lesquelles* may also be used for people; this usage, however, is less common. The following reflects more contemporary usage.

C'est le médecin à qui j'ai   **It is the doctor to whom**
   donné mes radios.   **I gave my x-rays.**

Compare that sentence with the following:

C'est le médecin auquel j'ai   **It is the doctor to whom**
   donné mes radios.   **I gave my x-rays.**

Here are some more examples of contemporary usage.

Voici le journal auquel il s'abonne.   **Here's the newspaper to which**
                                  he subscribes.

C'est la pièce à laquelle je m'intéresse.   **It's the play in which I am interested.**
J'ignore à quoi tu penses.   **I do not know what you are**
                                  thinking about.

C'est le comptable pour qui je travaille.   **It is the accountant for whom I work.**
C'est l'orchestre pour lequel il joue.   **It is the orchestra for which he plays.**
La beauté avec laquelle elle   **The beauty with which she**
   s'exprime est incomparable.   **expresses herself is incomparable.**

There is one exception: *qui* cannot be used with the preposition *parmi* (*among*).

*Il avait visité plusieurs villes,
    parmi lesquelles une dizaine de
    villes américaines.*
	**He had visited several cities,
	    among which were a dozen
	    American cities.**

Using Où

The relative pronoun *où* often replaces *dans lequel, sur lequel, par lequel.*

*La ville où elle habite est
    en Normandie.*
	**The town where she lives is
	    in Normandy.**

*Voici la rue où nous habitions après
    notre arrivée en France.*
	**Here is the street where we lived
	    after our arrival in France.**

Où is also used after expressions of time.

*Le jour où il ne pleuvra pas,
    nous irons à la plage.*
	**The day (when) it does not rain,
	    we'll go to the beach.**

*Le 24 novembre, c'est le jour
    où ils se sont mariés.*
	**November 24, it is the day
	    (when) they got married**

Exercise 2-18: Oral Practice

TRACK 10

Listen to each sentence and identify the relative pronouns.

1. ....   6. ....

2. ....   7. ....

3. ....   8. ....

4. ....   9. ....

5. ....   10. ....

The Relative Pronoun Dont

The relative pronoun *dont* acts as an object and can refer to people and things. It is used to refer to objects of verbs or adjectives that are followed by the preposition *de*. As with several other pronouns, the pronoun *dont* takes on different meanings.

For example, it can imply possession:

L'écrivain dont j'ai oublié le nom donne une lecture la semaine prochaine.	**The writer whose name I forgot will be giving a reading next week.**
Voici la danseuse dont nous connaissons la soeur.	**Here is the dancer whose sister we know.**

It can replace the preposition *de* and its object.

Le critique a parlé du nouveau spectacle à l'Olympia.	**The critic spoke about the new show at the Olympia.**
Le spectacle dont le critique a parlé est à l'Olympia.	**The show the critic talked about is at the Olympia.**
L'écrivain est content de son dernier roman.	**The writer is happy about his most recent novel.**
C'est un roman dont l'écrivain est content.	**It is a novel the writer is happy about.**
Son fils est fier de son exploit.	**His son is proud of his achievement.**
C'est un exploit dont son fils est fier.	**It is an achievement his son is proud of.**

In modern French, *dont* often replaces *duquel, de laquelle, desquels,* and *desquelles.* For example:

L'écrivaine anglaise dont je parle s'appelle Mary Wollstonecraft.	**The English writer I am talking about is Mary Wollstonecraft.**

This is preferable to:

L'écrivaine anglaise de laquelle je parle s'appelle Mary Wollstonecraft.	**The English writer I am talking about is Mary Wollstonecraft.**

Exercise 2-19: Do It with Dont

Formulate the sentences following the model, using the present tense of the verb.

document/avoir besoin (il) ⟶ *Voici le document dont il a besoin.*

1. *robe/avoir envie (elle)*

....

2. *film/parler (vous)*

....

3. *erreurs/avoir peur (je)*

....

4. *idées/se souvenir (ils)*

....

5. *travail/être fier (nous)*

....

6. *outils/se servir (tu)*

....

7. *frontières/s'approcher (ils)*

....

8. *mensonges/avoir honte (il)*

....

9. *exploits/se vanter (elle)*

....

10. *danger/se méfier (nous)*

....

Relative Pronouns and the Antecedent Ce

When there is no specific word or antecedent for the relative pronoun to refer to, the antecedent *ce* is added. *Ce qui, ce que, ce dont* and *ce à quoi*, all meaning *what*, refer to ideas, not to persons. They do not have a gender or number. As mentioned earlier, choosing the correct indefinite relative pronoun depends on the pronoun's function in the sentence: is it the subject, the direct object, or the object of a preposition?

Ce qui is used as the subject of the dependent clause.

Ce qui est arrivé est un miracle.	**What happened is a miracle.**
Je ne comprends pas ce qui se passe.	**I don't understand what's happening.**

Ce que is used as the direct object of the dependent clause.

Ce que vous dites est très sage.	**What you are saying is very wise.**
Il dit rarement ce qu'il pense.	**He rarely says what he thinks.**

Ce dont is used when verbs take the preposition *de.*

Elle ne sait pas ce dont ils ont besoin.	**She doesn't know what they need.**
Ce dont nous parlons est tout	**What we are talking about**
nouveau pour elle.	**is all new to her.**

Ce à quoi is used with verbs that take the preposition *à.*

Ce à quoi il aspire, c'est à une	**What he is aspiring to is an**
vie plus facile.	**easier life.**
Ce n'est pas ce à quoi il s'attendait.	**It is not what he expected.**

These indefinite relative pronouns, *ce qui, ce que, ce à quoi* and *ce dont,* are typically placed at the beginning of a sentence to mark an emphasis. When a verb requires a preposition, it is repeated in the second clause.

Ce qui me fascine, c'est la musique.	**What fascinates me is the music.**
Ce que nous regrettons, c'est le	**What we regret is the lack of interest.**
manque d'intérêt.	
Ce dont elle se plaint, c'est du bruit.	**What she is complaining about is noise.**
Ce à quoi nous nous intéressons,	**What we are interested in is**
c'est à votre point de vue.	**your point of view.**

Exercise 2-20: In Your Own Words

Follow the model and formulate sentences using the present tense of the verb and the appropriate indefinite relative pronoun.

> *aimer/vin français (elle)* ⟶ *Ce qu'elle aime, c'est le vin français.*

1. *s'intéresser/littérature (je)*

   ....

2. *avoir besoin/ordinateur (tu)*

   ....

3. *comprendre/situation (il)*

   ....

4. *se souvenir/fin du film (vous)*

   ....

5. *parler/fascinant (elle)*

....

6. *détester/désordre (nous)*

....

7. *se plaindre/pollution (ils)*

....

8. *s'attendre/problèmes (vous)*

....

9. *décrire/cauchemar (il)*

....

10. *se méfier/conseils (je)*

....

Part 3

The Present Tense

Before you start conjugating verbs in the present tense, let's go over some basics. In English, the infinitive is preceded by the preposition *to—to walk*, *to sing*. In French, verbs are divided into groups according to their endings— *-er, -ir, -re, -oir*.

Present Tense -er Verb Conjugations

Let's start with -er verbs. Regular verbs ending in -er follow the same conjugation. Remove the -er ending to get the root. For instance, the stem for parler (to speak) is parl. Then you add the endings corresponding to the subject pronouns. The endings for the -er regular verbs are: e, es, e, ons, ez, ent. The e, es, and ent endings of the verbs are all silent. The final s of nous, vous, ils, and elles links with verbs beginning with a vowel sound, making a z sound. That's what is called a liaison.

-er Verbs			
parler (to speak)			
je parle	I speak	nous parlons	we speak
tu parles	you speak	vous parlez	you speak
il/elle parle	he/she speaks	ils/elles parlent	they speak

As you probably remember, vous is used whenever you are talking to more than one person or when you are addressing one or more people with a certain degree of formality.

When Is the Present Tense Used in French?

The present tense is used to describe:

- An ongoing action and can be translated in different ways depending on the context

Il regarde un film.

He is watching (he watches, he does watch) a film.

- An action that will take place in the close future

Elle déménage samedi.

She'll be moving on Saturday.

- A habitual action

Tous les étés, ils vont à Nice.

They go to Nice every summer.

- A dramatic or historical fact

Le président démissionne et

l'entreprise fait faillite.

The president resigned and the

company went bankrupt.

Common Regular -*er* Verbs in the Present Tense

accepter	to accept
aimer	to like, to love
apporter	to bring
augmenter	to increase, to raise
bavarder	to chat
casser	to break
chercher	to look for
commander	to order
danser	to dance
déjeuner	to have lunch
demander	to ask
donner	to give
étudier	to study
gagner	to earn, to win
habiter	to live
manger	to eat
porter	to carry, to wear
regarder	to look at, to watch
travailler	to work
visiter	to visit

Exercise 3-1: Translation Exercise

Circle the correct translation for each verb form.

1. *nous regardons* (he watches, you watch, we watch)
2. *vous visitez* (you visit, he visits, I visit)
3. *il chante* (you sing, he sings, they sing)

4. *je donne* (she gives, we give, I give)
5. *elle gagne* (he wins, she wins, you win)
6. *tu acceptes* (you accept, I accept, they accept)
7. *ils acceptent* (he accepts, we accept, they accept)
8. *tu aimes* (you love, I love, she loves)
9. *vous mangez* (I eat, they eat, you eat)
10. *j'habite* (I live, they live, we live)

Exercise 3-2: The Right Form

Write the whole sentence using the correct verb form.

1. *Nous (apporter) des fleurs à l'hôtesse.*

   ....

2. *Elle (aimer) voyager avec ses amis.*

   ....

3. *Je (commander) une bouteille de vin.*

   ....

4. *Vous (regarder) un bon film à la télévision.*

   ....

5. *Ils (déjeuner) à la terrasse.*

   ....

6. *Tu (étudier) l'italien.*

   ....

7. *Je (chercher) mes clés.*

   ....

8. *Elle (porter) un chapeau noir.*

   ....

9. *Vous (gagner) beaucoup d'argent.*

   ....

10. *Tu (travailler) trop.*

   ....

Spelling Idiosyncrasies of the Regular -er Verbs

Some spelling changes occur with some -er verbs.

With verbs in -ger, like *changer* (to change), the g becomes *ge* before the letter o in the present tense.

je change	I change	*nous changeons*	we change
tu changes	you change	*vous changez*	you change
il/elle change	he/she changes	*ils/elles changent*	they change

Nous changeons d'avis.	**We are changing our mind.**
Nous mangeons des frites.	**We are eating French fries.**

Some spelling changes also occur with verbs in –cer. In *remplacer* (to replace), the c becomes ç before the letter o in the present tense. The *cedilla* (ç) under the c is needed to keep the soft pronunciation of the c in the infinitive form.

je remplace	I replace	*nous remplaçons*	we replace
tu remplaces	you replace	*vous remplacez*	you replace
il/elle remplace	he/she replace	*ils/elles remplacent*	they replace

Nous les remplaçons le jeudi.	**We replace them on Thursdays.**
Nous commençons la projection dans deux minutes.	**We are starting the screening in two minutes.**

Exercise 3-3: Spelling, Anyone?

Write the whole sentence using the correct verb form.

1. *Nous (encourager) les joueurs de cette équipe.*

   ....

2. *Nous (avancer) lentement dans la forêt.*

   ....

3. *Nous (placer) les invités autour de la table.*

   ....

4. *Nous (partager) un appartement à Paris.*

....

5. *Nous (prononcer) les mots correctement.*

....

6. *Nous (corriger) les fautes dans le texte.*

....

7. *Nous (effacer) le tableau.*

....

8. *Nous (renoncer) au projet.*

....

9. *Nous (mélanger) les souvenirs de notre voyage.*

....

10. *Nous (nager) dans la Méditerranée.*

....

More Spelling Changes

With verbs composed of *-e* + consonant + *-er* like *enlever* (*to remove*), an *accent grave* is added in all but the first and the second persons plural.

j'enlève	I remove	*nous enlevons*	we remove
tu enlèves	you remove	*vous enlevez*	you remove
il/elle enlève	he/she removes	*Ils/elles enlèvent*	they remove

Il enlève ses chaussures. — **He removes his shoes.**
Elle emmène son fils à l'école. — **She takes her son to school.**

With some verbs composed of *-é* + consonant + *-er*, like *préférer* (*to prefer*) changes may also occur. The *accent aigu* changes to an *accent grave* in all but the first and second persons plural.

je préfère	I prefer	*nous préférons*	we prefer
tu préfères	you prefer	*vous préférez*	you prefer
il/elle préfère	he/she prefers	*ils/elles préfèrent*	they prefer

Il gère les affaires de la famille.   **He manages the family business.**
Ils célèbrent leur dixième   **They are celebrating their**
  anniversaire de mariage.   **tenth anniversary.**

Some verbs composed of *–e + l + –er*, like *épeler* (*to spell*) sometimes take two *l*'s in all but the first and second persons plural. There are no fixed rules, so you need to memorize them.

j'épelle	I spell	*nous épelons*	we spell
tu épelles	you spell	*vous épelez*	you spell
il/elle épelle	he/she spells	*ils/elles épellent*	they spell

Exercise 3-4: Accent or No Accent?

Write the full sentence using the correct verb form.

1. *Il (lever) la main pour poser une question.*

   ....

2. *Je (ne pas exagérer) quand je dis qu'il est milliardaire.*

   ....

3. *Je lui (répéter) toujours la même chose.*

   ....

4. *Nous (préférer) passer nos vacances en Bretagne.*

   ....

5. *Elle (considérer) Léa comme sa soeur.*

   ....

6. *Ils (emmener) leur nièce à l'opéra.*

   ....

7. *Comment est-ce que tu (épeler) ton nom?*

   ....

8. *Où est-ce que tu (acheter) tes fruits et légumes?*

   ....

9. *Elle (renouveler) ses papiers d'identité tous les cinq ans.*

   ....

10. *Tu lui (rappeler) d'apporter sa raquette de tennis.*

    ....

The Interrogative Form

There are three ways of asking questions: inversion, the more familiar *est-ce que* form, or upward intonation.

Parlez-vous français?	**Do you speak French?**
Est-ce que vous parlez français?	**Do you speak French?**
Vous parlez français?	**Do you speak French?**

If the third person singular of a verb ends with a vowel, a *t* is added between the verb and the subject pronoun.

Travaille-t-elle le week-end?	**Does she work on weekends?**
Cherche-t-il un appartement?	**Is he looking for an apartment?**

The Negative Form

To make a sentence negative, place *ne . . . pas* around the conjugated verb.

Il n'aime pas l'hiver.	**He doesn't like winter.**
Nous ne comprenons pas votre explication.	**We do not understand your explanation.**

The negative form can be expressed with many other negations. For example:

Je ne veux rien.	**I don't want anything.**
Il ne connaît personne à Toulouse.	**He does not know anyone in Toulouse.**
Elle n'étudie plus le latin.	**She no longer studies Latin.**
Je ne prends jamais l'autobus.	**I never take the bus.**
Ce n'est guère difficile.	**It is hardly difficult.**

The negation *ni . . . ni* precedes the nouns it negates. When the definite article is used in the positive form, it remains in the negative. When the indefinite article is used, it is no longer used in the negative.

J'aime les framboises et les cerises.	**I like raspberries and cherries.**
Je n'aime ni les framboises ni les cerises.	**I like neither raspberries nor cherries.**
Il reçoit des cartes et des lettres.	**He receives cards and letters.**
Il ne reçoit ni cartes ni lettres.	**He receives neither cards nor letters.**

Exercise 3-5: In French!

Translate the following sentences using the *est-ce que* form when necessary.

1. He does not live in La Rochelle.

   ....

2. She is not looking for anything.

   ....

3. Does she speak Chinese?

   ....

4. How does he spell his name?

   ....

5. They never go to Paris.

   ....

6. She no longer loves Fabien.

   ....

7. I eat neither cheese nor bread.

   ....

8. We are encouraging you.

   ....

9. She does not like this town.

   ....

10. Is she studying in Berlin?

   ....

Être *and* Avoir

To be able to entertain any existential debate, you need to memorize the conjugation of the verbs of *être* (*to be*) and *avoir* (*to have*).

je suis	I am	*nous sommes*	we are
tu es	you are	*vous êtes*	you are
il/elle est	he/she is	*ils/elles sont*	they are

Il est écossais.		**He is Scottish.**	
Nous sommes satisfaits de son travail.		**We are satisfied with his work.**	

j'ai	I have	*nous avons*	we have
tu as	you have	*vous avez*	you have
il/elle a	he/she has	*ils/elles ont*	they have

Nous avons trois chats.		**We have three cats.**
Elle a un nouveau dictionnaire.		**She has a new dictionary.**

In the negative form, *un*, *une*, and *des* change to *de* or *d'*.

Je n'ai pas de rendez-vous ce matin.	**I don't have an appointment this morning.**
Vous n'avez pas de moutarde?	**You don't have any mustard?**

It is important to note that in some idiomatic expressions, English uses *to be* when French uses *avoir.*

j'ai besoin	I need	*j'ai de la chance*	I am lucky
j'ai chaud	I am warm	*j'ai faim*	I am hungry
j'ai froid	I am cold	*j'ai honte*	I am ashamed
j'ai mal aux pieds	my feet hurt	*j'ai peur*	I am afraid
j'ai raison	I am right	*j'ai soif*	I am thirsty
j'ai trente ans	I am thirty	*j'ai tort*	I am wrong

Exercise 3-6: Meet My Friends!

TRACK 11

Listen to the audio track and repeat. Then listen again and write down each sentence.

1. ....

2. ....

3. ....

4. ....

5. ....

6. ....

7. ....

8. ....

9. ....

10. ....

Exercise 3-7: Sentence Scramble

Match the sentences in the right-hand column with the corresponding sentences in the left-hand column.

1. *Elle est née en Italie.*	a. *Elle a peur.*
2. *Une souris est dans la salle.*	b. *Elle a soif.*
3. *Elle est jeune.*	c. *Elle a besoin de vacances.*
4. *Il fait très chaud*	d. *Elle a vingt ans.*
5. *Elle est fatiguée.*	e. *Elle est italienne.*

The -re Verbs

Now that you've mastered the *-er* verbs, let's take a look at the *-re* verbs. For regular *-re* verbs, remove the *-re* ending and follow the pattern below, illustrated by the verb *entendre* (*to hear*).

j'entends	I hear	*nous entendons*	we hear
tu entends	you hear	*vous entendez*	you hear
il/elle entend	he/she hears	*ils/elles entendent*	they hear

Nous attendons le train.　　　　**We are waiting for the train.**
Ils rendent visite à leur tante.　　**They visit their aunt.**

Some *-re* verbs are irregular. The most common are derivatives of *prendre* (*to take*). Again, it's a matter of memorizing them.

je prends	I take	*nous prenons*	we take
tu prends	you take	*vous prenez*	you take
il/elle prend	he/she takes	*ils/elles prennent*	they take

Tu apprends le français. **You are learning French.**
Je comprends votre point de vue. **I understand your point of view.**

Exercise 3-8: Getting It Right

Write the full sentence using the correct verb form.

1. *Elle (vendre) des bijoux fantaisie.*

   ....

2. *Ils (attendre) une réponse de l'agent immobilier.*

   ....

3. *Nous (prendre) des vacances en mai.*

   ....

4. *Il (descendre) l'escalier.*

   ....

5. *Vous (apprendre) vos leçons.*

   ....

6. *Il (répondre) aux questions.*

   ....

7. *Je (prendre) le petit déjeuner sur la terrasse.*

   ....

8. *Elle (surprendre) ses amis avec des recettes de cuisines incroyables.*

   ....

9. *Elle (perdre) toujours ses affaires.*

....

10. *J' (entendre) un bruit bizarre.*

....

The -ir Verbs

The *-ir* verbs are divided into two types and follow different conjugation patterns. For the first type, like *choisir (to choose)*, drop the *-ir* ending and add an *-iss* to the plural forms plus the proper endings.

je choisis	I choose	*nous choisissons*	we choose
tu choisis	you choose	*vous choisissez*	you choose
il/elle choisit	he/she chooses	*ils/elles choisissent*	they choose

Nous réfléchissons à votre proposition. **We are thinking about your proposal.**
Ils bâtissent une villa. **They are building a villa.**

Here other verbs that follow the same conjugation pattern.

accomplir	to accomplish	*agrandir*	to enlarge
applaudir	to applaud	*évanouir (s')*	to faint
finir	to finish	*grandir*	to grow
grossir	to put on weight	*investir*	to invest
maigrir	to lose weight	*obéir*	to obey
remplir	to fill	*réussir*	to succeed

The second type of *-ir* verbs follow a different pattern, like *partir (to leave)* and *sortir (to go out)*.

je pars	I leave	*nous partons*	we leave
tu pars	you leave	*vous partez*	you leave
il/elle part	he/she leaves	*ils/elles partent*	they leave

Tu sors ce soir?	**Are you going out tonight?**
Je pars à midi.	**I am leaving at noon.**

Other verbs have a mind of their own and follow no real pattern.

Irregular –*ir* Verbs

couvrir	to cover	*je couvre*	*nous couvrons*
cueillir	to pick	*je cueille*	*nous cueillons*
mourir	to die	*je meurs*	*nous mourons*
obtenir	to obtain	*j'obtiens*	*nous obtenons*
offrir	to offer	*j'offre*	*nous offrons*
ouvrir	to open	*j'ouvre*	*nous ouvrons*
souffrir	to suffer	*je souffre*	*nous souffrons*

Exercise 3-9: Which -ir Is It?

Rewrite the whole sentence using the correct verb form.

1. *Je (offrir) des chocolats à ma soeur.*

   ....

2. *Elle (cueillir) des roses dans le jardin.*

   ....

3. *Elle (souffrir) de rhumatismes.*

   ....

4. *Ses étudiants (réussir) toujours aux examens.*

   ....

5. *Je te (servir) un café?*

   ....

6. *Ils (remplir) les verres de vin.*

   ....

7. *Tu (dormir) bien?.*

....

8. *Ils (investir) dans une nouvelle affaire.*

....

9. *Je (mourir) de faim!*

....

10. *Ils (applaudir) les comédiens.*

....

The -oir Verbs

The *-oir* verbs fall into different categories. Let's start with the most commonly used ones, *vouloir (to want)* and *pouvoir (can, may)*. *Vouloir* expresses will and wishes.

je veux	I want	*nous voulons*	we want
tu veux	you want	*vous voulez*	you want
il/elle veut	he/she wants	*ils/elles veulent*	they want

Vous voulez une tasse de thé?   **Do you want a cup of tea?**
Elle veut vivre à Paris.   **She wants to live in Paris.**

Pouvoir expresses capacity, ability, and permission.

je peux	I can	*nous pouvons*	we can
tu peux	you can	*vous pouvez*	you can
il/elle peut	he/she can	*ils/elles peuvent*	they can

Je ne peux pas assister à la réunion.   **I can't attend the meeting.**
Pouvez-vous être à la gare à dix heures?   **Can you be at the station at ten?**

A more formal conjugation is also found for the first person singular.

| *Puis-je vous aider?* | **May I help you?** |
| *Puis-je vous accompagner?* | **May I go with you?** |

Many other -*oir* verbs have no regular conjugation pattern. Try to memorize a few at a time.

apercevoir	to see, to perceive	*j'aperçois*	*nous apercevons*
décevoir	to disappoint	*je déçois*	*nous décevons*
prévoir	to foresee	*je prévois*	*nous prévoyons*
recevoir	to receive	*je reçois*	*nous recevons*
voir	to see	*je vois*	*nous voyons*
falloir	to be necessary	*il faut*	
pleuvoir	to rain	*il pleut*	
valoir	to be worth	*cela vaut*	

The verb *devoir* (*must, to have to*) takes on various nuances according to the context and the intonation. It may involve a suggestion or an obligation.

je dois	I must	*nous devons*	we must
tu dois	you must	*vous devez*	you must
il/elle doit	he/she must	*ils/elles doivent*	they must

Tu dois arriver à l'heure.	**You must arrive on time.**
Il doit venir ce soir.	**He is supposed to come tonight.**
Combien est-ce que je vous dois?	**How much do I owe you?**

Exercise 3-10: Conjugating –oir Verbs

Rewrite the whole sentence using the correct verb form.

1. *Vous (voir) souvent Julien?*

   ....

2. *Ils (vouloir) une plus grande maison.*

   ....

3. *Nous (prévoir) un voyage en Inde.*

   ....

4. *Tu (recevoir) beaucoup de courrier?*

   ....

5. *Je (pouvoir) vous envoyer de la documentation.*

   ....

6. *L'avion (devoir) arriver à vingt heures.*

   ....

7. *Tu (vouloir) y aller?*

   ....

8. *Il (pleuvoir) à Paris aujourd'hui.*

   ....

9. *Il nous (devoir) mille euros.*

   ....

10. *Vous (ne pas devoir) vous inquiéter.*

    ....

Exercise 3-11: Connect the Dots

Make an appropriate sentence by matching the phrase in the right-hand column with the phrase in the left-hand column.

1. *Tu veux*   a. *combien d'argent?*
2. *Il faut absolument*   b. *tous ses amis.*
3. *Elle te doit*   c. *prendre une décision!*
4. *Il déçoit*   d. *assister à la réunion?*
5. *Vous ne pouvez pas*   e. *un café bien chaud?*

Savoir *and* Connaître

Savoir (to know) is another *-oir* verb that will come in handy. It means *to know a fact* or *to know how to do something from practice.* But knowledge is not that simple. It is essential to study *savoir*'s counterpart *connaître* with its different nuances. *Connaître* means *to know, to be acquainted with, to be familiar with.*

Let's start with *savoir.*

je sais	I know	*nous savons*	we know
tu sais	you know	*vous savez*	you know
il/elle sait	he/she knows	*ils/elles savent*	they know

Il sait parler français.   **He knows how to speak French.**
Je ne sais pas pourquoi il est en retard.   **I don't know why he is late.**

je connais	I know	*nous connaissons*	we know
tu connais	you know	*vous connaissez*	you know
il/elle connaît	he/she knows	*ils/elles connaissent*	they know

Vous connaissez Madame Villepin?   **Do you know Mrs. Villepin?**
Il connaît tous les restaurants   **He knows all the restaurants**
   de la région.   **in the region.**

Exercise 3-12: *What Do I Know?*

TRACK 12

Listen to the audio track and rewrite each sentence in the negative form.

1. ....
2. ....
3. ....
4. ....
5. ....
6. ....
7. ....
8. ....
9. ....
10. ....

Exercise 3-13: Which One Is Right?

Complete each sentence, using the correct form of *savoir* or *connaitre*.

1. *Maud* .... *jouer au basket-ball.*

2. *Il* .... *bien Laurence.*

3. *Tu* .... *parler allemand?*

4. *Ils* .... *nager.*

5. *Nous* .... *très bien Venise.*

6. *Elle* .... *faire marcher cet appareil.*

7. *Je* .... *la mère de Béatrice.*

8. *Tu* .... *s'il va assister à la réunion?*

9. *Vous* .... *un bon restaurant vietnamien dans le quartier?*

10. *Qui* .... *?*

The Pronominal Verbs

When a verb is preceded by *me*, *te*, *se*, *nous*, or *vous*, it is called a pronominal verb. There are four kinds of pronominal verbs: the reflexive, the reciprocal, the subjective, and the passive.

A pronominal verb is reflexive when the action is reflected on the subject and the action is done to oneself.

je me lève	I get up	*nous nous levons*	we get up
tu te lèves	you get up	*vous vous levez*	you get up
il/elle se lève	he/she gets up	*ils/elles se lèvent*	they get up

Elle s'habille pour sortir.	**She is getting dressed to go out.**
À quelle heure se couche-t-il?	**At what time does he go to bed?**
Ils ne se reposent jamais.	**They never rest.**

A pronominal verb is reciprocal when both the subjects act on one another.

Ils se téléphonent deux fois par jour.	**They call each other twice a day.**
Vous vous écrivez?	**Do you write to each other?**
Ils ne s'aiment plus.	**They no longer love each other.**

A pronominal verb is subjective when it is neither reflexive nor reciprocal. Its fate is to be a pronominal verb.

Il se rend compte de son erreur.	**He realizes his mistake.**
Je ne me souviens pas de lui.	**I don't remember him.**
Dépêche-toi!	**Hurry up!**

A pronominal verb is passive when the subject does not perform the action but is subjected to it.

La cuisine asiatique se mange avec des baguettes.	**Asian cuisine is eaten with chopsticks.**
Ça ne se fait pas.	**That is not done.**

Exercise 3-14: What's Your Pronominal Type?

Indicate if the pronominal verb is reflexive, reciprocal, subjective, or passive.

1. .... *Je me brosse les dents.*

2. .... *Ils se disent bonjour.*

3. .... *Nous nous promenons le long du canal.*

4. .... *Je ne m'en souviens plus.*

5. .... *Ça ne se dit pas en public.*

6. .... *Ils se détestent.*

7. .... *Le Sancerre se boit frais.*

8. .... *Il ne se rend pas compte de son arrogance.*

9. .... *Ils s'embrassent tendrement.*

10. .... *Les frites se mangent avec les doigts.*

Exercise 3-15: Reflexive, Reciprocal, Subjective, or Passive?

Match the sentences in the right-hand column with the corresponding sentences in the left-hand column.

1. *Ils se promènent.*
2. *Ils se disputent.*
3. *Ils s'embrassent.*
4. *Ils se dépêchent.*
5. *Ils se couchent tôt.*

a. *Ils s'aiment.*
b. *Ils aiment marcher.*
c. *Ils sont fatigués.*
d. *Ils ne sont pas d'accord.*
e. *Ils sont pressés.*

The Progressive Form

To express an action in progress, *en train de* + the infinitive form of the verb is used.

Ne me dérange pas, je suis en train de travailler.

Do not disturb me, I am working!

Elle est en train de faire la cuisine.

She is cooking.

Exercise 3-16: In Progress!

Answer the questions with the elements in parentheses using *en train de.*

1. *Qu'est-ce que tu lis? (un roman policier)*

....

2. *Qu'est-ce qu'ils mangent? (un couscous)*

....

3. *Qu'est-ce qu'elle regarde? (un film de science-fiction)*

....

4. *Qu'est-ce qu'il chante? (un aria de Bellini)*

....

5. *Qu'est-ce qu'elle boit? (un thé au citron)*

....

6. *Qu'est-ce que tu écris? (une lettre de recommandation)*

....

7. *Qu'est-ce que tu cueilles? (des framboises)*

....

8. *Qu'est-ce que vous cherchez? (mes lunettes)*

....

9. *Qu'est-ce qu'elle envoie? (des cartes postales)*

....

10. *Qu'est-ce que tu corriges? (les devoirs des étudiants)*

....

The -eindre and -aindre Verbs

To close this chapter on verbs in the present tense, let's look at yet another category: the verbs ending in *-eindre* and *-aindre*, like *craindre (to fear)*, follow this pattern:

je crains	I fear	*nous craignons*	we fear
tu crains	you fear	*vous craignez*	you fear
il/elle craint	he/she fears	*ils/elles craignent*	they fear

Qu'est-ce qu'ils peignent?	**What are they painting?**
Tu te plains tout le temps!	**You are always complaining!**
Ils se teignent les cheveux pour la pièce?	**They dye their hair for the play?**

Exercise 3-17: Practicing with –eindre and –aindre Verbs

Write the whole sentence, using the correct verb form.

1. *Tu (craindre) le froid.*

....

2. *Elle (se plaindre) sans cesse.*

....

3. *Ils (peindre) la façade de l'édifice.*

....

4. *Je (plaindre) le pauvre homme sans un sou.*

....

5. *Cela (enfreindre) le règlement.*

....

6. *Il (atteindre) toujours le sommet.*

....

7. *Qu'est-ce que tu (peindre)?*

....

8. *Elle (éteindre) la lumière avant de sortir.*

....

9. *Il (feindre) l'enthousiasme.*

....

10. *Les circonstances le (contraindre) à accepter leur offre.*

....

Let's Recap

Now let's review what you have learned.

Exercise 3-18: Conjugate the Verbs

Conjugate the following verbs in the present tense.

1. *regarder*

....

....

....

2. *commencer*

....

....

....

3. *servir*

....

....

....

4. *devoir*

....

....

....

5. *peindre*

....

....

....

6. *apprendre*

....

....

....

7. *sortir*

....

....

....

8. *nager*

....

....

....

9. *attendre*

....

....

....

10. *recevoir*

....

....

....

Exercise 3-19: Make Your Own Sentences

Translate the following sentences.

1. They live in a large apartment in Paris.

....

2. She remembers her first trip to Europe.

....

3. He does not know anyone in Nantes.

....

4. We are French.

....

5. She prefers roses.

....

6. He is hungry.

....

7. They take their niece to the theater once a year.

....

8. I am waiting for the bus.

....

9. Does he know how to swim?

....

10. They are investing in India.

....

Exercise 3-20: To Have or to Be?

Answer the following questions affirmatively, starting with *"Oui, . . ."*

1. *Est-ce que tu as un jardin?*

....

2. *Est-il français?*

....

3. *Est-ce qu'elle est contente de son travail?*

....

4. *Tu as besoin d'un nouvel ordinateur?*

....

5. *A-t-il un dictionnaire bilingue?*

....

6. *Ont-ils envie de déménager?*

....

7. *Êtes-vous libre ce week-end?*

....

8. *Est-ce que tu as froid?*

....

9. *Est-ce que tu as de la famille au Canada?*

....

10. *Il a quarante ans?*

....

Exercise 3-21: Make It Work

Make an appropriate sentence by matching the phrase in the right-hand column with the phrase in the left-hand column.

1. *Il éteint*
2. *Nous recevons*
3. *Elle peint*
4. *Ils se promènent*
5. *Nous devons*

a. *le long du canal.*
b. *des tableaux abstraits.*
c. *beaucoup d'emails*
d. *travailler demain.*
e. *la lumière.*

Part 4

The Past

What happened? Had he forgotten the rendez-vous? Did he used to be this way? Will he have left a note? After studying this section, you will be able to answer all these mysterious tense questions. You will also study *il y a*—*there is, there are*—and some expressions of time and space. What is past is past—but what verb form do we use to express it? In French there are several verb forms that can be used when speaking about the past. In this part, we will look at four of them: the simple past tense, the imperfect, the pluperfect, and the future perfect.

The Simple Past Tense: Le Passé Composé

The most common past tense is the *passé composé* or compound past. This tense is used for actions that occurred and were completed in the past.

Il a regardé la télévision hier soir.	**He watched television last night.**
J'ai appelé Noémie ce matin.	**I called Noémie this morning.**

Note that there are different ways to translate the *passé composé* in English. It all depends on the context.

Elle a acheté une bicyclette.	**She bought a bicycle.**
	She has bought a bicycle.
	She did buy a bicycle.

The *passé composé* combines the past participle of the verb you are using with the present tense of an auxiliary verb, *avoir* or *être*.

Forming the Past Participle

The past participle is formed by adding an ending to the verb stem. Regular past participles take the following endings:

-er Verbs Take -é			
parler (to speak)			
j'ai parlé	I spoke	*nous avons parlé*	we spoke
tu as parlé	you spoke	*vous avez parlé*	you spoke
il/elle a parlé	he/she spoke	*ils/elles ont parlé*	they spoke

-ir Verbs Take -i			
choisir (to choose)			
j'ai choisi	I chose	*nous avons choisi*	we chose
tu as choisi	you chose	*vous avez choisi*	you chose
il/elle a choisi	he/she chose	*ils/elles ont choisi*	he/she chose

-re Verbs Take *-u*

entendre (to hear)

j'ai entendu	I heard	*nous avons entendu*	we heard
tu as entendu	you heard	*vous avez entendu*	you heard
il/elle a entendu	he/she heard	*ils/elles ont entendu*	they heard

Here is a sample list of some verbs that have regular past participles.

Verbs ending in *-er*

acheter	to buy	*acheté*	bought
aimer	to love	*aimé*	loved
changer	to change	*changé*	changed
chercher	to look for	*cherché*	looked for
commencer	to begin	*commencé*	begun
créer	to create	*créé*	created
danser	to dance	*dansé*	danced
donner	to give	*donné*	given
embrasser	to kiss	*embrassé*	kissed
essayer	to try	*essayé*	tried
étudier	to study	*étudié*	studied
fermer	to close	*fermé*	closed
garder	to keep	*gardé*	kept
laver	to wash	*lavé*	washed
manger	to eat	*mangé*	eaten
marcher	to walk	*marché*	walked
oublier	to forget	*oublié*	forgotten
penser	to think	*pensé*	thought

refuser	to refuse	*refusé*	refused
sauver	to save	*sauvé*	saved
travailler	to work	*travaillé*	worked
trouver	to find	*trouvé*	found
visiter	to visit	*visité*	visited

Verbs ending in *-ir*

abolir	to abolish	*aboli*	abolished
agir	to act	*agi*	acted
bâtir	to build	*bâti*	built
consentir	to consent	*consenti*	consented
dormir	to sleep	*dormi*	slept
établir	to establish	*établi*	established
finir	to finish	*fini*	finished
fournir	to supply	*fourni*	supplied
frémir	to shiver	*frémi*	shivered
gémir	to moan	*gémi*	moaned
grandir	to grow up	*grandi*	grown up
mentir	to lie	*menti*	lied
obéir	to obey	*obéi*	obeyed
partir	to leave	*parti*	left
punir	to punish	*puni*	punished
réfléchir	to reflect	*réfléchi*	reflected
réussir	to succeed	*réussi*	succeeded
sentir	to feel	*senti*	felt
servir	to serve	*servi*	served

trahir	to betray	*trahi*	betrayed
vieillir	to age	*vieilli*	aged

Verbs ending in -re

battre	to beat	*battu*	beat
combattre	to fight	*combattu*	fought
conclure	to conclude	*conclu*	concluded
convaincre	to convince	*convaincu*	convinced
défendre	to defend	*défendu*	defended
dépendre	to depend on	*dépendu*	depended on
interrompre	to interrupt	*interrompu*	interrupted
mordre	to bite	*mordu*	bitten
perdre	to lose	*perdu*	lost
prétendre	to claim	*prétendu*	claimed
rendre	to give back	*rendu*	given back
répandre	to spread	*répandu*	spread
répondre	to answer	*répondu*	answered
rompre	to break	*rompu*	broken
tordre	to twist	*tordu*	twisted
vendre	to sell	*vendu*	sold

The Passé Composé with Avoir

Once you know the past participle, you have half of the equation. Now you must combine the past participle with an auxiliary verb. Most verbs in the *passé composé* are conjugated with *avoir*, so let's first review the present tense of the verb *avoir*.

j'ai	**I have**	*nous avons*	**we have**
tu as	**you have**	*vous avez*	**you have**
il/elle a	**he/she has**	*ils/elles ont*	**they have**

When *avoir* is the auxiliary verb used, the past participle does not agree in gender and number with the subject of the verb. The past participle does agree with the direct object is when it precedes the verb.

Elle a défendu sa position.	**She defended her position.**
Elle l'a défendue.	**She defended it.**
Ils ont refusé l'invitation.	**They declined the invitation.**
Ils l'ont refusée.	**They declined it.**

Many verbs conjugated with *avoir* in the *passé composé* have irregular past participles that you simply have to learn by heart.

J'ai écrit à ma soeur.	**I wrote to my sister.**
Nous avons compris la situation.	**We understood the situation.**

Here is a sample list of irregular past participles.

acquérir	to acquire	*acquis*	acquired
apprendre	to learn	*appris*	learned
avoir	to have	*eu*	had
boire	to drink	*bu*	drunk
comprendre	to understand	*compris*	understood
conduire	to drive	*conduit*	driven
craindre	to fear	*craint*	feared
devoir	must	*dû*	had to
dire	to say	*dit*	said
écrire	to write	*écrit*	written
être	to be	*été*	been
faire	to do, to make	*fait*	done, made
falloir	to have to	*fallu*	had to
lire	to read	*lu*	read

mettre	to put	*mis*	put
mourir	to die	*mort*	died
naître	to be born	*né*	born
offrir	to offer	*offert*	offered
ouvrir	to open	*ouvert*	opened
peindre	to paint	*peint*	painted
plaire	to please	*plu*	pleased
pleuvoir	to rain	*plu*	rained
pouvoir	can, to be able to	*pu*	could, been able to
prendre	to take	*pris*	taken
recevoir	to receive	*reçu*	received
résoudre	to resolve	*résolu*	resolved
rire	to laugh	*ri*	laughed
savoir	to know	*su*	known
suivre	to follow	*suivi*	followed
vivre	to live	*vécu*	lived
voir	to see	*vu*	seen
vouloir	to want	*voulu*	wanted

The Passé Composé with Être

Some verbs use *être* instead of *avoir* in the *passé composé*. There is no specific rule as to why this occurs, so you will simply have to memorize them. Fortunately, the list is short. First, let us review the present tense of the verb *être*.

je suis	I am	*nous sommes*	we are
tu es	you are	*vous êtes*	you are
il/elle est	he/she is	*ils/elles sont*	they are

Here are the verbs conjugated with *être* in the *passé composé*.

aller	to go
arriver	to arrive
descendre	to go down
devenir	to become
entrer	to enter
monter	to go up
mourir	to die
naître	to be born
partir	to leave
rentrer	to return
rester	to stay
revenir	to return
sortir	to go out
tomber	to fall
venir	to arrive

Unlike the past participle of verbs conjugated with *avoir*, the past participle of verbs conjugated with *être* always agrees in gender and number with the subject.

Il est arrivé en retard.	**He arrived late.**
Elle est arrivée en retard.	**She arrived late.**
Ils sont nés en Belgique.	**They were born in Belgium.**
Elles sont nées en Belgique.	**They were born in Belgium.**

Exercise 4-1: Memorizing Passé Composé Endings

TRACK 13

Listen to and repeat the *passé composé* conjugations of three verbs, all conjugated using *avoir* as the auxiliary verb: *donner* (*to give*), *finir* (*to finish*) and *perdre* (*to lose*).

donner

j'ai donné

tu as donné

il/elle a donné

nous avons donné

vous avez donné

ils/elles ont donné

finir

j'ai fini

tu as fini

il/elle a fini

nous avons fini

vous avez fini

ils/elles ont fini

perdre

j'ai perdu

tu as perdu

il/elle a perdu

nous avons perdu

vous avez perdu

ils/elles ont perdu

TRACK 14

Now listen to and repeat the *passé composé* conjugations of three verbs, all conjugated using *être* as the auxiliary verb: *arriver* (*to arrive*), *partir* (*to leave*) and *descendre* (*to go down*).

arriver

je suis arrivé (e)

tu es arrivé (e)

il/elle est arrivé(e)

nous sommes arrivé(e)s

vous êtes arrivé (e)(s)

ils/elles sont arrivé(e)s

partir

je suis parti(e)

tu es parti(e)

il/elle est parti(e)

nous sommes parti(e)s

vous êtes parti(e)(s)

ils/elles sont parti(e)s

descendre

je suis descendu(e)

tu es descendu(e)

il/elle est descendu(e)

nous sommes descendu(e)s

vous êtes descendu(e)(s)

ils/elles sont descendu(e)s

Exercise 4-2: Who Did It?

Translate the correct pronoun for each of the following sentences:

1. (I, he, they) .... *a vu le film.*

2. (He, we, they) .... *avons refusé l'invitation.*

3. (She, you, we) .... *as travaillé en Italie.*

4. (He, you, they) .... *sont allés au musée.*

5. (I, we, they) .... *ai acheté un appartement.*

6. (You, we, they) .... *ont voyagé en France.*

7. (He, we, I) .... *a loué une voiture.*

8. (You, she, they) .... *est arrivée tard.*

9. (She, you, we) .... *a acheté le livre*

10. (You, she, they) .... *as compris le message.*

Exercise 4-3: And What Did They Do?

Fill in the correct verb form using the *passé composé*.

1. *Mon frère* .... *(perdre) toute sa fortune.*

2. *Le public* .... *(applaudir) les musiciens.*

3. *Nous* .... *(marcher) toute la journée.*

4. *Le spectacle* .... *(finir) très tard.*

5. *Ils* .... *(attendre) l'autobus une demi-heure.*

6. *L'enfant* .... *(mentir).*

7. *Elle* .... *(trouver) un sac dans la rue.*

8. *Vous* .... *(grandir) en France?*

9. *Nous* .... *(manger) dans un restaurant vietnamien.*

10. *La librairie* .... *(vendre) beaucoup de livres.*

Exercise 4-4: To Be Noted

Fill in the correct verb form using the *passé composé*. All of the verbs use *être* as the auxiliary verb, so be sure that the past participle agrees in gender and number with the subject.

1. *Pierre (monter)* .... *par l'escalier.*

2. *Nous (rentrer)* .... *à minuit.*

3. *Sa voiture (tomber)* .... *en panne près de Lyon.*

4. *Il (descendre)* .... *du train.*

5. *Elles (revenir)* .... *de vacances dimanche.*

6. *Elle (partir)* .... *à Paris?*

7. *Ils (aller)* .... *au concert hier soir.*

8. *Sylvie (aller)* .... *au Canada l'été dernier.*

9. *Son fils (devenir)* .... *médecin.*

10. *Je (naître)* .... *en Normandie.*

The Imperfect Past Tense: L'Imparfait

The *imparfait* or imperfect is another tense that is used to refer to the past. The *passé composé* is used when you are speaking about an action that took place on a specific occasion in the past. But what if this action was continuous or habitual? That is when the *imparfait* is the perfect tense to use! Note that there are different ways to translate the *imparfait* in English. It all depends on the context.

Il travaillait.   **He was working./He used to work./He worked.**

The *imparfait* is simple to conjugate. Take the *nous* form of the present tense and remove the *-ons* ending. This gives you the stem. Then add the *imparfait* endings (*-ais, -ais, -ait, -ions, -iez, -aient*) to this stem. For example:

penser (to think): nous pensons ⟶ pens-

je pensais	I thought	*nous pensions*	we thought
tu pensais	you thought	*vous pensiez*	you thought
il/elle pensait	he/she thought	*ils/elles pensaient*	they thought

Always remember to use the *nous* form of the verb in the present tense as changes sometimes occur in the conjugation.

dire (to say): nous disons ⟶ dis-

je disais	I said	*nous disions*	we said
tu disais	you said	*vous disiez*	you said
il/elle disait	he/she said	*ils/elles disaient*	they said

Note that the *-ais, -ait, -aient* endings are pronounced alike.

Verbs with spelling changes in the present tense *nous* form, like *manger* and *commencer*, retain the spelling change only for the *je, tu, il, elle, ils,* and *elles* subject pronouns.

je partageais	I shared
tu voyageais	you traveled
ils mangeaient	they ate
je prononçais	I pronounced
elle effaçait	she erased
ils commençaient	they started

With the *nous* and *vous* forms in the *imparfait,* the extra *e* or the *ç* is not needed.

nous voyagions	we traveled
vous partagiez	you shared

Note that while the verb *avoir* is has a regular stem in the *imparfait* (*nous avons* ——→ *av-*), *être* has an irregular one (*nous sommes* ——→ *ét-*).

j'étais	I was	*nous étions*	we were
tu étais	you were	*vous étiez*	you were
il/elle était	he/she was	*ils/elles étaient*	they were

Exercise 4-5: Complete Conjugations

Conjugate the following verbs in the *imparfait*.

1. *donner* (to give)

   ....

   ....

   ....

2. *finir* (to finish)

   ....

   ....

   ....

3. *perdre* (to lose)

   ....

   ....

   ....

4. *manger* (to eat)

   ....

   ....

   ....

5. *commencer* (to begin)

   ....

   ....

   ....

6. *être* (to be)

....

....

....

The Subtle Imparfait

The *imparfait* is the tense of choice for describing repetitive or continuous action in the past, but it has other, more subtle uses as well. It can be used for background and description. Or it can be used to describe a situation that existed in the past.

For example:

Il faisait froid.	**The weather was cold.**
Il neigeait.	**It was snowing.**
Le métro était en retard.	**The subway was late.**
La musique était merveilleuse.	**The music was marvelous.**
Elle était triste.	**She was sad.**

The *imparfait* is also used to describe a continuous action that was going on in the past when another action interrupted it. The interruption is expressed by the *passé composé*. Take a look at the following examples:

Marie dormait quand le téléphone a sonné.	**Marie was sleeping when the phone rang.**
Je me promenais dans le parc quand il a commencé à pleuvoir.	**I was walking in the park when it began to rain.**

What if you want to make a suggestion or extend an invitation? Once again, the *imparfait* is the perfect choice. When used in this way, we typically use a *si + on + imparfait* construction. The informal *on* refers to two or more people and is conjugated as the third person singular, just like *il/elle*.

Si on allait à la plage?	**What about going to the beach?**
Si on prenait l'autobus?	**What about taking the bus?**

Exercise 4-6: The Perfect Form of the Imperfect Tense

Fill in the correct verb form using the imperfect tense.

1. *Il (pleuvoir).* ....

2. *Nous (être) très fatigués.* ....

3. *Il (faire) très froid* ....

4. *L'enfant (pleurer).* ....

5. *Son idèe (être) très originale.* ....

6. *Le train (avoir) trois heures de retard.* ....

7. *Elle (faire) du jogging tous les matins.* ....

8. *Je (travailler) le week-end.* ....

9. *Nous (habiter) Paris.* ....

10. *L'ascenseur ne (marcher) pas.* ....

Exercise 4-7: Everyone Is Imperfect!

Give the correct verb forms in the *imparfait*.

1. *savoir (tu)* ....

2. *donner (nous)* ....

3. *grandir (vous)* ....

4. *être (elles)* ....

5. *manger (je)* ....

6. *comprendre (ils)* ....

7. *boire (tu)* ....

8. *avoir (je)* ....

9. *choisir (vous)* ....

10. *aller (tu)* ....

Exercise 4-8: Perfecting Your Imperfect

Write the whole sentence, using the correct verb from in the imperfect tense.

1. *Les danseurs (être) magnifiques.*

....

2. *Tous les jours, le petit garçon (aller) à l'école.*

....

3. *Elle (prendre) un bain quand le téléphone a sonné.*

....

4. *Nous ne (connaître) pas sa famille.*

....

5. *Son père (être) écrivain à vingt-cinq ans.*

....

6. *Sa grand-mère (avoir) deux chats.*

....

7. *Elle (lire) lorsque sa soeur est arrivée.*

....

8. *Ils (adorer) écouter le jazz.*

....

9. *Je (ignorer) ses problèmes.*

....

10. *Il (faire) beau à la plage.*

....

Exercise 4-9: The Power of Suggestion

Suggest an activity to a friend using the form *si + on + imparfait*. Follow the example below.

> **aller à la plage** ⟶ **Si on allait à la plage?**

1. *faire un gâteau*

....

2. *prendre le train*

....

3. *acheter des billets pour le concert*

....

4. *inviter les Dumas a dîner*

....

5. *voyager en Inde*

....

The Imparfait *Versus the* Passé Composé

The *imparfait* is a frequent topic for serious—and often quite lively—discussion among French grammarians. "Why did Flaubert use an *imparfait* here, when he probably meant to use a *passé simple*!" "Why did Camus use an *imparfait* here when it is obvious he should have used a *passé composé*?" Why ask such questions? Because of the subtleties of the *imparfait*! Discussions can be endless.

But it is not just grammarians who are concerned with multiple past tenses. Think about it. In your everyday usage, almost any time you tell a story, you will have to use multiple tenses. The next time you are reading something, try to pay special attention to the verbs. Combining the *imparfait* and the *passé composé* will probably be one of the most difficult skills you will have to master in French grammar, so remember: flexibility is the key. Compare and study the following examples.

Elle est allée en Espagne en novembre.	**She went to Spain in November.**
Dans son enfance, elle allait en Espagne tous les étés.	**When she was young, she used to go to Spain every summer.**
Nous avons attendu le train pendant une heure.	**We waited an hour for the train.**
Nous attendions le train quand il a commencé à neiger.	**We were waiting for the train when it started to snow.**
Je me suis promenée dans le parc cet après-midi.	**I took a walk in the park this afternoon.**
Je me promenais dans le parc quand tout à coup j'ai vu un faucon.	**I was walking in the park when suddenly I saw a falcon.**
Son pére a travaillé dans cette usine pendant vingt ans.	**His father worked in this factory for twenty years.**

Mon père travaillait dans cette usine depuis vingt ans quand il a décidé de prendre sa retraite.	**My father had been working in this factory for twenty years when he decided to retire.**
Vous avez bien dormi?	**Did you sleep well?**
Il dormait quand soudain le chien a commencé à aboyer.	**He was sleeping when suddenly the dog started to bark.**

Exercise 4-10: Past Subtleties

Write the whole sentence using the correct verb form in the *imparfait* or *passé composé*. In deciding which tense to use, pay careful attention to whether the action is specific or continuous.

1. *Sylvie (lire) quand son frère (téléphoner).*

   ....

2. *Vous (manger) quand on (frapper) à la porte.*

   ....

3. *Nous (se promener) quand il (commencer) à pleuvoir.*

   ....

4. *Il (faire la lessive) quand son copain (arriver).*

   ....

5. *Nous (danser) quand la musique (s'arrêter).*

   ....

Verbs Conjugated with Être or Avoir in the Passé Composé

Remember the list of verbs that arbitrarily use *être* instead of *avoir* when conjugated in the *passé composé*? Well, six of those verbs—*sortir, rentrer, monter, descendre, passer,* and *retourner*—can also be conjugated using *avoir*. When this happens, the past participle remains the same but it follows the *avoir* rule of agreement: the past participle agrees with the direct object when it precedes the verb.

Il est descendu au sous-sol.	**He went down to the basement.**
Il a descendu les poubelles.	**He took down the garbage cans.**
Elle est sortie avec son frère.	**She went out with her brother.**
Elle a sorti le chien.	**She took out the dog.**

Nous sommes rentrés de vacances hier.	We came back from vacation yesterday.
Nous avons rentré les plantes dans la maison.	We brought the plants into the house.
J'ai passé trois semaines en Italie.	I spent three weeks in Italy.
Je suis passée devant la pâtisserie.	I passed by the pastry shop.
Elle a retourné l'omelette.	She turned over the omelette.
Elle est retournée à Tahiti.	She went back to Tahiti.
Nous sommes montés en haut de la Tour Eiffel.	We climbed to the top of the Eiffel Tower.
Nous avons monté les valises au grenier.	We took the suitcases to the attic.

Exercise 4-11: The Passé Composé

Make an appropriate sentence by matching the phrase in the right-hand column with the phrase in the left-hand column.

1.	*Tu as sorti*	a. *l'omelette.*
2.	*Il a retourné*	b. *devant la librairie.*
3.	*Nous sommes rentrés*	c. *pour la troisième fois.*
4.	*Vous êtes passés*	d. *très tard.*
5.	*Je suis retourné en Italie*	e. *les chaises de jardin.*

The Pluperfect Tense: Le Plus-Que-Parfait

The *plus-que-parfait* or pluperfect is another tense used when speaking about the past. It is used primarily when describing events that had been completed before another past event took place. (Read the preceding sentence again and see how we use it in English!) It is formed by combining the *imparfait* of one of the two auxiliary verbs, *être* or *avoir*, with the past participle of the main verb.

Plus-Que-Parfait of Avoir and Être

First let's review the *imparfait* of these two auxiliary verbs.

être (to be)

j'étais	I was	*nous étions*	we were
tu étais	you were	*vous étiez*	you were
il/elle était	he/she was	*ils/elles étaient*	they were

avoir (to have)

j'avais	I had	*nous avions*	we had
tu avais	you had	*vous aviez*	you had
il/elle avait	he/she had	*ils/elles avaient*	they had

Now, let's look at some examples:

Marc était déjà parti quand nous sommes arrivés.

Marc had already left when we got there.

Sonia a pensé que vous aviez besoin de renseignements.

Sonia thought you had needed some information.

Pronominal Verbs

Pronominal verbs were introduced in Part 3. In all past tenses, the pronominal verbs are conjugated with *être*; the reflexive *pronom* agrees in gender and number with the subject. In the negative, the *ne* and *pas* are placed around *être*.

Ils se sont promenés dans le parc. **They walked in the park.**
Vous êtes-vous habitué à votre nouveau travail? **Did you get used to your new job?**
Luc s'est rendu compte qu'il s'était trompé. **Luc realized he had made a mistake.**
La police a decouvert que le voleur s'était échappé. **The police discovered the thief had escaped.**

Using the Plus-Que-Parfait

Sometimes in English the *plus-que-parfait* is translated as a simple tense. However, in French, if there is any anteriority in a series of actions, the *plus-que-parfait* must be used.

Louise avait mangé la soupe que sa mère avait préparée.

Louise had eaten the soup that her mother (had) prepared.

Exercise 4-12: Past and Perfect

Give the correct verb forms in the *plus-que-parfait*.

1. *donner (nous)* ....

2. *s'amuser (elles)* ....

3. *sortir (je)* ....

4. *chanter (tu)* ....

5. *mentir (elle)* ....

Exercise 4-13: All Done, All Finished!

Fill in the correct verb forms, using the *plus-que-parfait*.

1. *Ma soeur* .... *(louer) un appartement quai Voltaire.*

2. *Il* .... *(apprendre) les nouvelles par la radio.*

3. *Je* .... *(s'arrêter) sur le bord de la route.*

4. *Nous* .... *(acheter) les billets mais la direction (annuler) le concert.*

5. *Ils* .... *(commencer) à manger sans nous attendre*

6. *Elle* .... *(s'habituer) enfin à la neige.*

7. *Ses parents (parler) toujours du restaurant où ils* .... *(se rencontrer).*

8. *Nous* .... *(refaire) tout le décor du salon*

9. *Il* ....*(commander) une énorme pizza.*

10. *Mon frère était en colère car tout le monde* .... *(oublier) son anniversaire.*

The Future Perfect: Le Futur Antérieur

The *futur antérieur* or future perfect describes an action that will take place and be completed before another future action. It is formed with the future tense of the auxiliary verbs *être* or *avoir* and the past participle of the main verb. Agreement rules are the same as for the *passé composé*. Although it is rarely used in English, its usage is fairly common in French.

Future Tense of Avoir and Être

First, let's review the future tense of the verbs *avoir* and *être*.

avoir (to have)

j'aurai	I will have	*nous aurons*	we will have
tu auras	you will have	*vous aurez*	you will have
il/elle aura	he/she will have	*ils/elles auront*	they will have

être (to be)

je serai	I will be	*nous serons*	we will be
tu seras	you will be	*vous serez*	you will be
il/elle sera	he/she will be	*ils/elles seront*	they will be

Forming the futur antérieur

Now, let's look at some examples of the *futur antérieur*.

finir (to finish)

j'aurai fini	I'll have finished
tu auras fini	you'll have finished
il/elle aura fini	he/she will have finished
nous aurons fini	we'll have finished
vous aurez fini	you'll have finished
ils/elles auront fini	they'll have finished

arriver (to arrive)

je serai arrivé	I'll have arrived

tu seras arrivé	you'll have arrived
il/elle sera arrivé(e)	he/she will have arrived
nous serons arrivé(e)s	we'll have arrived
vous serez arrivé(e)(s)	you'll have arrived
ils/elles seront arrivé(e)s	they'll have arrived.

Note the following examples.

Il aura passé toute sa vie à lire. **He'll have spent his whole life reading.**
D'ici 2050, la planète aura changé. **By 2050, the planet will have changed.**

Other Uses of the Futur Antérieur

The *futur antérieur* can also be used to express a probability of a past action.

J'aurai encore perdu mes clés. **I probably lost my keys again!**
Il aura raté le train. **He probably missed the train.**

The *futur antérieur* is also used after *si*, implying a completed action.

Elle se demande s'il aura terminé **She wonders whether he'll have finished**
à temps. **on time.**
Je me demande s'ils auront acheté **I wonder whether they'll have bought**
les billets. **the tickets.**

Exercise 4-14: Back to the Future

Listen to each sentence and identify the verb in the *futur antérieur*.

TRACK 15

1. ....
2. ....
3. ....
4. ....
5. ....
6. ....

7. ....
8. ....
9. ....
10. ....
11. ....
12. ....

Exercise 4-15: Perfect Future Ahead

Fill in the correct verb forms in the *futur antérieur*.

1. *Je me coucherai quand je* .... *(finir) le livre.*

2. *Elle achètera une grande maison quand elle* ....
   (gagner) à la loterie.

3. *Le public applaudira les acteurs quand ils* .... *(terminer)*
   la scène.

4. *Nous nous sentirons mieux dès que nous* .... *(résoudre)*
   ce problème.

5. *Ils regarderont la télé aussitôt que les enfants* ....
   (s'endormir).

Expressions of Time and Space

Past, present, or future? Now or later? Here or there? It is not only the tense of the verb that tells us when an action takes place. French has many expressions that are useful when talking about time or space. Here are a few of them.

Adverbs and Expressions of Time	
aujourd'hui	today
hier	yesterday
demain	tomorrow
avant-hier	the day before yesterday
après-demain	the day after tomorrow
la semaine dernière	last week
la semaine prochaine	next week
dans trois jours	in three days; three days from now
dans une quinzaine	in two weeks
dans un mois	in a month
dans un an	in a year

il y a trois jours	three days ago
il y a deux semaines	two weeks ago
il y a un mois	a month ago
il y a un an	a year ago

These adverbs are used when you are speaking with people directly. This is known as the direct style. When you relate a story or talk about past and future events, you'll use the *discours indirect* or indirect speech. Here are some expressions that will be useful then.

le jour même	the very day
la veille	the day before
le lendemain	the day after
l'avant-veille	two days before
le surlendemain	two days later
la dernière semaine	the last week (of a sequence)
la semaine suivante	the following week

Here are some additional adverbs or expressions of time.

Additional Adverbs or Expressions of Time

actuellement	presently
parfois	sometimes
autrefois	formerly
quelquefois	sometimes
chaque jour	every day
tous les jours	every day
un jour sur deux	every other day
une semaine sur deux	every other week

à l'heure actuelle	at the present time
ces temps-ci	these days
souvent	often
rarement	seldom
d'habitude	usually
tard	late
ne ... jamais	never
de temps à autre	from time to time
longtemps	for a long time
de temps en temps	from time to time
maintenant	now
tôt	early
en ce moment	at the present time
toujours	always, still
d'ordinaire	ordinarily
tous les jours	every day

Exercise 4-16: When Is It the Right Time?

Fill in the correct adverbs in the following sentences.

1. *Serge arrive.* .... (tomorrow)? *Oui, Serge*

   arrive .... (tomorrow morning).

2. *Vous êtes libres* .... (next week)? *Non, nous*

   ne sommes pas libres .... (next week).

3. *Où vas-tu* .... (today)? *Je vais à*

   la plage .... (today).
4. *Vous mangez de la viande* .... (every day)? *Non,*

   nous mangeons de la viande .... (every other day).

5. *Tu rentres* .... (late) *ce soir? Non,*

   ce soir je rentre .... (early).

6. *Est-ce qu'elle est* .... (often) *triste?*

   Non, elle est .... (rarely) *triste.*

7. *Est-ce que vous allez* .... (sometimes) *à l'opéra?*

   Non, je ne vais .... (never) *à l'opéra.*

8. *Tu as beaucoup de temps libre* .... (these days)?

   Non, je suis très occupé .... (more than ever).

Expressing Time with the Passé Composé

To express time with the *passé composé*, *pendant* (for, during) is commonly used. However, *pour* (for) is never used for the past.

J'ai habité cinq ans à Montréal.	**I lived five years in Montreal.**
J'ai habité pendant cinq ans à Montréal.	**I lived for five years in Montreal.**
Nous avons voyagé deux mois en Bretagne.	**We traveled two months in Brittany.**
Il a voyagé pendant deux mois en Bretagne.	**He traveled for two months in Brittany.**

Exercise 4-17: Time to Change

Rewrite each sentence, changing the verb to the *imparfait* and filling in the correct adverb.

1. *Nous voyageons* (often) *en France.*

   ....

2. *On dîne* (early) *chaque jour.*

   ....

3. *Ils sortent* (rarely) *le soir.*

   ....

4. *Elles écrivent des lettres* (from time to time).

....

5. *Ils lisent* (sometimes) *des journaux étrangers.*

....

Exercise 4-18: Time to Say It Yourself

Translate the following sentences using some of the expressions of time.

1. Yesterday was the first day of winter.

....

2. She rarely calls.

....

3. I was never on time.

....

4. They left last week.

....

5. His birthday is next month.

....

Adverbs and Expressions of Location

Not only is it important to know when an action occurs, it is often important to know where. Here are some words that are useful when talking about location.

ailleurs	elsewhere	*dessous*	under
auprés	next to, close to	*dessus*	on top
là-bas	over there	*devant*	in front of
à cet endroit	in this place	*ici*	here
à côté de	next to, beside	*là*	there
dedans	inside	*ça et là*	here and there

dehors	outside	*là-haut*	up there
derrière	behind	*loin*	far
partout	everywhere	*près*	near, close

Exercise 4-19: Animal Life

TRACK 16

Listen to the story and write down each adjective and adverb.

Adjectives: ....

....

Adverbs: ....

....

....

Exercise 4-20: Adverbs

Translate the following sentences using some of the expressions of location.

1. He sees mistakes everywhere.

....

2. Yesterday, we had dinner outdoors.

....

3. I lived here but I worked elsewhere.

....

4. She put her hand on top.

....

5. How about going to the beach? It is not too far.

....

6. He is in front of you.

....

7. He is behind us.

....

8. It is not far.

....

9. There is dust here and there.

....

10. She must be somewhere.

....

IL Y A

Il y a is a handy expression with many uses. It is a way of stating the existence of people and things: *there is, there are.* Look at the following examples.

Il y a du monde ici.	**There are a lot of people here.**
Y a-t-il un problème?	**Is there a problem?**
Est-ce qu'il y a une solution?	**Is there a solution?**
Non, il n'y a pas de solution.	**No, there is no solution.**

Il y a . . . que is a useful expression when you want to ask a question about the duration of an action that began in the past and continues in the present.

Here are some examples of the way in which it is used:

Il y a une heure que nous attendons.	**We have been waiting for an hour.**
Il y a deux jours que je travaille sur ce projet.	**I have been working on this project for two days.**
Il y a deux semaines que nous sommes en vacances.	**We have been on vacation for two weeks.**

Notice that in the examples, the French sentences use the present tense while the English version uses the past. Why the difference? The *imparfait* is the appropriate tense to use when we want to indicate habitual action in the past, so it would seem to be the logical choice here. However, because the action is continuing in the present, it is the present tense that is used in French.

Il y a is also a way to express the idea of *ago*, as in the following examples.

J'ai acheté ce livre il y a trois semaines.	**I bought this book three weeks ago.**
Il est parti en vacances il y a un mois.	**He left on vacation one month ago.**

When *il y a* is used in this way, the verb tense is in the *passé composé* because the action began in the past and was completed in the past.

Exercise 4-21: There Are Many Ways to Express Yourself

Translate the following sentences using the correct form of *il y a*.

1. There is a problem with the train this morning.

   ....

2. I have been waiting for an hour.

   ....

3. She went to Paris five years ago.

   ....

4. We have been living in New York for five years.

   ....

5. He left two hours ago.

   ....

Part 5

Future, Conditional, and Idiomatic Expressions

I n this part we will review the simple future, the future perfect, and the present and past conditional. With the different tenses, you will be able to refer to events that will take place, that will have taken place, that should take place, or that should have taken place. Once you become comfortable using them, you will no longer be limited to speaking of things only in terms of the immediate present or past. You will also review the verb *faire* and its idioms, the causative form, and the idiomatic expression *il s'agit de*. As you incorporate them into your spoken or written language, your French will become more nuanced and more precise.

The Simple Future

We reviewed the immediate future (*futur immédiat*) in Part 4. French has two other future tenses: the simple future (*futur simple*) and the future perfect (*futur antérieur*). To form the simple future of most verbs, use the infinitive as the stem and add the ending *ai, -as, -a, -ons, -ez,* or *-ont.* For verbs ending in *-re,* drop the *e* from the infinitive. Here are samples of the simple future of an *-er,* an *-ir,* and an *-re* verb.

donner (to give)

je donnerai	I'll give	*nous donnerons*	we'll give
tu donneras	you'll give	*vous donnerez*	you'll give
il/elle donnera	he/she will give	*ils/elles donneront*	they'll give

finir (to finish)

je finirai	I'll finish	*nous finirons*	we'll finish
tu finiras	you'll finish	*vous finirez*	you'll finish
il/elle finira	he/she will finish	*ils/elles finiront*	they'll finish

comprendre (to understand)

je comprendrai	I'll understand
tu comprendras	you'll understand
il/elle comprendra	he/she will understand
nous comprendrons	we'll understand
vous comprendrez	you'll understand
ils/elles comprendront	they'll understand

The simple future endings are the same for all verbs, but some verbs have irregular stems. Here are some examples.

j'irai	I'll go	*il pleuvra*	it'll rain
j'apercevrai	I'll notice	*je pourrai*	I'll be able to

j'aurai	I'll have	*je recevrai*	I'll recieve
je courrai	I'll run	*je saurai*	I'll know
je devrai	I'll have to	*je tiendrai*	I'll hold
j'enverrai	I'll send	*il vaudra*	it will be worth
je serai	I'll be	*je viendrai*	I'll come
je ferai	I'll do	*je verrai*	I'll see
il faudra	it will be necessary	*je voudrai*	I'll want

Some slight spelling modifications occur with some verbs:

appeler (to call)	*j'appellerai*
acheter (to buy)	*j'achèterai*
jeter (to throw)	*je jetterai*

There are many verbs that are irregular in the present tense but that are regular in the simple future. Here are a few examples.

je boirai	I'll drink	*je lirai*	I'll read
je conduirai	I'll drive	*je mettrai*	I'll put
j'écrirai	I'll write	*je prendrai*	I'll take

Exercise 5-1: Upcoming Events

Rewrite each sentence, changing the verb to the simple future tense.

1. *Je vais au musée.*

....

2. *Nous arrivons en retard.*

....

3. *Elle lit votre livre.*

....

4. *Vous apprenez le chinois.*

....

5. *Ils dînent chez leurs parents.*

....

6. *Nous partons en vacances.*

....

7. *Caroline travaille le week-end.*

....

8. *Tu prends le métro.*

....

9. *Robert fait du ski en hiver.*

....

Exercise 5-2: Find the Mistake

TRACK 17

Some sentences on this track use incorrect verb forms. Find the mistakes and write the sentence correctly.

1. ....

2. ....

3. ....

4. ....

5. ....

6. ....

7. ....

8. ....

9. ....

10. ....

Using the Simple Future

In a compound sentence, if the main clause is in the simple future, the dependent clause, introduced by certain conjunctions, will be also in the future. These conjunctions are:

quand	when
lorsque	when
dès que	as soon as
aussitôt que	as soon as
tant que	as long as

The simple future is used after certain conjunctions when expressing a future action; in English, the present tense is often used. For example:

Luc viendra à New-York quand il pourra.	**Luc will come to New York when he can.**
Lorsque j'aurai dix-huit ans, je voterai.	**When I am eighteen, I will vote.**

The simple future is also used in combination with a *si* clause in the present tense. For example:

Ils iront au musée si c'est possible.	**They'll go to the museum if it's possible.**
S'il pleut demain, je resterai chez moi.	**If it rains tomorrow, I'll stay home.**

In a narration, the simple future can be used to express a future idea from the standpoint of the past as shown in the following examples.

La plus belle femme du monde et elle ne se mariera jamais.	**The most beautiful woman in the world would never marry.**
Un des plus grands musiciens de son époque et il mourra sans un sou.	**One of the greatest musicians of his time would die without a penny.**

Exercise 5-3: Future x 2

Give the correct verb forms in the simple future.

1. *Le concert (commencer) quand tout le monde (être) assis.*

   ....

2. *Nous (prendre) beaucoup de photos quand nous (voyager) en France.*

   ....

3. *J'(acheter) le livre quand j' (aller) à la librairie.*

   ....

4. *Quand il (être) grand, il (devenir) médecin.*

   ....

5. *Dès que tu (arriver), je t' (expliquer) la situation.*

   ....

6. *Nous (prendre) une décision dès que nous (avoir) les faits.*

   ....

7. *Il (apprendre) le chinois quand il (habiter) en Chine.*

   ....

8. *Je (jouer) au tennis quand je (être) en vacances.*

   ....

9. *Dès que vous (finir) vous (partir).*

   ....

10. *Le musée (fermer) en avril quand la construction (commencer).*

    ....

The Future Perfect

As discussed in Chapter 4, the future perfect (*futur antérieur*) describes an action that will take place and be completed before another future action. It is formed with the future tense of *être* or *avoir* and the past participle of the main verb. Agreement rules are the same as for the *passé composé*. Although it is rarely used in English, its usage is fairly common in French.

lire (to read)

j'aurai lu	I'll have read	*nous aurons lu*	we'll have read
tu auras lu	you'll have read	*vous aurez lu*	you'll have read
il/elle aura lu	he/she will have read	*ils/elles auront lu*	they'll have read

Let's look at the following examples:

Il aura passé toute sa vie à voyager.   **He'll have spent his whole life traveling.**
D'ici lundi, il aura fini son roman.   **By Monday, he will have finished his novel.**

Exercise 5-4: The Future Is Perfect

Give the correct verb forms in the future perfect.

1. *Elle (étudier) l'anglais au Canada.* ....

2. *J'(finir) le projet avant la fin du mois* ....

3. *Nous (visiter) plusieurs pays en Asie* ....

4. *Les acteurs (jouer) dans une nouvelle pièce.* ....

5. *On (développer) un système plus efficace.* ....

6. *Vous (écrire) à toute la famille.* ....

7. *Nous (se reposer) des semaines à la campagne.* ....

8. *Elle (compléter) son stage de formation.* ....

9. *Son oncle (mourir) depuis longtemps.* ....

10. *Il ne (voir) jamais l'essentiel.* ....

Sometimes you have a choice between the simple future and the future perfect. When both clauses use the simple future, it is implied that both actions take place simultaneously.

Exercise 5-5: In the Future

Put the first verb in the simple future and the second verb in the future perfect.

1. *Nous (faire) le tour du monde quand nous (gagner) à la loterie.*

   ....

2. *Le public (applaudir) la chanteuse quand elle (terminer) sa chanson.*

   ....

3. *Je (se sentir) mieux dès que le temps (s'améliorer).*

   ....

4. *Les parents (regarder) la télé aussitôt que les enfants (s'endormir).*

   ....

5. *Tu (envoyer) un chèque quand tu (recevoir) l'argent.*

   ....

Using the Future Perfect

If you want to indicate that one action will have taken place before another in the future, use the future perfect. For example:

Elle vous écrira dès qu'elle aura fini ses devoirs	**She'll write you as soon as she finishes her homework.**
Dès que vous aurez accepté notre proposition, nous en discuterons plus longuement.	**As soon as you accept our proposal, we'll discuss it at length.**

The future perfect can also express a probability of a past action, in the same way that the simple future is used to express probability in the present.

Il aura encore échoué à ses examens.	**He probably failed his exams!**
Elle aura encore brûlé le gigot d'agneau!	**She probably burnt the leg of lamb!**
J'aurai manqué mon avion.	**I probably missed my plane.**
Mon frère aura encore fait des bêtises!	**My brother probably got in trouble again!**

The future perfect is also used after *si*, when it is used to mean *whether*. The future perfect is not used after *si* when it implies a condition.

Je me demande si j'aurai reçu sa lettre à temps.	**I am wondering whether I'll have received his letter in time.**
Si nous avons le temps, nous passerons vous voir.	**If we have time, we'll stop by to see you.**

Exercise 5-6: Will You Translate This?

Translate the following sentences into French.

1. We'll go to the movies.

   ....

2. He'll need to sell his car.

   ....

3. I'll take a literature course.

   ....

4. She'll visit Brittany when she is in France.

   ....

5. They'll go to Spain next summer.

   ....

6. We'll walk along the beach.

   ....

7. He'll study Italian when he is in Rome.

   ....

8. I'll see the Matisse exhibition when I am in Paris.

   ....

9. They'll travel to Asia when they have the time.

   ....

10. She'll become a lawyer.

    ....

Present Conditional

The present conditional (*conditionnel présent*) is formed by adding the endings of
the imperfect (*imparfait*) to the future stem of a verb. For the *-re* verbs, drop the *e*
from the infinitive. As we have seen, some verbs have an irregular future stem.

dire (to say)

je dirais	I would say	*nous dirions*	we would say
tu dirais	you would say	*vous diriez*	you would say
il/elle dirait	he/she would say	*ils/elles diraient*	they would say

aller (to go)

j'irais	I would go	*nous irions*	we would go
tu irais	you would go	*vous iriez*	you would go
il/elle irait	he/she would go	*ils/elles iraient*	they would go

Exercise 5-7: Would You Please . . .

Give the correct verb forms in the present conditional.

1. *aller (je)* ....

2. *comprendre (il)* ....

3. *lire (vous)* ....

4. *avoir (nous)* ....

5. *chanter (elle)* ....

6. *vendre (tu)* ....

7. *être (elles)* ....

8. *anticiper (vous)* ....

9. *défendre (ils)* ....

10. *savoir (nous)* ....

Uses of the Present Conditional

The present conditional has many uses. It is used to express a wish or a suggestion.

Je voudrais partir aussitôt que possible.	**I would like to leave as soon as possible.**

It can be used to make a statement or a request more polite.

Voudriez-vous venir nous voir ce soir?	**Would you like to come and see us this evening?**
Est-ce qu'elle pourrait te donner un coup de main?	**Could she give you a hand?**

It can also be used when a condition is implied. When the main clause is in the present conditional, the *si* clause is in the imperfect (*imparfait*).

Elle prendrait un taxi si elle était pressée.	**She would take a cab if she were in a hurry.**

The present conditional is also used to express unconfirmed or alleged information. In this case, it is called the journalistic conditional (*conditionnel journalistique*) and you will often see it used when reading the newspaper or listening to the news.

Le président se rendrait aux États-Unis vendredi.	**The president is reportedly going to the United States on Friday.**
Son porte-parole démissionnerait lundi.	**His spokesman is reportedly going to resign on Monday.**

Exercise 5-8: Nothing but Conditions!

TRACK 18

Listen to the audio track and repeat. Then listen again and reverse the sentence, each starting with the *si* clause. Write the new sentence.

1. ....

2. ....

3. ....

4. ....

5. ....

6. ....

7. ....

8. ....

9. ....

10. ....

Exercise 5-9: Make It Conditional

Translate the following sentences into French, conjugating the verbs in parentheses using *tu* when necessary and inversion.

1. Would you *(aller)* to Mongolia?

....

2. Would he *(passer)* to your home?

....

3. Would you *(changer)* the time of your departure?

....

4. Would you *(aimer)* to come with us?

....

5. Would he *(refuser)* to see it?

....

6. Would you *(nourrir)* my dog?

....

7. Would he *(prendre)* a flight later?

....

8. Would you *(suivre)* a dance course with me?

....

9. Would we *(discuter)* this project in the spring?

....

10. Would they *(accepter)* our offer?

....

Exercise 5-10: It's All Conditional

Put the first verb in the present conditional and the second verb in the imperfect.

1. *Ils (être) contents si nous (venir).*

....

2. *J' (aller) à la plage s'il (faire) chaud.*

....

3. *Elle (prendre) des vacances en été si elle (pouvoir).*

....

4. *Nous (emmener) Louise au Musée d'Orsay si elle (venir) à Paris.*

....

5. *Il y (avoir) moins de violence si les hommes (être) plus raisonnables.*

....

6. *Il (étudier) la danse s'il (être) plus souple.*

....

7. *J'(acheter) un parapluie s'il (pleuvoir).*

....

8. *Tu lui (donner) de l'argent s'il en (avoir) besoin.*

....

9. *Nous (être) ravis si tu nous (inviter).*

....

10. *Je (venir) si tu le me (demander).*

....

Exercise 5-11: What If?

Put the verbs in the *si* clause in the imperfect and those in the main clause in the conditional.

1. *Si j' (avoir) plus d'argent, je (travailler) moins.*

....

2. *Si elle (attendre), elle (obtenir) un meilleur prix pour son appartement.*

....

3. *Si tu (planter) plus de fleurs, tu (avoir) un plus beau jardin.*

....

4. *Si je (vendre) ce tableau, je (pouvoir) acheter cette sculpture.*

....

5. *Si nous (pouvoir), nous (partir) la semaine prochaine.*

....

6. *Si vous les (inviter), nous (être) très contents.*

....

Exercise 5-12: Demanding Conditions

Translate the following sentences using *vous* when necessary.

1. We would go to Paris if we had more time.

....

2. She would buy this dress if it were less expensive.

....

3. I would be grateful if you accompanied me to the station.

....

4. He would write a letter if you needed it.

....

5. The prime minister is reportedly in India today.

....

The Past Conditional

The past conditional (*conditionnel passé*) expresses what would have happened if another event had taken place or if certain conditions had not been present. It is formed with the present conditional of *être* or *avoir* and the past participle of the main verb. The rules of agreement common to all compound tenses still apply.

donner (to give)

j'aurais donné	I would have given
tu aurais donné	you would have given
il/elle aurait donné	he/she would have given
nous aurions donné	we would have given
vous auriez donné	you would have given
ils auraient donné	they would have given

Exercise 5-13: I Would Have Said It!

Listen to the audio track and repeat. Then listen again and write down each verb in the past conditional.

TRACK 19

1. ....

2. ....

3. ....

4. ....

5. ....

6. ....

7. ....

8. ....

9. ....

10. ....

Uses of the Past Conditional

The past conditional has a number of uses. It can be used to express regret or reproach.

Elle aurait voulu y assister.	**She would have liked to attend.**
J'aurais aimé le féliciter.	**I would have liked to congratulate him.**
Cela aurait été tellement plus facile.	**It would have been so much easier.**

The past conditional is usually found with a *si* clause in the pluperfect (*plus-que-parfait*).

Il aurait fini plus tard si tu ne l'avais pas aidé.	**He would have finished later if you had not helped him.**
Nous serions arrivés à l'heure s'il y avait eu moins de circulation.	**We would have arrived on time if there had been less traffic.**

The past conditional, like the present conditional, is used as a journalistic conditional (*conditionnel journalistique*) to make a statement not confirmed by authorities. In most cases where the word *allegedly* or *reportedly* is used in English, the conditional will be used.

Le tremblement de terre aurait fait des milliers de victimes au Mexique.	**The earthquake reportedly killed thousands of people in Mexico.**
Il aurait volé la voiture de son voisin.	**He allegedly stole his neighbor's car.**

The conditional or the past conditional are also used with *au cas où* (*in case*).

Au cas où ce livre ne vous plairait pas, dites-le-moi.	**In case you do not like this book, let me know.**
Au cas où tu n'aurais pas retrouvé tes clés, mon frère s'occupera de toi.	**In case you did not find your keys, my brother will take care of you.**

Exercise 5-14: Past Conditional and Pluperfect

Put the first verb in the past conditional and the second verb in the pluperfect.

1. *Nous (aller) avec vous si nous (pouvoir).*

   ....

2. *Il (visiter) cette ville s'il (avoir) plus de temps.*

   ....

3. *Elles (voir) ce film s'il (être) sous-titré.*

   ....

4. *J' (inviter) Luc s'il (ne pas travailler) ce soir-là.*

   ....

5. *Il (écrire) une pièce sur ce sujet s'il (trouver) les acteurs pour le jouer.*

   ....

6. *Elle (vendre) leur appartement si ses enfants (décider) de déménager.*

   ....

7. *Vous (arriver) en retard si votre voiture (tomber) en panne.*

   ....

Exercise 5-15: Pluperfect and Conditional

Put the first verb in the pluperfect and the second verb in the past conditional.

1. *Si elle (finir) ses devoirs, elle (pouvoir) sortir le week-end.*

   ....

2. *Si tu (mettre) ton manteau, tu (ne pas avoir) si froid.*

   ....

3. *Si la victime (pouvoir) témoigner au tribunal, la situation (être) différente.*

   ....

4. *Si on (ne pas guillotiner) le roi, l'histoire du pays (prendre) une tournure différente.*

   ....

5. *Si nous (étudier) la grammaire, nous (faire) moins de fautes.*

   ....

Exercise 5-16: Conditional Past and Present

Rewrite each sentence, changing the verbs from the present conditional to the past conditional, and from the imperfect to the pluperfect.

1. *Le chat mangerait s'il avait faim.*

   ....

2. *J'assisterais au concert si j'étais en ville.*

   ....

3. *Nous jouerions au tennis s'il ne pleuvait pas.*

   ....

4. *Il vous enverrait un message s'il n'était pas si occupé.*

   ....

5. *Tu lui expliquerais la décision s'il te contactait.*

   ....

Exercise 5-17: Our Sources Tell Us . . .

Translate the following sentences using the present or past journalistic conditional.

1. The President reportedly went to China last week.

   ....

2. The victim allegedly gave the police a complete description.

   ....

3. The snowstorm reportedly killed several people in the Alps.

   ....

4. The director reportedly resigned.

   ....

5. The fire has reportedly destroyed dozens of houses.

   ....

6. Unemployment is reportedly going to increase next year.

   ....

7. The President reportedly signed the agreement.

   ....

8. Many species are reportedly in danger because of global warming.

....

9. A bank employee allegedly stole the money.

....

10. The writer reportedly refused to sign the contract.

....

Exercise 5-18: Just in Case

Make an appropriate sentence by matching the phrase in the right-hand column with the phrase in the left-hand column.

1. *Au cas où il pleuvrait*   a. *tu viendrais avec moi.*
2. *Au cas où vous l'auriez oublié*   b. *elle pourrait se servir des miennes.*
3. *Au cas où ta voiture serait en panne* c. *prenez un parapluie.*
4. *Au cas où elle aurait perdu ses lunettes* d. *prévenez la police.*
5. *Au cas où quelque chose aurait été volé* e. *c'est mon anniversaire vendredi.*

Could, Would, and Should

Could, would, and should have different meanings in English and are translated in several ways in French. Every time you come across one of these words, make sure to examine its nuance in English.

Could

When *could* refers to a single, unique action in the past, the *passé composé* of *pouvoir* is used.

Je n'ai pas pu venir.   **I could not come.**

When "could" refers to a description or a habitual action, the imperfect of *pouvoir* is used.

À cette époque-là, les femmes ne   **At that time, women**
pouvaient pas travailler en dehors   **could not work outside**
de la maison.   **the home.**

When *could* refers to a future idea, a hypothesis, or a suggestion, the present conditional of *pouvoir* is used.

Pourriez-vous venir me voir la semaine prochaine?	**Could you come and see me next week?**

Should

When *should* means *ought to*, the present or past conditional is used.

Ils devraient être moins bruyants.	**They should be less noisy.**

When *should* refers to a hypothetical situation, the imperfect is used.

Si vous aviez besoin de quoi que ce soit, n'hésitez pas à me contacter.	**If you should need anything, do not hesitate to contact me.**

Would

When *would* refers to a repeated action in the past, the imperfect is used.

Quand j'étais jeune, j'allais à la plage tous les jours en été.	**When I was young, I would go to the beach every day in the summer.**

When *would* refers to a polite request, the conditional is used.

Voudriez-vous baisser le volume?	**Would you mind turning down the volume?**

When *would* refers a future idea, a hypothesis, or a suggestion, the main verb is in the present conditional.

Il s'inscrirait à ce cours s'il y avait de la place.	**He would sign up for this course if there were some space.**

Exercise 5-19: I Would If I Could

Translate the following sentences, using *tu* and the inversion.

1. Could you help me?

   ....

2. He should have not told you the ending of the film.

   ....

3. Would you mind coming later?

   ....

4. We would go to Rome if we had the time.

   ....

5. I should not have eaten so much chocolate!

   ....

The Verb Faire

The verb *faire* (*to do, to make*) is an important one, and it is used in many idiomatic expressions. Let's first review its irregular conjugation.

je fais	I do	*nous faisons*	we do
tu fais	you do	*vous faites*	you do
il/elle fait	he/she does	*ils/elles font*	they do

Faire is used in most expressions relating to the weather.

Quel temps fait-il?	**What's the weather like?**
Il fait beau.	**It is nice.**

Faire is also used in expressions relating to chores, activities, and sports.

Elle fait la cuisine.	**She is cooking.**
Son mari fait la vaisselle.	**Her husband is doing the dishes.**

Exercise 5-20: Julie's Sunday

TRACK 20

Listen to Julie's story and then describe what Julie decides to do on Sunday afternoon.

....

....

....

....

Exercise 5-21: Make a Match

Match the phrases in the right-hand column with the corresponding sentences in the left-hand column.

1. *Elle aime préparer à manger.*
2. *J'aime dormir l'après-midi.*
3. *Nous aimons marcher à la montagne.*
4. *Ils aiment explorer des pays.*
5. *Tu aimes acheter des choses.*

a. *faire un voyage*
b. *faire une randonnée*
c. *faire les courses*
d. *faire la cuisine*
e. *faire la sieste*

The Causative Form: Using Faire + Infinitive

The verb *faire* may be followed by an infinitive to express the idea of having something done by someone or of causing something to happen. It is formed using the verb *faire* followed by the infinitive form of another verb.

Je répare l'objet cassé moi-même.	**I repair the broken object myself.**
Je fais réparer l'objet cassé par un professionel.	**I have the broken object repaired by a professsional.**
Il lave la voiture.	**He washes the car.**
Il fait laver la voiture.	**He has the car washed.**
Vous plantez les fleurs vous-même?	**Do you plant the flowers yourself?**
Non, je fais planter les fleurs par le jardinier.	**No, I have the flowers planted by the gardener.**

Exercise 5-22: How Do You Do . . .

TRACK 21

Listen to the audio track and repeat. Then listen again and answer the questions using the causative form and integrating the element in parentheses.

EXAMPLE
You see: (un jardinier)
You hear: Est-ce que tu plantes les fleurs toi même?
You write: Non, je fais planter les fleurs par un jardinier

1. *(un architecte)*

   ....

2. *(un chef)*

   ....

3. *(une couturière)*

   ....

4. *(un peintre professionnel)*

   ....

5. *(mon secrétaire)*

   ....

Exercise 5-23: Whodunit

Rewrite each sentence, changing the verb to the causative form.

EXAMPLE: *Je lave ma voiture.* ⟶ *Je fais laver ma voiture.*

1. *Vous écrivez la lettre.*

   ....

2. *Je fais la cuisine.*

   ....

3. *Il répare la voiture.*

   ....

4. *Tu envoies le message.*

   ....

5. *Nous préparons le dîner.*

....

6. *Vous lisez le dossier.*

....

7. *Il investit sa fortune.*

....

8. *Vous remplacez l'employé malade.*

....

9. *Le professeur corrige les examens des étudiants.*

....

10. *Je chante la chanson.*

....

Using the Idiom Il S'agit De

Another frequently used French idiom is *il s'agit de* (*it is a matter of, it is about*). Take a look at the following examples.

De quoi s'agit-il?	**What is it about?**
Il s'agit d'amour.	**It is a question of love.**
Il s'agit de vengeance.	**It is about revenge.**

Exercise 5-24: What's It All About?

Translate the following sentences using *il s'agit de*.

1. This novel is about an artist.

....

2. This film is about gangsters in Chicago.

....

3. This book is about politics.

....

4. This film is about love.

....

Part 6

Adjectives and Adverbs

Adjectives and adverbs are keys to describing objects, people, places, or actions. Adjectives modify nouns and adverbs modify verbs. Their purpose is to better describe the objects or actions they modify. Using them in your speech allows you to create much more complex—and interesting—statements. Adjectives agree in gender and number with the nouns they modify, while adverbs do not change form.

Qualifying Adjectives

Qualifying adjectives help to describe things and people. They agree in gender and number with the noun they modify. To form the feminine you usually need to add an *e* to the masculine form.

Il est content. Elle est contente.	**He is happy. She is happy.**
Il est français. Elle est française.	**He is French. She is French.**
Le jardin est petit. La ville est petite.	**The garden is small. The city is small.**
Marc est grand. Laura est grande.	**Marc is tall. Laura is tall.**

The final consonant *d* of *grand* is silent while the *d* of *grande* is pronounced in the feminine. When an adjective ends with an *e* in the masculine form, the feminine form remains the same.

Henri est malade. Marie est malade.	**Henry is sick. Marie is sick.**
Il est fantastique. Elle est fantastique.	**He is fantastic. She is fantastic.**
Cet exercice est facile. Cette leçon est facile.	**This exercise is easy. This lesson is easy.**

In many cases, the feminine of an adjective can take various forms. You will notice some patterns in the following examples (*–ien* becomes *–ienne*; *–if* becomes *–ive*), but there are many exceptions to these patterns.

Jean est péruvien. Marie est péruvienne.	**John is Peruvian. Mary is Peruvian.**
Gilles est amoureux. Alice est amoureuse.	**Gilles is in love. Alice is in love.**
Thierry est sportif. Eléonore est sportive.	**Thierry likes sports. Eleanor likes sports.**
Ce document est faux.	**This document is false.**
Cette pièce est fausse.	**This is a fake coin.**
Il est roux. Elle est rousse.	**He has red hair. She has red hair.**

Some adjectives are irregular.

Laurent est beau. Noëlle est belle.	**Laurent is good-looking. Noëlle is good-looking.**
Cet homme est fou. Cette femme est folle.	**This man is crazy. This woman is crazy.**

Exercise 6-1: Which Adjective?

Circle the right form.

1. *Steven est américain/américaine.*
2. *Cette rue est bruyant/bruyante.*
3. *La voisine de Sarah est gentil/gentille.*
4. *L'appartement est grand/grande.*
5. *Cette fleur est violet/violette.*
6. *Ma bicyclette est bleu/bleue.*
7. *Cette peinture est beau/belle.*
8. *Papa est fatigué/fatiguée.*
9. *Cet homme est fou/folle.*
10. *Cette histoire est long/longue.*

Exercise 6-2: Masculine to Feminine

Rewrite each sentence, replacing Boris with Élodie and using the feminine form of the adjective.

1. *Boris est russe.*
2. *Boris est élégant.*
3. *Boris est drôle.*
4. *Boris est beau.*
5. *Boris est frileux.*
6. *Boris est capricieux.*
7. *Boris est bavard.*
8. *Boris est petit.*
9. *Boris est amusant.*
10. *Boris est amoureux.*

Position of the Adjectives

In French, most qualifying adjectives follow the noun.

Il aime le chocolat chaud.	**He likes hot chocolate.**
C'est un musée d'art contemporain.	**It's a museum of contemporary art.**
Il a un travail intéressant.	**He has an interesting job.**
Patrick aime les légumes crus.	**Patrick likes raw vegetables.**

Some adjectives precede the noun. You will have to memorize them.

J'ai lu un bon livre.	**I read a good book**
D'où vient cette mauvaise odeur?	**Where does this bad smell come from?**
Frédéric a acheté une belle maison.	**Frédéric bought a beautiful house.**
Ce jeune homme s'appelle Mathias.	**This young man is called Mathias.**
C'est une longue aventure.	**This is a long adventure.**
Jérémie a un petit chien.	**Jérémie has a small dog.**
Bertrand a un nouveau travail.	**Bertrand has a new job.**
C'est une vieille histoire.	**It's an old story.**
Mon oncle a un gros camion.	**My uncle has a big truck.**

Exercise 6-3: Let's Figure Out the Adjectives!

TRACK 22

Listen to the audio track and repeat. Then listen again and write down each adjective with the gender and number.

1. Adjective: .... Gender: .... Number: ....

   Adjective: .... Gender: .... Number: ....

2. Adjective: .... Gender: .... Number: ....

   Adjective: .... Gender: .... Number: ....

3. Adjective: .... Gender: .... Number: ....

4. Adjective: .... Gender: .... Number: ....

   Adjective: .... Gender: .... Number: ....

   Adjective: .... Gender: .... Number: ....

5. Adjective: .... Gender: .... Number: ....

   Adjective: .... Gender: .... Number: ....

6. Adjective: .... Gender: .... Number: ....

   Adjective: .... Gender: .... Number: ....

   Adjective: .... Gender: .... Number: ....

7. Adjective: .... Gender: .... Number: ....

   Adjective: .... Gender: .... Number: ....

   Adjective: .... Gender: .... Number: ....

8. Adjective: .... Gender: .... Number: ....

   Adjective: .... Gender: .... Number: ....

9. Adjective: .... Gender: .... Number: ....

   Adjective: .... Gender: .... Number: ....

10. Adjective: .... Gender: .... Number: ....

    Adjective: .... Gender: .... Number: ....

Change of Meaning

Some adjectives can either precede or follow a noun: their meanings change according to the position.

ma propre soeur/une chemise propre	**my own sister/a clean shirt**
cette pauvre Marie!/un homme pauvre	**that poor Mary!/a poor man**
le mois dernier/le dernier mois	**last month/the last month**
sa chère mère/	**his dear mother/**
un restaurant cher	**an expensive restaurant**
une chaussette sale/une sale histoire	**a dirty sock/a nasty story**
mon ancien quartier/	**my old neighborhood/**
une montre ancienne	**an antique watch**

Exercise 6-4: Where to Place It?

Place the adjective in the right place.

1. *un spectacle/beau* ....

2. *une ferme/vieille* ....

3. *des yeux/bleus* ....

4. *l'art/moderne* ....

5. *un appartement/grand* ....

6. *la cuisine/française* ....

7. *une distance/grande* ....

8. *un prix/bon* ....

9. *un pull/chaud* ....

10. *un chat/gros* ....

Exercise 6-5: Beginning to End

Make an appropriate sentence by matching the phrase in the right-hand column with the phrase in left-hand column.

1. *Je suis partie en Asie*   a. *à sa chère grand-mère.*
2. *Cette pauvre Denise*   b. *l'hiver dernier.*
3. *Nous avons acheté*   c. *a beaucoup de problèmes!*
4. *Elle a rendu visite*   d. *un petit studio.*
5. *Je l'ai rencontré*   e. *le dernier jour de mes vacances.*

Comparisons

In French, comparisons of adjectives take three different forms: *plus . . . que (more . . . than), moins . . . que (less . . . than)* and *aussi . . . que (as . . . as).*

Stéphanie est plus courageuse que moi.	**Stéphanie is more courageous than I.**
Le film est moins intéressant que le livre.	**The movie is less interesting than the book.**
Cet été est aussi chaud que l'été dernier.	**This summer is as hot as last summer.**

As in English, some adjectives are irregular in the comparative form.

Ton choix est meilleur que le mien.	**Your choice is better than mine.**
Cet hiver est pire que l'hiver dernier.	**This winter is worse than last winter.**
Il n'a pas montré la moindre émotion.	**He didn't show the slightest emotion.**

Exercise 6-6: What's the Order?

Form sentences with the following elements. Use a comparative form of the adjective as indicated.

1. *Pierre / Luc / sportif / +*

   ....

2. *Carole / sa mère / grande / =*

   ....

3. *Manuel / Vincent / gentil / +*

   ....

4. *Ce livre-ci / ce livre-là / intéressant / –*

   ....

5. *L'hiver à Paris / l'hiver à New York / froid / –*

   ....

6. *Le cinéma / la télévision / intéressant / +*

   ....

7. *Le chocolat / le café / amer / –*

   ....

8. *Martine / Marianne / compétente / =*

   ....

9. *Le poisson / la viande / bon / +*

   ....

10. *Ma belle-mère / ta belle-mère / généreuse / =*

    ....

Exercise 6-7: Practicing Comparisons

Translate the following sentences into English.

1. *La campagne est plus calme que la ville.*

   ....

2. *Ma connexion Internet est plus rapide que la tienne.*

   ....

3. *Isabelle est aussi généreuse que Bertrand.*

....

4. *Ton idée est meilleure que celle de Sara.*

....

5. *Je n'ai pas eu le moindre problème.*

....

6. *Son nouvel appartement est plus petit que son ancienne maison.*

....

7. *La fille est aussi grande que la mère.*

....

8. *Je n'ai pas la moindre envie de t'accompagner.*

....

9. *Ce pauvre Denis n'est pas plus heureux que Dominique.*

....

10. *Philippe n'est pas plus courageux que Jean.*

....

Superlatives

In French, the superlative form (*the most, the worst, the best, the least,* etc.) is simply formed by adding the definite article to the comparative form, followed by *de* (*in* or *of* in English).

C'est la plus belle ville du pays.	**It's the most beautiful city in the country.**
J'étais la plus jeune de tous.	**I was the youngest of all.**
C'est l'histoire la moins drôle que j'aie jamais entendue.	**It's the least funny story I ever heard.**

Irregular forms follow the same rule.

C'est le meilleur résultat de toute l'année.	**It's the best result of the year.**
Ce sont les pires vacances que j'ai jamais passées.	**They are the worst holidays I ever spent.**
C'est la moindre des choses que tu puisses faire.	**It's the least you can do.**

Exercise 6-8: Can You Guess?

Translate the following sentences into French.

1. I don't have the slightest idea.

   ....

2. It is the worst thing I ever heard.

   ....

3. It is one of the poorest countries in the world.

   ....

4. This is the best show I have ever seen!

   ....

5. My uncle is the funniest man in the family.

   ....

6. This is her best movie.

   ....

7. My brother is the kindest person in the world.

   ....

8. Kéda is the best cook I have ever known.

   ....

9. He was the richest man in town.

   ....

10. Angélique is the least talented of your group.

    ....

Adjectives of Color

To describe things, you may need adjectives of colors.

rouge	red	*bleu*	blue
vert	green	*jaune*	yellow
noir	black	*blanc*	white
gris	grey	*rose*	pink

violet	violet	*orange*	orange
pourpre	purple	*marron*	brown
bordeaux	burgundy	*beige*	beige
ocre	ochre	*roux* (hair)	red
bleu foncé	dark blue	*bleu clair*	light blue
bleu ciel	sky blue	*bleu marine*	navy blue
vert olive	olive green	*vert pomme*	apple green
vert bouteille	bottle green		

When using adjectives describing colors, you usually need to make them agree in gender and number with the noun they modify.

Il y a quelques nuages gris.	**There are a few grey clouds.**
Tu veux une pomme verte ou jaune?	**Do you want a green or a yellow apple?**
J'ai acheté des fleurs roses.	**I bought pink flowers.**
Elle a les cheveux roux.	**She has red hair.**

When the adjective comes from the noun of a fruit or a plant, it always remains in the masculine singular form.

Elle porte une robe marron.	**She is wearing a brown dress.**
Les murs sont orange.	**The walls are orange.**
Il a les cheveux châtain.	**He has light brown hair.**
Ces rideaux indigo seront parfaits.	**These indigo curtains will be perfect.**

When adjectives are combined to specify a color, they all remain in the masculine singular form.

Sa veste est rouge clair.	**His jacket is light red.**
Elle a les yeux bleu foncé.	**She has dark blue eyes.**
Ma voiture est vert olive.	**My car is olive green.**
L'eau était bleu marine.	**The water was navy blue.**

Exercise 6-9: *It Comes in All Colors*

Make the adjectives agree in gender and number.

1. *Mon chat est (gris)* ....

2. *La porte de sa maison est (bleu clair)* ....

3. *J'aime les fleurs (jaune)* ....

4. *Elle était (vert)* ....

5. *Ma bicyclette est (marron)* ....

6. *Les cerises sont (rouge)* ....

7. *Ces coussins sont (orange)* ....

8. *J'ai acheté une voiture (noir)* ....

9. *Mon appartement est tout (blanc)* ....

10. *Le chapeau de Caroline est (rose bonbon)* ....

Exercise 6-10: *What Color?*

Make an appropriate sentence by matching the phrase in the right-hand column with the phrase in the left-hand column.

1. *J'aime les films*   a. *verte.*
2. *Le ciel est*   b. *marron.*
3. *Les pommes sont*   c. *en noir et blanc.*
4. *L'herbe est*   d. *bleu.*
5. *Le tronc des arbres est*   e. *vertes, rouges, ou jaunes.*

Adverbs of Time

We studied the adverbs of time in Part 4. Let's review them a little.

Je suis partie la veille de son arrivée.   **I left the day before he arrived.**
Elle a emménagé la semaine suivante.   **She moved in the following week.**
Il est arrivé le jour même de mon mariage.   **He arrived the very day of my wedding.**

Exercise 6-11: Today, Tomorrow, or Another Time

TRACK 23

Listen to Grégoire's story, then write a sentence to summarize the content.

....

....

....

....

....

....

There are many other adverbs or expressions of time. Here are a few more.

toujours	still/always
chaque jour	every day
tous les jours	every day
tous les deux jours	every other day
en ce moment	at this present time
maintenant	now
actuellement	presently
souvent	often
d'habitude	usually
d'ordinaire	ordinarily
jamais	never
rarement	rarely/seldom
longtemps	for a long time
tard	late
tôt	early

parfois	sometimes
quelquefois	sometimes
de temps en temps	from time to time
de temps à autre	from time to time
tout le temps	all the time
autrefois	formerly

Je serai toujours là pour toi.	**I will always be there for you.**
En ce moment, elle est à Moscou.	**At this present time, she is in Moscow.**
Tu n'es jamais à l'heure.	**You are never on time.**
J'ai longtemps hésité.	**I hesitated for a long time.**
C'est parfois difficile.	**Sometimes it's difficult.**
Il me rend quelquefois visite.	**He sometimes comes for a visit.**
Elle pleure tout le temps.	**She cries all the time.**

Exercise 6-12: What's the Adverb?

Translate the adverbs into French.

1. *Tu le vois* (from time to time) ....

2. *Vous devez être* (on time) ....

3. *Pourquoi n'y vas-tu pas plus* (often) ....

4. *Il m'appelle* (every day) ....

5. *Nous allons* (sometimes) .... *au cinéma.*

6. .... (yesterday), *j'ai trouvé un cadeau pour maman.*

7. *Jeanne arrive* (in two days) ....

8. *Il pleut* (every other day) ....

9. *Elle est plus heureuse que* (last year) ....

10. (At this present time) ...., *je suis en voyage d'affaires en Asie.*

Adverbs of Manner

To describe actions, you can use adverbs of manner. Here are a few of them.

exprès	on purpose
volontiers	with pleasure, gladly
plutôt	rather
comme	like
ainsi	that way
bien	well/good
mal	badly/not well

Il le fait exprès.	**He does it on purpose.**
Je t'inviterais volontiers.	**I would invite you with pleasure.**
Je préfère plutôt aller au cinéma.	**I would rather go to the movies.**
Il a réagi comme ça.	**He reacted like that.**
Il parle ainsi.	**He speaks that way.**
Il a bien travaillé.	**He worked well.**
Il a mal dormi.	**He didn't sleep well.**

Exercise 6-13: All Manners!

Translate the following sentences.

1. He is rather stupid.

   ....

2. Did he do it on purpose?

   ....

3. Why do you treat them this way?

   ....

4. Can you help me? / With pleasure.

   ....

5. He behaved badly.

   ....

Adverbs of Quantity

To express quantity, you will need specific adverbs.

beaucoup	very much/a lot
trop	too much
assez	enough
peu	little/few

J'aime beaucoup mon oncle.	**I like my uncle very much.**
Il parle trop.	**He talks too much.**
Fait-il assez de sport?	**Does he take enough exercise?**
Il mange peu.	**He eats little.**

Some of these adverbs can be combined in order to emphasize quantity.

beaucoup trop	way too much
bien assez	quite enough
bien trop	way too much
bien trop peu	way too little

Il travaille beaucoup trop.	**He works way too much.**
Il mange bien assez.	**He eats quite enough.**
Elle parle bien trop.	**She talks way too much.**
Il dort trop peu.	**He sleeps too little.**

Exercise 6-14: A Lot of Translation Practice

Translate the following sentences, using *vous* when necessary.

1. He eats too little.

   ....

2. She smiles a lot.

   ....

3. You talk too much.

....

4. She doesn't read enough.

....

5. I thank you very much.

....

6. You work enough.

....

7. Don't worry much!

....

8. She walks a lot.

....

9. He sleeps way too little.

....

10. She laughs a lot.

....

Position of the Adverb

In most tenses, most adverbs are placed after the verb.

Elle travaille beaucoup.	**She works a lot.**
Il vient tous les jours.	**He comes every day.**
Il conduit bien.	**He drives well.**
Tu souris peu.	**You don't smile a lot.**
Marie rit beaucoup.	**Marie laughs a lot.**

In the *passé composé*, adverbs of quantity, quality, and frequency are placed between *avoir* or *être* and the past principle.

Elle rit beaucoup./Elle a beaucoup ri.	**She laughs a lot./She laughed a lot.**
Il m'appelle souvent./	**He often calls me./**
Il m'a souvent appelé.	**He often called me.**
Il conduit bien./Il a bien conduit.	**He drives well./He drove well.**

Elle mange peu./
   Elle a peu mangé.

She doesn't eat a lot./
   She didn't eat much.

Exercise 6-15: Past Events

Rewrite each sentence, changing the verb to the *passé composé*.

1. *Frédéric dépense trop.*

2. *Marine travaille assez.*

3. *Pascal réagit mal.*

4. *Valérie voyage souvent en Asie.*

5. *Nous rions beaucoup.*

6. *Christine m'appelle rarement.*

7. *Samuel ne s'amuse pas assez en vacances.*

8. *Tu parles bien.*

9. *Éric ne séjourne pas souvent à Paris.*

10. *Isabelle dort assez.*

Exercise 6-16: Translation Time

Translate the following sentences.

1. He has beautiful white teeth.

2. Martine is always nice and in a good mood.

....

3. He plays with a big orange balloon.

....

4. Elisa is a beautiful little girl.

....

5. This poor Juliette is sick all the time.

....

6. My young brother has a new girlfriend.

....

7. Tomorrow, we are leaving for Amsterdam.

....

8. Last year, I was the best student in my school.

....

9. It is the worst thing I have ever heard.

....

10. I bought a big red car.

....

Exercise 6-17: How Do You Say It?

Rewrite the sentences, using the specified adjectives and adverbs.

1. *Tu as la nationalité* (American)? *Non, j'ai* (always) *eu la nationalité* (French).

....

2. *Vous êtes arrivés* (yesterday)? *Non, nous sommes arrivés* (here) (last week).

....

3. *Tu travailles* (every day)? *Non, je travaille* (from time to time).

....

4. *Élodie est* (tall)? *Oui, elle est* (taller than) *son mari.*

....

5. *Ton travail est* (interesting)? *Non, il est* (more boring than) *celui de l'* (last year).

   ....

6. *Tu te sens* (good) (today)? *Oui, je suis en* (better) *forme qu'* (yesterday).

   ....

7. *Il se marie* (next week)? *Oui, il se marie avec son amie* (Italian).

   ....

8. *Tu pars en week-end* (sometimes)? *Oui, je vais voir ma* (best) *amie* (every month).

   ....

9. *Tu crois qu'elle est* (crazy)? *Non, je crois qu'elle travaille* (too much).

   ....

10. *C'est un* (long) *voyage? Oui, nous arriverons* (in two days).

   ....

Exercise 6-18: The Matching Exercise

Make an appropriate sentence by matching the phrase in the right-hand column with the phrase in the left-hand column.

1. *Pierre voyage souvent*   a. *de sa soeur adorée.*
2. *Marie parle beaucoup*   b. *loin de chez lui.*
3. *Victor aime bien*   c. *à son avenir.*
4. *Valérie s'est mariée*   d. *les beaux livres d'art antique.*
5. *Pauline pense peu*   e. *l'année dernière avec un homme charmant.*

Exercise 6-19: It's Happening Now

Write sentences with the following elements, using the present tense.

1. *Françoise / beaucoup / voyage*

   ....

2. *Elisabeth / moins de talent / Muriel/a*

   ....

3. *Pierre / bien / dessine*

   ....

4. *Donne-moi / la clé / petite*

....

5. *plus/Martin / Thierry / est / paresseux*

....

6. *Anna / trop / travaille*

....

7. *André / mange / trop*

....

8. *Il aime / la cuisine / bonne*

....

9. *Noah / calcule / mal*

....

10. *Léopold / bien / joue*

....

Part 7

The Infinitive, the Imperative, and Object Pronouns

Now the plot thickens. You will learn how to mix and match different parts of speech. What happens when an infinitive or an imperative meets an object pronouns? What happens if this object is direct or indirect? Let's take a look.

Direct Objects

We studied pronouns in Part 2 and will review them here to see how to use them with infinitives and the imperative.

Je l'aperçois au loin.	**I can see it (him/her) in the distance.**
Marc nous regarde.	**Marc is looking at us.**
Pascal vous félicite.	**Pascal congratulates you.**

Using the Direct Object Pronoun in the Past Tense

In a sentence with auxiliary or compound verbs, the direct object pronoun comes before the verb to which it refers.

J'ai pris le sac.	**I took the bag.**
Je l'ai pris.	**I took it.**
Elle n'a pas fermé la porte	**She did not close the door.**
Elle ne l'a pas fermée.	**She did not close it.**

Using Direct Object Pronouns with Inversions

In the interrogative form, using inversion, the direct object pronoun comes immediately before the verb.

Achèteras-tu cet appartement?	**Will you buy this apartment?**
L'achèteras-tu?	**Will you buy it?**
Prend-il ses médicaments?	**Does he take his pills?**
Les prend-il?	**Does he take them?**

Using Direct Object Pronouns with Infinitives

When an infinitive has a direct object, the direct object pronoun immediately precedes the infinitive.

Tu peux donner mon adresse.	**You can give my address.**
Tu peux la donner.	**You can give it.**
Elle saura trouver le chemin.	**She will know how to find the way.**
Elle saura le trouver.	**She will know how to find it.**

Using Direct Object Pronouns in the Imperative

In the positive imperative, the direct object pronoun follows the verb. There is a hyphen between the verb and the direct object pronoun.

Arrose les plantes tous les jours!	**Water the plants every day!**
Arrose-les tous les jours!	**Water them every day!**
Soutenez vos joueurs!	**Support your players!**
Soutenez-les!	**Support them!**

In the negative imperative, the direct object pronoun remains before the verb.

Ne prends pas ta voiture!	**Do not take your car!**
Ne la prends pas!	**Do not take it!**
Ne punis pas ton fils!	**Do not punish your son!**
Ne le punis pas!	**Do not punish him!**

Exercise 7-1: What's the Pronoun?

Rewrite each sentence, replacing the words in bold with a direct object pronoun.

1. *Elle a accepté **ma proposition**.*

   ....

2. *Nous devons prendre **cet itinéraire**.*

   ....

3. *Il est en train de lire **ce livre**.*

   ....

4. *Tu devrais appeler **le médecin**.*

   ....

5. *Claire aime **les contes de fées**?*

   ....

6. *Nous voulons louer **cette maison**.*

   ....

7. *Prenez **votre douche** maintenant!*

   ....

8. *Ouvrez **les rideaux**!*

....

9. *Il va conduire **la voiture de Jean**.*

....

10. *Ne regarde pas **les gens** comme ça!*

....

Exercise 7-2: In the Past

Answer the following questions, replacing the words in bold with a direct object pronoun. Don't forget to make the past participles with the direct object pronouns agree in number and gender.

1. *Il a pris **les bouteilles de vin**?*

   Oui,...

2. *Elle a rangé **la harpe** dans sa chambre?*

   Oui,...

3. *As-tu lu **son roman**?*

   Non,...

4. *A-t-il nourri **le chat**?*

   Oui,...

5. *A-t-il remercié **vos parents**?*

   Non,...

6. *Avez-vous trouvé **la solution à vos problèmes**?*

   Oui,...

7. *A-t-il ouvert **la porte**?*

   Non,...

8. *As-tu écouté **les ballades de Chopin**?*

   Oui,...

9. *Il a accepté **la décision**?*

   Non,...

10. *As-tu remis **les clés** à la gardienne?*

    Oui,...

Using Direct Object Pronouns with Voici and Voilà.

Voici and *voilà* are used to announce or show something or someone. You can use the direct object pronouns to designate the person(s) or the thing(s).

Où est Fanny?/La voilà!	**Where is Fanny?/Here she is!**
Où sont mes valises?/Les voici!	**Where are my suitcases?/Here they are!**
Où êtes-vous?/Nous voici!	**Where are you?/Here we are!**

Exercise 7-3: Voici! Voilà!

Answer the following questions using *voici* or *voilà*.

1. *Où est ton frère?* ....

2. *Où sont tes amis?* ....

3. *Où est ta femme?* ....

4. *Où te caches-tu?* ....

5. *Où est Isabelle?* ....

6. *Où est le plan de la ville?* ....

7. *Où êtes-vous* (plural)? ....

8. *Où sont tes affaires?* ....

9. *Où sont nos cadeaux?* ....

10. *Où est notre chambre?* ....

Are you okay with the *objet direct*? Now, let's take a look at the *objet indirect*.

Indirect Objects

In French, the indirect object pronoun replaces animate indirect objects (people, animals). The object is called indirect because it is preceded by a preposition—usually *à*—telling to whom or for whom something is done. Let's look at a few examples.

Je lui raconte une histoire.	**I tell him a story.**
Ils t'ont apporté des fleurs.	**They brought you flowers.**

Vous donne-t-il entière satisfaction?	**Does he give you full satisfaction?**
Je ne lui ai pas prêté mon appartement.	**I did not lend him my apartment.**
Ouvre-moi ta porte!	**Open your door!**
Parle-moi de ta vie!	**Tell me about your life!**
Ne lui dis rien!	**Don't tell him anything!**

Exercise 7-4: Indirect Objects in Action

Translate the following sentences, using *tu* and inversion.

1. Did you tell her the story?

   ....

2. She gave me her opinion.

   ....

3. They did not mention the incident to us.

   ....

4. I spoke to her about the meeting.

   ....

5. Did you return the video to him?

   ....

6. This house belongs to them.

   ....

7. His grandmother donated her entire collection to you.

   ....

8. Did you borrow some money from her?

   ....

9. When will you tell me the truth?

   ....

10. We cannot pay you the rent.

    ....

Exercise 7-5: Pronoun Switch!

Rewrite each sentence, replacing each singular indirect object pronoun with the plural one and each plural indirect object with the singular one.

1. *Elle m'a téléphoné hier.*

   ....

2. *Je lui ai appris la bonne nouvelle.*

   ....

3. *Ils t'ont donné combien de temps?*

   ....

4. *Pourquoi nous a-t-il menti?*

   ....

5. *Vas-tu me dire la vérité?*

   ....

6. *Rapportez-nous les livres!*

   ....

7. *Commande-moi un café, s'il te plaît!*

   ....

8. *Elle vous a apporté des biscuits.*

   ....

9. *Je leur ai demandé pardon.*

   ....

10. *Elles lui ont fait un beau cadeau.*

    ....

Placement of the Indirect Object Pronoun with Some Specific Verbs

There are always exceptions! With some verbs with prepositions, the indirect object follows the preposition when replacing an animate thing, whatever the tense or the mode of the verb. In this case, the indirect object pronoun is replaced by the disjunctive pronoun, also known as the stressed or tonic pronoun.

Here is the list of the disjunctive pronouns:

moi	me	*nous*	us
toi	you	*vous*	you
lui	him	*eux*	them
elle	her	*elles*	them

Here are a few verbs governed by this rule. You will need to memorize them.

penser à	to think about	*songer à*	to think about
parler de	to talk about	*avoir besoin de*	to need
avoir peur de	to be scared of	*faire attention à*	to pay attention to
tenir à	to be attached to/to care about		

Il pense à sa petite amie.	**He thinks about his girlfriend.**
Il pense à elle.	**He thinks about her.**
Je tiendrai toujours à mes proches.	**I will always be attached to my relatives.**
Je tiendrai toujours à eux.	**I will always be attached to them.**
Pense à ta fille!	**Think about your daughter!**
Pense à elle!	**Think about her!**

The same rule applies with reflexive verbs: the indirect object pronoun is placed after the preposition, whatever the tense or the mode of the verb. It is also replaced by the disjunctive pronoun.

Il se souvient de son grand-père.	**He remembers his grandfather.**
Il se souvient de lui.	**He remembers him.**
Ils s'intéressent à nous.	**They are interested in us.**

Exercise 7-6: Question and Answer

Match the question in the left column with the appropriate answer in the right column.

1. *Il a peur de son patron?*
2. *Il a peur de sa voisine?*
3. *Il a peur de ses collègues?*
4. *Il a peur de vous?*
5. *Il a peur de ses cousines?*

a. *Non, il n' a pas peur de nous.*
b. *Non, il n'a pas peur d'eux.*
c. *Non, il n'a pas peur de lui.*
d. *Non, il n' a pas peur d'elles.*
e. *Non, il n'a pas peur d'elle.*

The Pronoun Y

Y is an indirect object pronoun that replaces an inanimate thing, a place, an idea, a concept, an action, and so on. The object is indirect because it is preceded by a preposition, usually the preposition *à. Y* is placed right before the verb with most tenses and modes.

Elle obéit aux ordres.	**She obeys the orders.**
Elle y obéit.	**She obeys them.**
Nous nous habituons à la pluie.	**We are getting used to the rain.**
Nous nous y habituons.	**We are getting used to it.**
Il réfléchit à ce qu'on lui a dit.	**He is thinking about what he was told.**
Il y réfléchit.	**He is thinking about it.**

Using the Pronoun Y in the Past Tense

In the past tense the indirect object pronoun *y* is placed before the auxiliary verb. Note that the past participle does not agree in gender and number with the indirect object.

J'ai répondu à ta lettre.	**I replied to your letter.**
J'y ai répondu.	**I replied to it.**
Il n'a rien compris à mes suggestions.	**He understood nothing of my suggestions.**
Il n'y a rien compris.	**He understood nothing.**

Using the Pronoun Y with the Imperative

With the positive imperative, the indirect object pronoun *y* is placed right after the verb with a hyphen.

Réponds à ma question!	**Answer my question!**
Réponds-y!	**Answer it!**
Pensez à votre avenir!	**Think about your future!**
Pensez-y!	**Think about it!**

With the negative imperative, the indirect object pronoun *y* is placed right before the verb.

Ne renonce pas à tes rêves!	**Do not give up your dreams!**
N'y renonce pas!	**Do not give them up!**
Ne croyez pas à ce qu'il raconte!	**Do not believe what he says!**
N'y croyez pas!	**Do not believe it!**

Using the Pronoun Y with the Interrogative

With inversion, the indirect object pronoun *y* is placed right before the verb.

A-t-il réfléchi à ce qu'il veut?	**Did he think about what he wants?**
Y a-t-il réfléchi?	**Did he think about it?**
Ne penses-tu pas à ton avenir?	**Don't you think about your future?**
N'y penses-tu pas?	**Don't you think about it?**

Exercise 7-7: All about Y!

Rewrite each sentence, replacing the indirect object in bold with *y*.

1. *As-tu pensé **à porter plainte**?*

   ....

2. *Ne m'oblige pas **à me mettre en colère**!*

   ....

3. *Il tenait beaucoup **à cette maison**.*

   ....

4. *Prends garde **au gros chien**!*

   ....

5. *Nous ne voyons pas d'inconvénient **à ce que tu viennes avec nous**.*

   ....

6. *A-t-il goûté **à mon canard à l'orange**?*

   ....

7. *Nous devons réfléchir **à votre proposition**.*

   ....

8. *Ils ne s'intéressent pas **à ce genre de films**.*

   ....

9. *Je m'habitue assez bien **à sa présence**.*

   ....

10. *Elles ont renoncé **à leurs avantages**.*

    ....

The Pronoun En

When a verb is used with the preposition *de*, the pronoun *en* can replace an inanimate object. The pronoun *en* usually immediately precedes the verb.

Elle a besoin de ton aide.	**She needs your help.**
Elle en a besoin.	**She needs it.**
Je m'occupe de votre propriété.	**I am taking care of your property.**
Je m'en occupe.	**I am taking care of it.**

Using the Pronoun En in the Past Tense

In the past tense the pronoun *en* is placed before the auxiliary verb. The past participle does not agree in gender and number with *en*.

Il s'est souvenu de ce jour.	**He remembered that day.**
Il s'en est souvenu.	**He remembered it.**
Je me suis inquiété de ne pas avoir de tes nouvelles.	**I was worried not to hear from you.**
Je m'en suis inquiété.	**I was worried about it.**

Using the Pronoun En with the Interrogative

In a question using inversion, the pronoun *en* precedes the verb.

As-tu parlé de ce qui t'est arrivé?	**Did you talk about what happened to you?**
En as-tu parlé?	**Did you talk about it?**
N'a-t-il pas envie de rester?	**Doesn't he feel like staying?**
N'en a-t-il pas envie?	**Doesn't he feel like it?**

Using the Pronoun En with the Imperative

In positive commands, the pronoun *en* follows the verb.

Mets du beurre dans tes pâtes!	**Put some butter in your pasta!**
Mets-en dans tes pâtes!	**Put some in your pasta!**
Servez-vous de mon téléphone!	**Use my phone!**
Servez-vous en!	**Use it!**

Exercise 7-8: Listen Carefully!

TRACK 24

Listen to the audio track and repeat. Then listen again and answer each question in the affirmative form, using the pronoun *en* to replace the phrase introduced by *de*.

1. ....

2. ....

3. ....

4. ....

5. ....

6. ....

7. ....

8. ....

9. ....

10. ....

Exercise 7-9: Is It Y or En?

Rewrite each sentence, replacing the words in bold with *y* or *en*.

1. *Elle a parlé **de ses soucis** toute la soirée.*

....

2. *Je vais réfléchir **à ce que tu viens de me dire**.*

....

3. *Il a très envie **de fêter son anniversaire avec tous ses amis**.*

....

4. *Voyez-vous un inconvénient **à ce que je dorme chez vous ce soir**?*

....

5. *Ne te décharge pas sur moi **de toute ta colère**!*

....

6. *Elle a besoin **de prendre du repos**.*

....

7. *As-tu remédié **au problème**?*

....

8. *Ils ont la preuve **de sa culpabilité**.*

....

9. *Elle s'est approchée **de l'ascenseur**.*

....

10. *Nous devons obéir **aux ordres qu'ils nous ont donnés**.*

....

Are you ready to combine direct and indirect object pronouns in the same sentence? *Allons-y!*

Direct and Indirect Objects Combined

When a direct and an indirect pronoun are combined in a sentence, the indirect object pronoun usually comes first.

Il te montre le chemin.	**He shows you the way.**
Il te le montre.	**He shows it to you.**
Ils nous apportent leurs dossiers.	**They bring us their files.**
Ils nous les apportent.	**They bring them to us.**

If the direct (*lui, leur*) and indirect (*le, la, les*) pronouns are in the third person, the direct object pronoun comes first.

Elle lui donne la réponse.	**She gives him the answer.**
Elle la lui donne.	**She gives it to him.**
Nous adresserons les requêtes	**We will send the requests**
aux deux avocats.	**to the two attorneys.**
Nous les leur adresserons.	**We send them to them.**

Combining Object Pronouns in the Past Tense

When used with the past tense, the direct object pronoun is placed before the auxiliary verb. The past participle must agree in number and gender with the direct object placed before the verb.

J'ai tendu la main à Gautier.	**I held out my hand to Gautier.**
Je la lui ai tendue.	**I held it out to him.**
Nous avons envoyé la lettre à nos voisins.	**We sent the letter to our neighbors.**
Nous la leur avons envoyée.	**We sent it to them.**

Combining En and an Indirect Object

When combined with an indirect object pronoun, *en* is always in second position.

J'envoie des fleurs à Sylvie.	**I send some flowers to Sylvie.**
Je lui en envoie.	**I send her some.**
Il prêtera des livres à ton fils.	**He will lend some books to your son.**
Il lui en prêtera.	**He will lend him some.**

The past participle does not agree in number and gender with *en*.

Il a emprunté des chaises à ses voisins.	**He borrowed some chairs from his neighbors.**
Il leur en a emprunté.	**He borrowed some from them.**
Nous avons envoyé des roses à ta mère.	**We sent some roses to your mother.**
Nous lui en avons envoyé.	**We sent her some.**

Exercise 7-10: From Noun to Pronoun

Match the question in the left column with the appropriate answer in the right column.

1. *Tu as donné ta démission à ton patron?*
2. *Tu as donné le sac à ta mère?*
3. *Tu as donné des nouvelles à Patrick?*
4. *Tu as donné ta parole à tes amis?*
5. *Tu as donné des conseils à tes collaborateurs?*

a. *Oui, je leur en ai donné.*
b. *Oui, je la leur ai donnée.*
c. *Oui, je la lui ai donnée.*
d. *Oui, je lui en ai donné.*
e. *Oui, je le lui ai donné.*

Exercise 7-11: What Pronoun?

Rewrite each sentence, replacing the words in bold with a pronoun.

1. *Elle nous a apporté **des bonbons**.*

....

2. *Je ne vous donnerai pas **de conseils**.*

....

3. *Il leur a ouvert **la porte**.*

....

4. *Elles lui offriront **ce beau foulard**.*

....

5. *Tu nous as raconté **des mensonges**.*

....

6. *Il nous a raconté **son histoire**.*

....

7. *Vous leur avez vendu **votre maison**?*

....

8. *Je lui ai dit **ce que je pensais d'elle**.*

....

9. *Il m'a demandé **ce que je voulais faire pour les vacances**.*

....

10. *Ils nous avaient recommandé **cet hôtel**.*

....

Exercise 7-12: Twosome

Rewrite each sentence, replacing both the direct and indirect objects in bold with the appropriate pronouns.

1. *Il a parlé **de son travail à sa femme**.*

....

2. *Je te conseille **d'envoyer tes meilleurs vœux à ta grand-tante**.*

....

3. *J'enverrai **ma lettre de démission au directeur des ressources humaines**.*

....

4. *Il a apporté **des marrons glacés à ses collègues**.*

....

5. *Donne **la main à ta sœur**!*

....

6. *Nous avons raconté **nos aventures à Vincent et Stella**.*

....

7. *Ils ont prêté **leur voiture à Isabelle**.*

....

8. *Avez-vous rendu **les clés à la propriétaire**?*

....

9. *Il a cédé **sa place à son petit frère**.*

....

10. *Nous devrions parler **de cette histoire à tes parents**.*

....

Imperative

The imperative is used to give orders, to make suggestions, or to give advice. To put a verb in the imperative, you take the *tu*, *nous*, and *vous* form of the present tense and drop the subject pronoun.

pense	think	*pensons*	let's think	*pensez*	think
choisis	choose	*choisissons*	let's choose	*choisissez*	choose
vois	see	*voyons*	let's see	*voyez*	see
va	go	*allons*	let's go	*allez*	go
fais	do	*faisons*	let's do	*faites*	do

Note that for the *-er* verbs, the *s* of the *tu* form is dropped.
Here are a few examples:

Passe ton permis de conduire d'abord!	**Get your driver's license first!**
Réalise tes rêves!	**Make your dreams come true!**
Bois quelque chose!	**Drink something!**
Viens avec moi!	**Come with me!**
Allons au cinéma!	**Let's go to the movies!**
Répondez à mes questions!	**Answer my questions!**

For negative commands, place *ne. . . pas* around the verb.

Ne me parle plus!	**Don't talk to me anymore!**
Ne perdez pas le chien!	**Don't lose the dog!**
Ne nous disputons pas pour si peu!	**Let's not argue for so little!**

There are some irregular imperatives, among which are *être*, *avoir*, and *savoir*.

Irregular Imperatives			
être:	to be	*sois*	be
soyons	let's be	*soyez*	be
avoir:	to have	*aie*	have
ayons	let's have	*ayez*	have
savoir:	to know	*sache*	know
sachons	let's know	*sachez*	know

Sois heureux!	**Be happy!**
Sache que je t'aime!	**Know that I love you!**
Ayez bon espoir!	**Be optimistic!**
Ne soyez pas triste!	**Don't be sad!**

The verb *vouloir* (*to want*) uses the imperative form only with *vous*.

Veuillez me suivre!	**Please follow me!**
Veuillez accepter mes excuses!	**Please accept my apologies!**

The Imperative of Pronominal Verbs

Note the position of the reflexive pronoun in the imperative of pronominal verbs.

Tu te promènes.	**You are taking a walk.**
Promène-toi!	**Take a walk!**

Ne te promène pas!	**Do not take a walk!**
Vous vous coiffez.	**You do your hair.**
Coiffez-vous!	**Do your hair!**
Ne vous coiffez pas!	**Do not do your hair!**

Idiomatic Expressions with the Imperative

There are many idiomatic expressions using the imperative.

Sois sage!	**Be good!**
Fais attention!	**Be careful!**
Laisse tomber!	**Forget it! / Drop it!**
Dépêche-toi!	**Hurry up!**
Allons-y!	**Let's go!**
Voyons, ne sois pas stupide!	**Come on, don't be stupid!**
Allez-vous-en!	**Go away!**
Soyez gentil!	**Be nice!**

Exercise 7-13: Listen to Me!

Write down commands based on the infinitive phrases and cues.

1. *Ne pas manger si vite (tu).*

   ....

2. *Se dépêcher (vous).*

   ....

3. *Ne pas fermer les yeux (nous).*

   ....

4. *Aller au zoo avec les enfants (tu).*

   ....

5. *Prendre place à mes côtés (vous).*

   ....

6. *Être fier de lui (vous).*

   ....

7. *Boire deux litres d'eau par jour (vous).*

   ....

8. *Prendre soin d'elle (tu).*

   ....

9. *Se réconcilier (nous).*

   ....

10. *Savoir que je serai toujours là (tu).*

    ....

Exercise 7-14: It's Imperative

Make an appropriate sentence by matching the phrase in the right-hand column with the phrase in the left-hand column.

1. *Veuillez*
2. *Réfléchis bien*
3. *Passe*
4. *Ne te fâche pas*
5. *Emmène-moi*

a. *de très bonnes vacances.*
b. *au restaurant.*
c. *agréer mes sincères salutations.*
d. *à ce que tu dis.*
e. *pour si peu de choses.*

Present Infinitive

A verb in the infinitive mode is by definition not conjugated. In English the infinitive is often replaced by a present participle. In French, the infinitive is used in many ways. You are going to look into a few of the usual ones. But first, let's look at the negative infinitive. With an infinitive, the *ne pas* or other negative expression precedes the verb.

Je lui ai demandé de ne pas dire un mot.   **I asked him not to say a word.**
Elle a promis de ne plus te déranger.   **She promised not to disturb you any longer.**
Il m'a dit de ne pas m'inquiéter.   **He told me not to worry.**

The Infinitive as a Subject of a Verb

The infinitive can be the subject of a verb.

Photographier les animaux, c'est son métier.   **Photographing animals is his job.**
Y aller en voiture serait plus pratique.   **Going there by car would be more practical.**

The Infinitive for General Instructions

In French, the infinitive is used to express general instructions, prescriptions, public notices, and proverbs. In English, the imperative is used.

Conserver au réfrigérateur.	**Keep refrigerated.**
Propriété privée. Ne pas entrer.	**Private property. Do not enter.**
Éteindre votre téléphone portable.	**Turn off your cell phone.**

If you are into French cuisine, you will often find the infinitive in recipe books.

Ajouter du sel et du poivre.	**Add salt and pepper.**
Mélanger puis mettre au four.	**Mix, then put in the oven.**

The Infinitive in Interrogatives

The infinitive can be used in the interrogative.

Pourquoi partir maintenant?	**Why leave now?**
Que faire?	**What is there to do?**
Où chercher?	**Where to look?**

The Infinitive after Verbs of Perception

In French, the infinitive is used after verbs of perception. In English, you will find a present participle.

Il regarde le train partir.	**He watches the train leaving.**
Il a senti la casserole brûler.	**He smelled the pan burning.**

The Infinitive after the Verbs Faire and Laisser

After the verbs *faire* (*to do*) and *laisser* (*to let*), you need the infinitive.

J'ai fait expertiser ce tableau.	**I had this painting appraised.**
Laisse-le parler.	**Let him talk.**
Nous lui avons fait prendre conscience de ses erreurs.	**We let him realize his mistakes.**

Let's look now at the causative form *faire* + infinitive.

Tu t'es fait faire une belle coupe des cheveux.	**You had your hair beautifully cut.**
Ils se sont fait construire un garage à côté de la maison.	**They had a garage built by the house.**

The Infinitive after Certain Verbs

Some verbs are followed directly by the infinitive. You will have to memorize them.

Il n'ose pas donner son avis.	**He does not dare give his opinion.**
Tu devrais rentrer chez toi.	**You should go home.**
Nous voulons te voir.	**We want to see you.**

The Infinitive after Expressions of Time and Position

The infinitive is used with expressions of how one passes the time.

Je passe mon temps à m'amuser.	**I spend my time having fun.**
Elle passe sa vie à se plaindre.	**She spends her life complaining.**

The infinitive is also used after expressions of position. It is preceded by the preposition *à*.

Il est assis à ne rien faire.	**He sits doing nothing.**
Nous étions allongés par terre à bavarder.	**We were lying on the floor chatting.**

Exercise 7-15: Using Infinitives

Translate the following sentences using *tu* when necessary.

1. Do not enter.

   ....

2. They were leaning against the wall listening to some music.

   ....

3. She asked me to return to my place.

   ....

4. I was sitting looking at her painting.

   ....

5. Add garlic and mix.

....

6. What is there to say?

....

7. Leaving before 7 A.M. would be a good idea.

....

8. I saw the man walking up the stairs.

....

9. You spend your life working.

....

10. She is squatting in the middle of the room doing yoga.

....

Exercise 7-16: *What's the Deal?*

TRACK 25

Listen to the audio track and repeat. Then listen again and write each sentence in the *passé composé*.

1. ....

2. ....

3. ....

4. ....

5. ....

Past Infinitive

The past infinitive is used to mark an action that occurred before the action of the main verb in a sentence. It is formed with the infinitive of *être* or *avoir* and the past participle of the verb.

Je regrette de n'avoir pas pu être là. — **I regret I could not be there.**
Il te remercie de l'avoir aidé. — **He thanks you for having helped him.**
Nous espérons ne pas avoir été — **We hope we were not**
  trop bruyants hier soir. — **too loud last night.**

The Past Infinitive as a Subject of a Verb

Just like the present infinitive, the past infinitive can be the subject of a verb.

Avoir menti n'était pas bien.	**Lying was not good.**
Lui avoir parlé était un soulagement.	**Talking to him was a relief.**

The past infinitive can also be used in interrogatives.

Pourquoi avoir dit la vérité?	**Why did [you] tell the truth?**
Comment avoir oublié ça?	**How could one have forgotten that?**

Exercise 7-17: Still Infinitive!

Rewrite the sentences, replacing the present infinitive with the past infinitive.

1. *Tu es gentille de venir jusqu'ici.*

   ....

2. *Il s'excuse de partir avant la fin.*

   ....

3. *Elle nous remercie de penser à elle.*

   ....

4. *Corinne regrette de ne pas avoir de magnétoscope chez elle.*

   ....

5. *Laure espère ne pas rater son examen.*

   ....

6. *Jean-Louis souhaite récupérer son canapé avant le mois prochain.*

   ....

7. *Pascale nous remercie de garder son chat en son absence.*

   ....

8. *Quel dommage de quitter ce quartier!*

   ....

9. *Pardonnez-nous d'être en retard!*

   ....

10. *Jure-moi de tout faire comme je te l'ai demandé!*

    ....

Verbal Constructions with Avant and Après

When introducing an action with the preposition *avant*, the present infinitive is preceded by the preposition *de*. In this case, the subjects of the main clause and of the infinitive clause are the same.

Passe-moi un coup de fil avant de partir!	**Give me a call before leaving!**
Elle a pris une grande respiration avant d'entrer dans la salle d'examen.	**She took a deep breath before entering the exam room.**
Elle l'a déposé à son hôtel avant de l'emmener au restaurant.	**She dropped him off at his hotel before taking him to the restaurant.**

The past infinitive is used when introducing a past action with the preposition *après*.

Après avoir mangé, il est sorti.	**After eating, he went out.**
Il a été renvoyé après s'être opposé aux décisions du Conseil d'administration.	**He was fired after opposing the decisions of the Board of Trustees.**
Après avoir travaillé vingt ans dans une banque parisienne, je me suis installée à la campagne.	**After working twenty years in a Parisian bank, I settled down in the countryside.**

Exercise 7-18: Time Will Tell

Rewrite the sentences, replacing *avant* with *après* and changing the present infinitive into the past infinitive.

1. *Il a ouvert la porte avant d'entendre la sonnette.*

   ....

2. *Le boulanger fait cuire le pain avant d'ouvrir la boulangerie.*

   ....

3. *Je suis partie avant de lui dire que je l'aimais.*

   ....

4. *Elles riaient avant de découvrir la surprise.*

   ....

5. *Avant de manger, fais une petite sieste.*

   ....

6. *Viens me chercher avant d'aller au supermarché.*

....

7. *Elle prépare le dessert avant de servir le plat principal.*

....

8. *Vous dînerez avant d'aller au cinéma.*

....

9. *Il peint avant de coller les morceaux de textile sur la toile.*

....

10. *Elle se douche avant de prendre son petit-déjeuner.*

....

Let's Recap

Now that you are a champion of object pronouns and the imperative and infinitive forms, let's recap!

Exercise 7-19: All in Order!

Put all the sentence elements in order and make any necessary changes.

1. *Clara / demande / nous / une explication.*

....

2. *Je / vais apporter / en / ce soir.*

....

3. *Ma tante / invite / me / pour le réveillon de Noël.*

....

4. *L'enfant/ a tiré / leur / la langue.*

....

5. *Donne / nous / le!*

....

6. *Ne regarde pas / les!*

....

7. *Tu/as envoyé / à tes parents / les?*

....

8. *Marion / veut / rendre / lui / les.*

....

9. *Elle / pense / y / beaucoup?*

....

10. *Boris / ne s'est pas excusé / en.*

....

Exercise 7-20: Which One Is It?

Replace the words in bold with the appropriate pronouns.

1. *Vas-tu te plaindre **de ce qu'il vient de faire**?*

....

2. *Ne mange pas **ces cochonneries**!*

....

3. *Il va réfléchir **à ta proposition**.*

....

4. *Il apporte un gros gâteau **à sa tante**.*

....

5. *Avez-vous peur **de sa réaction**?*

....

6. *A-t-elle pensé **à interrompre cet imbécile**?*

....

7. *A-t-elle pensé **à Ludovic**?*

....

8. *Ne rêvez pas trop **d'une augmentation de salaire pour cette année**!*

....

9. *Pense **à ta chère Élise**!*

....

10. *Elle a envoyé **le colis à son amie**.*

....

Exercise 7-21: Mixing It Up

Make an appropriate sentence by matching the phrase in the right-hand column with the phrase in the left-hand column.

1. Fais attention	*a. avant de prendre cette décision.*
2. Réfléchissez bien	*b. tu devrais te reposer.*
3. Marche devant	*c. à ne pas casser ma théière.*
4. Ne sors pas ce soir,	*d. faisons tout notre possible pour gagner!*
5. Ne partons pas battus,	*e. et montre-nous le chemin.*

Exercise 7-22: Translate These Sentences!

Translate the following sentences, using *vous* and inversion.

1. Draw the curtains before going to bed!

....

2. Do not forget to send her an e-mail before you leave!

....

3. After hearing the news, he burst into tears.

....

4. It is nice of you to call me.

....

5. Have you thought about it enough before asking them the question?

....

6. Can you buy some bread before coming home?

....

7. Promise me not to open that letter before getting on the plane!

....

8. Does she get dressed before putting on makeup?

....

9. I do not accept being treated like that.

....

10. She should negotiate before signing the contract.

....

Exercise 7-23: Let's Go to Avignon!

TRACK 26

Listen to the audio track and write down each sentence.

1. ....

2. ....

3. ....

4. ....

5. ....

6. ....

7. ....

8. ....

9. ....

10. ....

Part 8

The Subjunctive

In the previous part, you studied infinitives and the imperative mood. Most of what you have learned so far has been in the indicative mood, which states an objective fact, a certainty. The subjunctive mood deals with the domain of subjectivity and expresses emotions, wishes, doubt, and anything hypothetical. Although it is rare in English,—"I wish I were a king,"—it is standard in French. Note that the subjunctive is only used when the subjects of the main clause and the dependent clause are different. If the subjects are the same, use the infinitive.

The Present Subjunctive

For most verbs, the present of the subjunctive is formed by adding *e, es, e, ions, iez,* or *ent* to the stem. For *je, tu, il, elle, ils,* and *elles,* drop the *-ent* ending from the third person plural of the present indicative. For *nous* and *vous,* drop the *-ons* ending from the first person plural of the present indicative and add *–ions* and *–iez,* respectively.

regarder (to watch, to look at)

je regarde	I watch	*nous regardions*	we watch
tu regardes	you watch	*vous regardiez*	you watch
il/elle regarde	he/she watches	*ils/elles regardent*	they watch

Il veut que tu écrives une lettre de remerciement.	**He wants you to write a thank you letter.**
Je doute qu'il boive du café.	**I doubt he drinks coffee.**

Exercise 8-1: Present Subjunctive Practice

Give the correct verb forms in the subjunctive.

1. *dire:*   *nous* ....
2. *chanter:*   *elle* ....
3. *prendre:*   *je* ....
4. *voir:*   *je* ....
5. *croire:*   *vous* ....
6. *répondre:*   *vous* ....
7. *mettre:*   *il* ....
8. *finir:*   *tu* ....
9. *comprendre:*   *vous* ....
10. *choisir:*   *je* ....

Not That Regular

Some verbs are partially irregular like *aller* (*to go*) and *vouloir* (*to want*), and some are totally irregular like *être* (*to be*), *avoir* (*to have*), *savoir* (*to know*), *pouvoir* (*can*), and *faire* (*to do*). The verb table in the back of the book will help you sort out all the conjugations.

Il veut que tu y ailles.	**He wants you to go there.**
Je ne crois pas que tu puisses le convaincre.	**I don't think you can convince him.**
Elle préfère que tu sois à la réunion.	**She prefers you to be at the meeting.**
Je doute qu'il le sache.	**I doubt he knows it.**
Je regrette que vous ayez tant d'ennuis.	**I am sorry you are having so many problems.**

Uses of the Subjunctive

The subjunctive is used after verbs expressing will, desire, and wishes.

Je veux que tu ailles voir un médecin.	**I want you to see a doctor.**
Elle préfère que nous arrivions avant midi.	**She prefers us to arrive before noon.**

The subjunctive is used after expressions of emotion.

Il est triste que tu ne puisses pas venir ce soir.	**He is sad you can't come tonight.**
Nous regrettons qu'elle ne travaille plus ici.	**We are sorry she no longer works here.**

The subjunctive is used after expressions of doubt.

Tu ne crois pas qu'il soit compétent?	**You don't think he is competent?**
Elle doute que ce soit la bonne solution.	**She doubts it is the right solution.**

Exercise 8-2: In the Mood

Indicate if each verb is in the present indicative or present subjunctive.

1. .... *vous mangiez*

2. .... *tu dis*

3. .... *vous parliez*

4. .... *il puisse*

5. .... *vous pensiez*

6. .... *j'écris*

7. .... *vous allez*

8. .... *elle réponde*

Exercise 8-3: Let's Talk Subjunctive!

Put the verbs in parentheses in the present subjunctive.

1. *Nous voulons que Marc (prendre) ses responsabilités.*

....

2. *Je ne crois pas qu'elle (savoir) la nouvelle.*

....

3. *Vous doutez que ce reportage (être) authentique.*

....

4. *J'ai peur que leur système (avoir) un virus.*

....

5. *Mathilde aimerait bien qu'Ulysse (pouvoir) l'aider.*

....

6. *Il regrette que vous (ne pas assister) à la fête ce soir.*

....

7. *Nous somme déçus qu'il (venir) tout seul,*

....

8. *Je suis si contente que vous (préparer) le dîner.*

....

Impersonal Expressions

The subjunctive is also used after certain impersonal expressions. In the same manner that some verbs are followed by the indicative and others by the subjunctive, some impersonal expressions are followed by one mood or the other. In most cases, the expressions followed by the subjunctive express will, obligation, necessity, emotion, judgment, and doubt.

Il est rare qu'il soit en colère.   **It is rare for him to be angry.**

Here are some impersonal expressions followed by the indicative:

il est certain	it is certain	*il est évident*	it is obvious
il est sûr	it is sure	*il est vrai*	it is true
il est probable	it is probable	*il me (lui) semble*	it seems to me (to him/her)

Here are some impersonal expressions followed by the subjunctive:

il faut	one must	*il est essentiel*	it is essential
il est indispensable	it is essential	*il est juste*	it is fair
il est possible	it is possible	*il se peut*	it may be
il est important	it is important	*il vaut mieux*	it is better
il est préférable	it is preferable	*il est souhaitable*	it is desirable
il est naturel	it is natural	*il est normal*	it is normal

Exercise 8-4: Yes It Is!

Put the verbs in parentheses in the present subjunctive.

1. *Il est dommage que la librairie (être) fermée aujourd'hui.*

   ....

2. *Il est douteux qu'il (vouloir) rester à Paris.*

   ....

3. *Il est étonnant que ce magasin (avoir) si peu de clients.*

   ....

4. *Il est possible que cette mission (être) dangeureuse.*

   ....

5. *Mathilde aimerait bien qu'Ulysse (pouvoir) l'aider.*

   ....

6. *Il est rare que vous (avoir) raison.*

   ....

7. *Il est étrange qu'il (ne pas répondre) au téléphone.*

....

8. *Cela vaut la peine qu'elle (faire) ce voyage.*

....

9. *Il faut que tu (aller) à Lyon avant jeudi.*

....

10. *Il est important que vous lui (parler) demain matin.*

....

The Subjunctive and Superlatives

The subjunctive is used after superlatives like *le plus grand* (*the largest*) and *le moins cher* (*the least expensive*) and after adjectives expressing a superlative idea, like *premier* (*first*), *dernier* (*the last*), and *seul* (*only*).

C'est la seule chanson que je sache par coeur.   **It's the only song I know by heart.**

Exercise 8-5: Superlative!

Put the verbs in parentheses in the present subjunctive.

1. *C'est le village le plus pittoresque que je (connaître).*

....

2. *C'est le premier livre ancien que vous (posséder).*

....

3. *C'est le seul ami qu'il (avoir) à Paris.*

....

4. *C'est l'ordinateur le plus performant qui (être) sur le marché.*

....

5. *C'est le restaurant le moins cher que nous (connaître) dans ce quartier.*

....

6. *Ce sont les premiers investissements que nous (faire) dans ce pays.*

....

7. *C'est la seule recette qu'elle (savoir) faire.*

....

8. *C'est la seule veste qui lui (aller).*

   ....

9. *C'est la personne la plus gentille que nous (fréquenter) dans l'immeuble.*

   ....

10. *C'est l'unique souci qu'il (avoir).*

    ....

The Subjunctive with Conjunctions

With impersonal expressions, you had to decide between the indicative and the subjunctive mood. It's the same scenario with conjunctions. Some are followed by the indicative. Others are followed by the subjunctive.

Appelle-moi dès que tu arriveras.   **Call me as soon as you arrive.**

Here are some of the conjunctions followed by the subjunctive.

afin que	so that, in order to	*pour que*	so that, in order to
de peur que	for fear that	*de crainte que*	for fear that
avant que	before	*jusqu'à ce que*	until
bien que	although	*quoique*	although

Nous partirons avant qu'il fasse nuit.   **We'll leave before dark.**

When the subjects of the main clause and the dependent clause are the same, the infinitive is used. However there are no corresponding prepositions with *jusqu'à ce que, bien que, quoique,* and *pourvu que.*

Il étudie afin de réussir l'examen.   **He studies to pass the exam.**
Elle met un autre pull de peur   **She puts on another sweater**
    d'avoir froid.   **for fear of being cold.**

Exercise 8-6: Spell It Out!

Listen to the audio track and down each sentence.

1. ....

TRACK 27

2. ....

3. ....

4. ....

5. ....

6. ....

7. ....

8. ....

9. ....

10. ....

Exercise 8-7: What Do You Think?

Make an appropriate sentence by matching the phrase in the right-hand column with the phrase in the left-hand column.

1. *Elle ira au travail demain*
2. *Elle louera une villa*
3. *Elle est efficace*
4. *Elle prendra une décision*
5. *Elle insistera*

a. *afin que ses amis en profitent.*
b. *jusqu'à ce que vous acceptiez.*
c. *avant qu'il soit trop tard.*
d. *quoiqu'elle soit un peu lente.*
e. *à moins qu'il y ait une grève des transports.*

There's Always Hope!

The conjunction *pourvu que* (*provided that*) is also used to say *let's hope*. If you are with French friends who are a bit anxious about this or that, you'll often hear this expression.

Elle ira en Asie pourvu que sa collègue l'accompagne.	**She'll go to Asia provided her colleague goes with her.**
Pourvu qu'il y ait beaucoup de neige dans les Alpes!	**Let's hope there is a lot of snow in the Alps!**

Exercise 8-8: Let's Hope!

Translate the following sentences using *pourvu que* with the subjunctive. Use the *vous* form when necessary.

1. Let's hope it does not rain tomorrow!

   ....

2. Let's hope the shop is open!

   ....

3. Let's hope they do not arrive before us!

   ....

4. Let's hope you can buy this house!

   ....

5. Let's hope he comes alone!

   ....

6. Let's hope they are happy!

   ....

7. Let's hope you are right!

   ....

8. Let's hope they are on time!

   ....

9. Let's hope he can attend the meeting!

   ....

10. Let's hope she goes to Paris this summer!

    ....

The Past Subjunctive

When the action of the dependent clause is anterior to the action of the main clause, the past subjunctive is used. The past subjunctive is formed with *être* or *avoir* in the subjunctive plus the past participle of the verb.

comprendre (to understand)

j'aie compris	I understood
tu aies compris	you understood
il/elle ait compris	he/she understood
nous ayons compris	we understood

vous ayez compris	you understood
ils/elles aient compris	they understood

Je suis content que vous ayez reçu le document à temps.	**I am happy you got the document in time.**
Je regrette que tu ne sois pas venu.	**I am sorry you did not come.**

Exercise 8-9: It All Happened!

TRACK 28

Listen to the audio track and repeat. Then listen again and identify the tense of the verb. It will be either *subjonctif présent* or *subjonctif passé*.

1. ....
2. ....
3. ....
4. ....
5. ....

6. ....
7. ....
8. ....
9. ....
10. ....

Exercise 8-10: It's All Behind Us!

Rewrite the sentences, changing the verb in the dependent clause from the present to the past subjunctive.

1. *Je suis contente que tu puisses venir.*

   ....

2. *J'ai peur qu'elle ne prenne pas la bonne décision.*

   ....

3. *Il ne pense pas que tu fasses assez d'effort.*

   ....

4. *Nous sommes désolés que tu n'acceptes pas cette offre.*

   ....

5. *C'est la seule recette qu'il sache faire.*

   ....

6. *Il est incroyable qu'il dise des choses pareilles.*

   ....

7. *Je doute qu'il envoie son C.V.*

   ....

8. *Tu es surpris qu'il ne dise rien?*

   ....

9. *Je ne crois pas qu'ils comprennent le problème.*

   ....

10. *Il est naturel qu'elle aille chez sa grand-mère.*

    ....

Whatever, Wherever, Whoever

You will encounter the present and past subjunctive in expressions such as *whatever, wherever, whoever.*

When *whatever* is followed by a verb, the neutral form *quoi que* is used.

Quoi qu'il pense, elle est
    d'accord avec lui.
	Whatever he thinks, she
	    agrees with him.

Quoi que tu lui dises, il n'écoute jamais.	**Whatever you tell him, he never listens.**

When *whatever* is followed by a noun, *quel que* is used. It agrees in gender and number with the subject.

Quel que soit le prix, nous l'achèterons.	**Whatever the price, we'll buy it.**
Quelles que soient vos opinions,	**Whatever your opinions,**
je serai toujours votre ami.	**I'll always be your friend.**
Où qu'il soit, je le trouverai.	**Wherever he is, I'll find him.**
Qui que vous soyez, dites-nous la vérité.	**Whoever you are, tell us the truth.**

Exercise 8-11: Find the Ending, Wherever It Is

Make an appropriate sentence by matching the phrase in the right-hand column with the phrase in the left-hand column.

1. *Qui que vous soyez*	a. *avance avec prudence.*
2. *Quel que soit ton objectif*	b. *ne dépense pas trop d'argent.*
3. *Où que tu ailles*	c. *soyez tolérant.*
4. *Quoi que tu achètes*	d. *je te suivrai.*
5. *Quelles que soient ses faiblesses*	e. *identifiez-vous.*

The Present Participle

The present participle can be used as a verb, as noun or as an adjective. The present participle is formed with the *nous* form of the present indicative. Simply drop the *-ons* ending and add *-ant*.

parler	*parlant*	speaking
prendre	*prenant*	taking

Some present participles have an irregular form.

être	*étant*	being
avoir	*ayant*	having
savoir	*sachant*	knowing

As a verb, the present participle does not change form.

Ne sachant pas quoi dire, elle est partie.   **Not knowing what to say, she left.**

When an action precedes another one, the present participle can take on a combined form.

ayant dîné	having dined	*étant arrivé*	having arrived

Ayant compris son erreur, il s'est excusé.   **Having understood his mistake, he apologized.**

As an adjective, the present participle agrees with the noun it qualifies.

C'était un endroit charmant.   **It was a charming place.**

As a noun, the present participle agrees in gender and number with the noun to which it refers.

Bernard, c'est un battant.   **Bernard is a fighter.**

Exercise 8-12: Present Participles

Write out the present participle of each verb.

1. *protéger* ....
2. *apprendre* ....
3. *savoir* ....
4. *lire* ....
5. *se promener* ....
6. *influencer* ....
7. *voir* ....
8. *fasciner* ....
9. *être* ....
10. *choisir* ....

Exercise 8-13: Make a Sentence

Make an appropriate sentence by matching the phrase in the right-hand column with the phrase in the left-hand column.

1. *Sachant la vérité*	a. *il a pris un taxi.*
2. *Traversant la région*	b. *il a appelé la police.*
3. *Ayant faim*	c. *il a cherché une solution.*
4. *Comprenant le problème*	d. *il a acheté un sandwich.*
5. *Étant en retard*	e. *il en a profité pour visiter des châteaux.*

Gerunds

A gerund is formed with *en* + the present participle. It can express simultaneity, manner, condition, or causality between two actions.

Elle tricote en regardant la télévision.   **She knits while watching television.**

When a tension, a contradiction, between two actions needs to be underlined, use *tout en* + the present participle.

Tout en pleurant, il riait.   **While crying, he was laughing.**

Exercise 8-14: While Doing This . . .

Put the verbs in parentheses in the gerund form.

1. *Elle a perdu un talon en (traverser) la rue.*

   ....

2. *Elle a fait la connaissance d'Ève en (voyager) à Bali.*

   ....

3. *C'est en (faire) plus d'exercice que vous resterez en forme.*

   ....

4. *Tu peux acheter une baguette en (revenir) du travail?*

   ....

5. *Sonia a claqué la porte en (sortir).*

   ....

6. *Elle s'est cassé le bras en (patiner) sur le lac.*

   ....

7. *Tout en (écrire) son C.V., il regardait un match de foot à la télé.*

   ....

8. *Appelle-moi en (arriver) à l'aéroport.*

   ....

9. *En (accepter) un tel marché, vous risquez de vous ruiner.*

   ....

10. *(Être) sur le point de partir, il s'est rendu compte qu'il n'avait pas son passeport.*

    ....

Exercise 8-15: Listening Comprehension

Listen to the audio track and repeat. Then listen again and indicate whether you hear in each sentence an *adjectif*, a *participe présent*, or a *gérondif*.

TRACK 29

1. ....
2. ....
3. ....
4. ....
5. ....

6. ....
7. ....
8. ....
9. ....
10. ....

The Passive Voice

A sentence can be either in the active or the passive voice. In the active voice, the subject performs an action; in the passive voice, the subject is acted upon.

Les pirates découvrent le trésor.	**The pirates discover the treasure.**
Le trésor est découvert par les pirates.	**The treasure is being discovered by the pirates.**
Le pharaon a construit la pyramide.	**The pharaoh built the pyramid.**
La pyramide a été construite par le pharaon.	**The pyramid was built by the pharaoh.**

The passive voice is much more common in English than in French. In French, the passive voice can be used to put an emphasis on the subject or to avoid specifying the agent of an action in order to remain vague.

La preuve de son innocence a été dissimulée par la police.	**The proof of his innocence was concealed by the police.**
Aucune décision n'a été prise.	**No decision was made.**

Common forms of the passive voice are expressed in different ways.

Ici, on parle anglais.	**English is spoken here.**
On vous demande au téléphone.	**You are wanted on the phone.**

Exercise 8-16: Something Is Being Done!

TRACK 30

Listen to the audio track and write down each sentence.

1. ....

2. ....

3. ....

4. ....

5. ....

6. ....

7. ....

8. ....

9. ....

10. ....

Exercise 8-17: Let's Be Passive!

Translate the following sentences using the passive voice.

1. The castle is being built by the king.

   ....

2. Her painting will be sold on Saturday.

   ....

3. This wine is drunk cool.

   ....

4. A new computer is being installed.

   ....

5. Dinner will be served on the terrace.

   ....

Let's Recap

Now let's review what you have learned!

Exercise 8-18: Setting the Mood

Indicate if each verb is in the present indicative or present subjunctive.

1. .... *vous regardiez*

2. .... *tu dis*

3. .... *nous allons*

4. .... *vous appeliez*

5. .... *je voie*

6. .... *elle sache*

7. .... *tu aies*

8. .... *nous traversons*

9. .... *elles soient*

10. .... *vous connaissez*

Exercise 8-19: What's the Deal?

Put each verb in parentheses into the present indicative or the present subjunctive.

1. *Je regrette que vous (ne pas pouvoir) rester plus longtemps.*

....

2. *Elle veut que tu (apprendre) le chinois.*

....

3. *Il est ravi que vous (aimer) son gâteau.*

....

4. *Le consul a peur que la situation (devenir) trop dangereuse.*

....

5. *C'est la seule veste qui lui (aller).*

....

6. *Elle dit que son nouveau travail (être) très intéressant.*

....

7. *Nous doutons que l'avion (être) à l'heure.*

....

8. *Il écrit que son poste (être) en péril.*

....

9. *Nous souhaitons que vous (réussir).*

....

10. *Il sait qu'elle (avoir) raison.*

....

Exercise 8-20: All Impersonals Are Not Equal

Put each verb in parentheses following an impersonal expression into the present indicative or the present subjunctive.

1. *Il est étrange que tu (recevoir) tant de courrier.*

....

2. *Il est certain qu'elle (dire) toujours ce qu'elle pense.*

....

3. *Il est incroyable qu'ils (ne pas pouvoir) nous donner une réponse.*

....

4. *Il vaut mieux que vous (faire) vite.*

....

5. *Il est dommage qu'ils (être) si têtus.*

....

6. *Il est indispensable que vous (trouver) un appartement avant mai.*

....

7. *Il est bon que tu (être) présent pour cet entretien.*

....

8. *Il semble qu'elle (savoir) ce qu'elle fait.*

....

9. *Il est naturel que vous (hésiter) avant de prendre cette décision.*

....

Exercise 8-21: How to Say?

Translate the following sentences using the *vous* form when necessary.

1. I'll be in the park unless it is raining.

....

2. I'll send you her book so that you can read it before the meeting.

....

3. Jean can call her before you arrive.

....

4. I doubt she knows how to contact him.

....

5. You must cook for us!

....

6. Whatever you prepare, I'll eat it.

....

7. Although he is not rich, he is very generous.

....

8. Wherever you are, I'll be there.

....

9. Whatever his opinions, they'll vote for him.

....

Exercise 8-22: Talking About the Past

Put the verbs in parentheses into the past subjunctive.

1. *Je suis étonné qu'il (ne pas téléphoner).*

....

2. *Nous ne pensons pas qu'ils (vendre) leur maison de campagne.*

....

3. *Je doute qu'ils (arriver) à temps.*

....

4. *Il est bizarre que vous (laisser tomber) une telle occasion.*

....

5. *Il a peur qu'ils (avoir) des problèmes graves.*

....

6. *Il est dommage qu'il (ne rien dire) avant.*

....

7. *Je ne crois pas qu'elle (visiter) l'Argentine.*

....

8. *Il est possible qu'il (perdre) l'ordonnance du médecin.*

....

Exercise 8-23: *This Is the Way It Goes*

Translate the following sentences using *vous* and the active voice when necessary.

1. This meat is served with red wine.

....

2. They met while traveling on a boat.

....

3. Having learned Italian, he decided to learn French.

....

4. She found the answer while surfing the Internet.

....

5. This red wine is to be served cool.

....

6. This verb is followed by the indicative.

....

7. He had his hair cut in Paris.

....

8. The king is building a new castle.

....

9. Chinese is spoken here.

....

10. This is not to be repeated.

....

Part 9

Prepositions

Prepositions are one of the major obstacles in learning French. In this part, you will study different uses of prepositions. Let's start with prepositions used with geographical names. They will be most useful if you are going to France, *si vous allez en France*. One thing to keep in mind is the gender of geographical names, which you studied in Part 1.

Prepositions with Geographical Names

To tell someone what city you are in or what city you are traveling to, use the preposition *à*.

Il habite à Toulouse.	**He lives in Toulouse.**
Elle vont à Londres.	**They are going to London.**

A few cities like *Le Havre, Le Caire, La Rochelle, Le Touquet, Le Mans,* and *La Havane* are preceded by an article.

Ils sont en vacances au Caire.	**They are on vacation in Cairo.**
Elle est allée à La Nouvelle-Orléans.	**She went to New Orleans.**

With countries, regions, states, provinces, and continents, the preposition varies according to gender. You may want to review the gender of geographical names in Part I. The basic rule is as follows:

en	feminine
en	masculine beginning with a vowel
au	masculine singlular
aux	masculine and feminine plural

Elle travaille en France.	**She is working in France.**
Nous voyageons en Arkansas.	**We are traveling in Arkansas.**
Ce musée est au Japon.	**This museum is in Japan.**
Vous habitez aux États-Unis?	**Do you live in the United States?**

The five continents are feminine. Provinces, states, and countries are usually feminine with some exceptions; for example, *le Mexique (Mexico)* and *le Cambodge (Cambodia)*. In some cases, *dans le* replaces *au*, like *dans le Midi, dans le Languedoc, dans le Roussillon*.

When countries are islands, the preposition may vary.

à Cuba	in Cuba	*à Tahiti*	in Tahiti
à La Réunion	in Reunion	*à Madagascar*	in Madagascar
à la Jamaïque	in Jamaica	*en Haïti*	in Haiti

Exercise 9-1: What's the Preposition?

Indicate the right preposition to use with each geographical name.

1. .... *Pérou*   6. .... *Vietnam*

2. .... *Italie*   7. .... *Espagne*

3. .... *États-Unis*   8. .... *Canada*

4. .... *France*   9. .... *Paris*

5. .... *Le Caire*   10. .... *Californie*

Exercise 9-2: Where Are They All Going?

Write the whole sentence using the correct preposition.

1. *Je voyagerai . . . Grèce.*

....

2. *Ils sont allés . . . Strasbourg.*

....

3. *Nous allons envoyer notre fils . . . Irlande.*

....

4. *Tu iras . . . Luxembourg?*

....

5. *Elle fera du ski . . . Colorado.*

....

6. *L'agent de voyages leur a conseillé d'aller . . . Inde.*

....

7. *Son nouvel emploi sera . . . Chine.*

....

8. *Ils passeront leurs vacances . . . Turquie.*

....

9. *Je voudrais aller . . . Mexique.*

....

10. *Nous sommes invités à un mariage . . . Hongrie.*

....

Exercise 9-3: Where Are They Working?

Write complete sentences combining the elements below and using the verb *travailler* in the present tense.

1. *Marc / Paris / France*

   ....

2. *Jèrôme / Boston / États-Unis*

   ....

3. *Pedro / Buenos Aires / Argentine*

   ....

4. *Aziz / Carthage / Tunisie*

   ....

5. *Maria / Porto / Portugal*

   ....

6. *Chloé / Amsterdam / Hollande*

   ....

7. *Aruna / Bangkok / Thaïlande*

   ....

8. *Fatiha / Casablanca / Maroc*

   ....

9. *Nora / Shangai / Chine*

   ....

10. *Pierre / Ottawa / Canada*

    ....

Exercise 9-4: What Are They Saying?

TRACK 31

Listen to the audio track, noting that some incorrect prepositions are used. Decide what corrections are needed and write down each sentence correctly.

1. ....

2. ....

3. ....

4. ....

5. ....

6. ....

7. ....

8. ....

9. ....

10. ....

For feminine geographical entities, origin is expressed by *de* without a definite article. For masculine and plural ones, *de* is used with the definite article.

Il rentrera d'Allemagne demain.	**He'll return from Germany tomorrow.**
Elle est originaire du Brésil.	**She comes from Brazil.**
Ils ont rapporté cette sculpture	**They brought back this sculpture**
des États-Unis.	**from the United States.**

Exercise 9-5: Where Are They From?

Write the whole sentence using *de, d', du, de la* or *des*.

1. *Il est originaire . . . Belgique.*

....

2. *Cette sculpture provient . . . Mali.*

....

3. *Elle est revenue . . . Jordanie hier soir.*

....

4. *Cette sculpture vient . . . Vietnam.*

....

5. *Ça vient . . . Colorado.*

....

6. *Rapporte-moi un souvenir . . . Argentine.*

....

7. *Ils rentrent tout juste . . . Chine.*

....

8. *Qu'est-ce que tu as rapporté . . . Turquie?*

....

9. *Elle est originaire . . . Japon.*

....

10. *Cette horloge vient . . . Suède.*

....

Common Prepositions

En, à, and *de* are not used only with geographical names. They are very common prepositions. Here are a few additional prepositions that you will have to memorize.

à	at, in	*après*	after
avant	before	*avec*	with
chez	at, with	*contre*	against
dans	in	*de*	of, from
derrière	behind	*dès*	from
devant	in front of	*durant*	during
en	in	*entre*	between
envers	toward	*hormis*	apart from
hors	except, apart from	*malgré*	in spite of
par	by, through	*parmi*	among
pendant	during	*pour*	for
sans	without	*sauf*	except
selon	according to	*sous*	under
suivant	according to	*sur*	on
vers	toward	*vu*	considering, given

Vincent est venu chez moi.   **Vincent came to my place.**
Selon eux, c'est arrivé à 20 heures 30.   **According to them, it**
           happened at 8:30 P.M.

*Parmi les invités, il y avait son
nouveau petit ami.
Malgré la pluie, nous avons fait
une promenade agréable.*

**Among the guests was her
new boyfriend.
In spite of the rain, we had
a nice walk.**

Exercise 9-6: Elizabeth's Crazy Vacation

TRACK 32

Listen to the audio track and answer the questions.

1. *Où va Elizabeth?*

    ....

2. *Quel est l'objectif de ce voyage?*

    ....

3. *Est-ce que sa mère approuve ce voyage?*

    ....

4. *Est-ce qu'Elizabeth parle espagnol?*

    ....

5. *Quelle est l'opinion de la soeur d'Elizabeth?*

    ....

Exercise 9-7: Traductions

Translate the following sentences, using *vous* when necessary.

1. She came with me.

    ....

2. The cat is hiding under the cupboard.

    ....

3. According to me, you are wrong.

    ....

4. Hélène is leaning against the wall.

    ....

5. He came without his wife.

    ....

6. She went for a walk despite the snow.

    ....

7. Considering the circumstances, I think you made the right choice.

....

8. You can stay at my place.

....

9. Wait for me in front of the train station!

....

10. They paid for everything except the taxi.

....

Now let's look in detail at the most common prepositions: *à*, *de*, *chez*, and *sur*.

The Preposition À

The preposition *à*, when combined with the definite article, can take on different forms.

à + le = au	
Pierre est au bureau.	**Pierre is at the office.**
à + la = à la	
Anne est à la plage.	**Anne is at the beach.**
à + les = aux	
Il est allé aux toilettes.	**He went to the restroom.**

We have already seen how to use *à* with geographical names or with indirect objects. The preposition *à* can also express nature, function, or purpose.

une machine à écrire	a typewriter
une machine à laver	a washing machine
une machine à coudre	a sewing machine
une machine à sous	a slot machine
un métier à tisser	a loom
un moulin à café	a coffee grinder

un moulin à poivre	a pepper mill
un moulin à vent	a windmill
un moulin à paroles	a chatterbox
un verre à eau	a water glass
un verre à vin	a wine glass
une flûte à champagne	a champagne flute
une mousse au chocolat	a chocolate mousse
une glace à la myrtille	a blueberry ice cream
un sorbet à la banane	a banana sorbet
un gâteau à la carotte	a carrot cake
une tasse à café	a coffee cup

J'ai fait une tarte aux olives.   **I baked an olive tart.**

Sylvie est un vrai moulin à paroles!   **Sylvie is a real chatterbox!**

Il n'a pas de machine à laver chez lui.   **He does not have a washing machine at home.**

Tu préfères une glace à la vanille ou un sorbet au citron?   **Do you prefer a vanilla ice cream or a lemon sorbet?**

The Preposition De

Like the preposition *à*, the preposition *de* can take different forms when combined with the definite article.

de + le = du

J'ai rêvé du Père Noël.   **I dreamed about Santa Claus.**

de + la = de la

Le journaliste parle de la météo.   **The journalist is talking about the weather.**

de + les = des

Il a peur des araignées.   **He is afraid of spiders.**

Like *à*, *de* is used with geographical names and indirect objects. To express possession, you also need the preposition *de* combined with a noun.

Aujourd'hui c'est l'anniversaire de Marie.	**It's Marie's birthday today.**
Je travaille dans la librairie de mon oncle.	**I work in my uncle's bookstore.**
La maison des Perriard est vide.	**The Perriards' house is empty.**

When describing an action, you also need the preposition *de*.

Elle l'a salué d'un air aimable.	**She greeted him with a friendly look.**
Il a rayé ton nom d'un trait de plume.	**He erased your name with one stroke of the pen.**
D'un geste lent, il lui a pris la main.	**With a slow gesture, he took her hand.**

The preposition *de* can also denote contents or composition.

un verre de lait	a glass of milk
une bouteille de bordeaux	a bottle of claret
une tasse de café	a cup of coffee
un bol de chocolat chaud	a bowl of hot chocolate
une boîte de haricots	a can of beans
une poignée de framboises	a handful of raspberries

Je prendrai un bol de soupe.	**I'll have a bowl of soup.**
Il a ouvert une boîte de lentilles.	**He opened a can of lentils.**
Servez-moi une tasse de thé!	**Give me a cup of tea!**
Donnez-moi une poignée de noisettes!	**Give me a handful of hazelnuts!**

Exercise 9-8: A Tea Cup or a Cup of Tea?

Write the whole sentence using the correct preposition: *à* or *de*.

1. *À Las Vegas, nous avons passé des heures devant les machines . . . sous.*

   ....

2. *Tu veux un bol . . . potage?*

   ....

3. *Va chercher des verres . . . limonade dans le buffet!*

4. *Elle a ouvert une boîte . . . cassoulet.*

5. *Nous avons bu une bouteille . . . eau.*

6. *Nous venons d'acheter une machine . . . sécher le linge.*

7. *Regarde le vieux moulin . . . vent!*

8. *Je prendrai une assiette . . . crudités.*

9. *Il refuse d'utiliser sa vieille machine . . . écrire.*

10. *Ils apportent un panier . . . fruits.*

The Preposition Chez

Chez can mean different things. Let's look at a few examples.

Elle a fêté son anniversaire chez nous.	**She celebrated her birthday at our house.**
Chez Clément est une chaîne de restaurants.	**Chez Clément is a restaurant chain.**
J'ai acheté mon ordinateur chez Apple.	**I bought my computer at the Apple store.**
Ce que j'aime chez Chateaubriand, c'est son romantisme.	**What I like about Chateaubriand is his romanticism.**
Qu'est-ce qui ne va pas chez ta soeur?	**What is wrong with your sister?**

The Preposition **Sur**

The preposition *sur* also takes on different meanings. *Sur* is not always translated with the word *on* in English.

Les livres sont sur l'étagère.	**The books are on the shelf.**
Ma maison donne sur la rivière.	**My house looks out on the river.**
L'hôtel donne sur la plage.	**The hotel faces the beach.**
J'ai versé 200 euros sur ton compte.	**I transferred 200 euros to your account.**
Je n'ai plus que 15 euros sur mon compte.	**I only have 15 euros left in my account.**
Je n'ai pas mon portable sur moi.	**I don't have my cell phone with me.**
Ma chambre fait trois mètres sur quatre.	**My bedroom measures three meters by four.**
Ils répondent au téléphone vingt-quatre heures sur vingt-quatre.	**They answer the phone twenty-four hours a day.**
Le magasin est ouvert sept jours sur sept.	**The shop is open seven days a week.**
Je voudrais travailler seulement quatre jours sur sept.	**I would like to work only four days out of seven.**
Il a une chance sur deux d'être accepté.	**He has one chance out of two to be accepted.**

The English word *on* is not always translated as *sur* in French. That would be too easy! See the following examples.

Je l'ai rencontré dans la rue.	**I ran into him on the street.**
Élise ne travaille pas le mercredi.	**Élise does not work on Wednesdays.**
Ils habitent au dixième étage.	**They live on the tenth floor.**
À ta droite, tu peux voir le Panthéon.	**On your right, you can see the *Panthéon*.**

Translating the Preposition **With**

There are many different ways to translate the preposition *with* in French. Let's see a few examples.

Nous sommes sortis avec Marie.	**We went out with Marie.**
Il est parti avec sa valise.	**He left with his suitcase.**

In English, *with* is used to refer to an attribute of someone or something. In French, you would use *à* + the definite article.

Il regarde la femme aux yeux noirs.	**He's looking at the woman with dark eyes.**
Apporte-moi la malle aux poignées dorées!	**Bring me the trunk with golden handles!**
L'homme au manteau gris a pris la fuite.	**The man with the grey coat ran away.**

In French, the preposition is omitted when describing a way of doing things or a way of carrying oneself.

Il m'écoutait, les bras ballants.	**He listened to me with his arms swinging.**
Elle avançait, les yeux fermés.	**She moved forward with her eyes closed.**

With some adjectives, *with* in English is translated by *de* in French.

Elle est heureuse de sa nouvelle vie.	**She is happy with her new life.**
Il est content de son travail.	**He is happy with his job.**

Exercise 9-9: Identify the Correct Preposition

Write the whole sentence using the correct preposition.

1. *Elle a dormi . . . son oncle et sa tante.*

   ....

2. *Le supermarché est ouvert six jours . . . sept.*

   ....

3. *Apporte-moi des pinces . . . cheveux!*

   ....

4. *Hier, nous avons dîné . . . Juliette.*

   ....

5. *Elle a apporté une bouteille . . . champagne.*

   ....

6. *Je n'ai plus rien . . . mon compte en banque.*

   ....

7. *Il est parti . . . tous mes dossiers.*

   ....

8. *Il y a quelque chose d'étrange . . . ce garçon.*

9. *Tu n'as pas de machine . . . laver la vaisselle?*

10. *Elle lui a offert un bouquet . . . fleurs.*

Exercise 9-10: Let's Get Reconciled with Prepositions!

Translate the following sentences, using *tu* and inversion.

1. The girl with red hair is my niece.

2. Are the shops here open on Sundays?

3. My living room measures ten meters by five.

4. On your left there is the Eiffel Tower.

5. The woman with the yellow sweater is looking at us.

6. Julien works on the third floor.

7. My bedroom faces the street.

8. What is the problem with him?

9. Their new house faces the ocean.

10. You can call me twenty-four hours a day.

Using En *and* Dans

En and *dans* are both used to express time.
    Dans is used to express an action that is about to begin.

Nous partons dans dix minutes.	**We are leaving in ten minutes.**
Le spectacle commence dans quinze minutes.	**The show will begin in fifteen minutes.**

    En is used to express the length of time that an action has taken, takes, or will take.

Il a peint toute la cuisine en deux jours.	**He painted the whole kitchen in two days.**
Elle va essayer de faire sa thèse en trois ans.	**She will try to do her thesis in three years.**

    In the following examples, *en* is used in a general meaning, while *dans* is more specific.

Stéphane va au travail en voiture.	**Stéphane drives to work.**
Monte dans la voiture!	**Get in the car!**
Il est venu en métro.	**He came by subway.**
Ils se sont rencontrés dans le métro.	**They met in the subway.**
José vit en Floride.	**José lives in Florida.**
Dans le Paris des années 1930, il y avait moins de circulation.	**In 1930s Paris, there was less traffic.**

Using En *and* À

In expressions of time, hours of the day are expressed with *à*, and months, years, and seasons are expressed with *en* except for spring.

Le film commence à 20 heures.	**The movie starts at 8 P.M.**
Passe me voir à midi.	**Come and see me at noon.**
Mon grand-père est né en 1937.	**My grandfather was born in 1937.**
L'homme a marché sur la lune en 1969.	**Man walked on the moon in 1969.**

J'aime prendre mes vacances en automne.	**I like to take my vacation in the fall.**
Il fait très chaud dans le Sud de la France en été.	**Summer is very hot in the South of France.**
Ma fille est née au printemps.	**My daughter was born in the spring.**

To express means of transportation, the prepositions *à* and *en* are used.

aller à bicyclette (à/en vélo)	to go by bicycle
aller à cheval	to ride a horse
aller à pied	to go on foot, to walk
aller en autobus	to go by bus
aller en autocar	to go by bus (intercity)
aller en avion	to go by plane, to fly
aller en bateau	to go by boat
aller en métro	to go by subway
aller en péniche	to go by barge
aller en train	to go by train
aller en voiture	to go by car, to drive

Il est venu à pied.	**He came on foot.**
Gilles est rentré chez lui à pied.	**Gilles walked home.**
Henriette va au travail en voiture.	**Henriette drives to work.**
Elle est rentrée à vélo.	**She biked home.**

Exercise 9-11: En or Dans?

Write the whole sentence using the correct preposition.

1. *Ils sont partis vivre . . . Afrique.*

....

2. *Tu es venu . . . avion?*

....

3. *Marianne a préparé le repas . . . une demi-heure.*

....

4. *Ils sont montés . . . l'avion avec deux heures de retard.*

....

5. *Notre train part . . . quinze minutes.*

....

6. *Montez . . . le train tout de suite!*

....

7. *. . . la France de Louis XIV, le peuple était asservi.*

....

8. *Je préférerais y aller . . . voiture.*

....

9. *. . . le Paris des années folles, les gens s'amusaient beaucoup.*

....

10. *Elle a envie de vivre . . . Amérique du Nord.*

....

Exercise 9-12: À or En?

Translate the following sentences into French using the proper preposition: *à* or *en*. Use the *vous* form when necessary.

1. Pierre bikes to work every day.

....

2. Vincent van Gogh died in 1890 in Auvers-sur-Oise.

....

3. My flight arrives at 12:30 P.M.

....

4. They decided to bike to Chartres.

....

5. In the winter, I like to stay at home.

....

6. The guests arrived at midnight.

....

THE EVERYTHING FRENCH PRACTICE BOOK

7. Roses are in full bloom in the spring.

....

8. Can you drive to work?

....

9. She walked to the zoo.

....

10. Julie started working here in 2002.

....

Exercise 9-13: Which Preposition to Choose?

Write the whole sentence using the correct preposition.

1. *Georges vit toujours . . . sa mère.*

....

2. *Je vais à Madrid . . . le train de nuit.*

....

3. *Floriane nous rendra visite . . . printemps.*

....

4. *On dit que Christophe Colomb a découvert l'Amérique . . . 1492.*

....

5. *Appelle-moi . . . midi!*

....

6. *Ne me regarde pas . . . cet air-là!*

....

7. *J'irai toute seule, . . . toi.*

....

8. *. . . Mozart, j'aime tout.*

....

9. *Le salon fait six mètres . . . quatre.*

....

10. *Je te rappelle . . . dix jours.*

....

Compound Prepositions

Prepositions can be two- or three-word compounds. These are called prepositive locutions. You will have to memorize them one by one!

à cause de	because of
à côté de	beside, next to
à défaut de	for lack of
à force de	by dint of
à la faveur de	thanks to, owing to
à la merci de	at the mercy of
à l'égard de	toward, with regard to
à l'exception de	except for
à l'instar de	following the example of
à l'insu de	without somebody's knowing
à même	straight from, next to
à même de	in a position to do something
à partir de	from
à raison de	at the rate of
à travers	across, through
au bas de	at the bottom of, at the foot of
au bord de	by, on the verge of, on the brink of
au coin de	at the corner of
au-delà de	beyond
au-dessous de	under, below
au-dessus de	above, on top of
au lieu de	instead of

au milieu de	in the middle of
au moyen de	by means of
au nord de	north of
auprés de	next to, with
au prix de	at the cost of
au sud de	south of
autour de	around
aux alentours de	in the vicinity of
aux dépens de	at the expense of
aux environs de	in the vicinity of
d'après	according to
de façon à	so as to
de peur de	for fear of
en bas de	at the bottom of
en dehors de	outside of, apart from
en dépit de	inspite of
en face de	in front of, opposite
en guise de	by way of
en haut de	at the top of
en raison de	because of, owing to
face à	against, facing
faute de	for lack of, for want of
grâce à	thanks to
le long de	along
loin de	far from

lors de	at the time of, during
par rapport à	in comparison with, in relation to, with regard to
près de	close to
quant à	as for, as to

Louis a perdu la voix lors
  d'une conférence.
Quant à moi, je préfère aller au cinéma.

Jean a cédé de peur d'être renvoyé.
À force de dire des bêtises,
  tu vas finir par les croire.
La boucherie est au coin de la rue.

À l'instar de son prédécesseur, le
  nouveau patron a pris rendez-vous
  avec tous les cadres de son équipe.

Il a acheté une nouvelle voiture à
  l'insu de sa femme.
En raison de la grève, le métro ne
  circule pas aujourd'hui.

Louis lost his voice
  during a conference.
As far as I am concerned,
  I prefer going to the movies.
Jean gave in for fear of being fired.
If you keep on saying stupid things,
  you will end up believing them.
The butcher's shop is at the
  corner of the street.
Following the example of his
  predecessor, the new boss made an
  appointment with all the
  managers of his team.
He bought a new car without
  his wife knowing.
Because of the strike, the
  subway doesn't run today.

Exercise 9-14: Putting Your Knowledge to the Test

Translate the following sentences, using the *tu* form.

1. According to the weather forecast, it will be sunny all weekend

....

2. Despite your opinion, I am going to go to that meeting.

....

3. Renée lives far away from the city.

....

4. He bought a house by a lake.

....

5. You can call me in the middle of the night if you need to.

....

6. Apart from you, I don't know anyone here.

....

7. I didn't write for lack of time.

....

8. Instead of looking at people having fun in the water, why don't you go yourself?

....

9. Barbara smokes without her parents knowing.

....

10. Thanks to my friend Roselyne, I found a new apartment very quickly.

....

Special Prepositions

There are subtle differences between some prepositive locutions with similar meanings.

Grâce à is positive, *à cause de* is negative, and *en raison de* is more neutral.

Il a découvert le théâtre grâce à son professeur de littérature.	**He discovered acting thanks to his literature teacher.**
Elle a échoué à cause de son manque de confiance en elle.	**She failed because of her lack of self-confidence.**
L'école est fermée en raison d'une épidémie de grippe.	**The school is closed because of a flu epidemic.**

À même can mean different things.

Ne mange pas à même la casserole!	**Don't eat straight out of the saucepan!**
J'aime porter mes pulls à même la peau.	**I like to wear my sweaters next to my skin.**
L'enfant s'est endormi à même le sol.	**The child fell asleep on the bare floor.**

When followed by a verb, *à même de* means "in a position to do something."

Le chauffeur sera à même de répondre à votre question.	**The driver will be in a position to answer your question.**

Je ne suis pas à même de te dire	**I am not in a position to**
ce qu'il faut faire.	**tell you what to do.**

The word *fleur* (flower) is used in the prepositive locution *à fleur de*, as in the following examples.

J'ai les nerfs à fleur de peau.	**I am all on edge.**
Il a une sensibilité à fleur de peau.	**He's very touchy.**
L'écueil est à fleur d'eau.	**The reef is just above the water.**

Exercise 9-15: Which Is Correct?

Write the whold sentence, using the appropriate prepositive locution.

1. *Jérôme a dû partir plus tôt . . . du mauvais temps.*

   ....

2. *Natacha s'est assise . . . de Laurent.*

   ....

3. *Nous avons skié . . . la forêt.*

   ....

4. *Ma tante possède une maison . . . la mer.*

   ....

5. *. . . le réprimander tout le temps, tu ferais mieux d'essayer de comprendre pourquoi ton fils agit ainsi.*

   ....W.

6. *. . . les dernières nouvelles, il y aurait des survivants à la catastrophe aérienne.*

   ....

7. *. . . prendre la voiture, je préfère y aller en train.*

   ....

8. *C'est . . . discours du président que nous avons appris qu'il avait été promu.*

   ....

9. *Elle n'a rien dit à Pierre . . . le décevoir.*

   ....

10. *Philippe habite une ferme . . . champs de blé.*

    ....

Exercise 9-16: What Do You Hear?

TRACK 33

Listen to the audio track and repeat. Then listen again and translate each sentence into English.

1. ....

2. ....

3. ....

4. ....

5. ....

6. ....

7. ....

8. ....

9. ....

10. ....

The Preposition À with Verbs

Some verbs need prepositions. Many are followed by the preposition *à* when they precede an infinitive. You can learn the following list of examples.

aider à	to help
s'accoutumer à	to get accustomed to
s'amuser à	to enjoy
apprendre à	to learn, to show how
arriver à	to manage
aspirer à	to aspire
s'attendre à	to expect
chercher à	to try, to attempt
commencer à	to start
consentir à	to agree, to consent

continuer à	to continue, to keep on
se décider à	to make up one's mind
encourager à	to encourage
faire attention à	to pay attention
s'habituer à	to get used
hésiter à	to hesitate
s'intéresser à	to get interested in
inviter à	to invite
se mettre à	to start, to begin
parvenir à	to manage
préparer à	to get ready
renoncer à	to give up
se résigner à	to resign oneself
réussir à	to succeed
tenir à	to insist, to be eager
viser à	to aim at

Soudain, Anna s'est mise à rire. **Suddenly, Anna started to laugh.**
Prépare-toi à serrer beaucoup de mains. **Get ready to shake a lot of hands.**
Il m'encourage à poursuivre **He encourages me to continue**
 mes recherches. **my research.**

Exercise 9-17: Practice with Preposition À

Translate the following sentences using the *vous* form when necessary.

1. You should learn how to drive.

   ....

2. Henri managed to get the job.

   ....

3. Jocelyn is very eager to know you.

....

4. Pay attention to price!

....

5. He tried to call you all day.

....

6. Don't expect to see me at the party!

....

7. I am getting used to Marc, my new colleague.

....

8. I insist on talking to you!

....

9. Janine got interested in philosophy when she was sixteen.

....

10. Everyone aspires to a better world.

....

The Preposition De with Verbs

Now that you have memorized some of the *à* verbs, let's look at some verbs followed by the preposition *de* when they precede an infinitive.

accepter de	to accept
accuser de	to accuse
s'arrêter de	to stop
avoir besoin de	to need to
avoir envie de	to feel like
avoir l'intention de	to intend to
avoir peur de	to be afraid of
cesser de	to stop, to cease
choisir de	to choose

conseiller de	to advise
convaincre de	to convince
craindre de	to fear
défendre de	to forbid
demander de	to ask
se dépêcher de	to hurry
s'efforcer de	to try hard
empêcher de	to prevent
s'empêcher de	to refrain from
envisager de	to contemplate
essayer de	to try
éviter de	to avoid
s'excuser de	to apologize
faire semblant de	to pretend
feindre de	to feign, to pretend
finir de	to finish, to end
interdire de	to forbid
menacer de	to threaten
mériter de	to deserve
offrir de	to offer
oublier de	to forget
permettre de	to allow, to permit
persuader de	to persuade, to convince
se plaindre de	to complain
projeter de	to plan
promettre de	to promise

refuser de	to refuse
regretter de	to regret
remercier de	to thank
reprocher de	to reproach
soupçonner de	to suspect
se souvenir de	to remember

Élisabeth regrette de ne pas avoir étudié plus longtemps.	**Élisabeth regrets not having studied longer.**
Le coq m'a empêché de dormir.	**The rooster prevented me from sleeping.**
Il nous a convaincus d'aller voir ce film.	**He convinced us to go see that movie.**
Merci d'être venu.	**Thank you for coming.**

Exercise 9-18: À or De?

Write the whole sentence, using the appropriate preposition.

1. *Le policier nous a conseillé . . . prendre une autre route.*

   ....

2. *Laurent ne parvient pas . . . joindre Sophie par téléphone.*

   ....

3. *Ma tante s'attend . . . nous voir arriver vers 15 heures.*

   ....

4. *Ne commence pas . . . .m'énerver!*

   ....

5. *Mon ami m'a promis . . . m'écrire dès son arrivée à Bali.*

   ....

6. *Les parents interdisent à leurs enfants . . . regarder la télévision le week-end.*

   ....

7. *Il s'est amusé . . .changer les noms sur les boîtes aux lettres.*

   ....

8. *Tu devrais faire attention . . . ne pas trop manger.*

....

9. *Elle soupçonne son petit frère . . . faire des bêtises dans son dos.*

....

10. *J'hésite . . . appeler ma grand-mère si tôt.*

....

Exercise 9-19: No Guessing with the Preposition!

Translate the following sentences using the appropriate preposition and *tu* when necessary.

1. Keep on studying!

....

2. He should learn how to sing.

....

3. He invited me to come with him to the countryside.

....

4. I advise you to stop smoking.

....

5. The landlord refused to sign the bill of sale.

....

6. Nicolas contemplates traveling around the world for a year.

....

7. I feel like going to the swimming pool.

....

8. The people in charge were accused of letting the situation get worse.

....

9. His father helped him move his things.

....

10. I invite you to join us.

....

Other Prepositions with Verbs

Avant de (*before*), is followed by the present infinitive.

Embrasse-moi avant de partir.	**Kiss me before leaving.**
Il prend ses médicaments	**He takes his medicines**
avant de se coucher.	**before going to bed.**

Après (*after*), is followed by the past infinitive. The past infinitive is formed with *avoir* or *être* plus the past participle of the verb.

Marie se sentait plus légère après	**Marie felt lighter after**
avoir pris sa décision.	**making her decision.**
Valérie a pris un mois de vacances après	**Valérie took a month's vacation after**
avoir travaillé dur pendant une année.	**working hard for a year.**
Elle s'est effondrée en larmes après	**She burst into tears after**
avoir entendu la mauvaise nouvelle.	**hearing the bad news.**

Exercise 9-20: Before or After?

Rewrite the sentence, replacing *avant de* + present infinitive with *après* + past infinitive.

1. *Elle a éclaté de rire avant de finir de nous raconter son histoire.*

   ....

2. *Grégoire a avalé un sandwich avant de prendre la route.*

   ....

3. *Lucie a pris un bain avant d'aller à la soirée.*

   ....

4. *Fabienne est venue me parler avant de prendre sa décision.*

   ....

5. *Arnaud est tombé malade juste avant de partir en vacances.*

   ....

6. *Patricia a prévenu le gardien de la fuite d'eau avant d'appeler le plombier.*

   ....

7. *Les touristes lisent le guide avant d'arriver à destination.*

   ....

8. *Le peintre prépare ses couleurs avant de commencer un nouveau tableau.*

   ....

9. *Le président annonce une augmentation de salaire avant d'acheter une autre voiture.*

   ....

10. *Elle dit bonjour avant de commencer son discours.*

   ....

Same Verbs/Different Prepositions

Another important thing to remember is that the same verb can be used with no preposition, just followed by a direct object, or it can be followed by different prepositions. Let's look at a few examples.

finir

Le réalisateur a fini son film.	**The filmmaker has finished his movie.**
Ils ont fini de manger.	**They have finished eating.**
Elle a fini par se décider à l'épouser.	**She ended up deciding to marry him.**

commencer

Elle commence son nouveau travail demain.	**She'll start her new job tomorrow.**
Il a commencé à pleuvoir hier soir.	**It started to rain last night.**
Ils ont commencé par nous souhaiter la bienvenue.	**They started by welcoming us.**

décider

Elles n'ont encore rien décidé.	**They have not decided anything yet.**
J'ai décidé d'arrêter de fumer.	**I decided to stop smoking.**
Karim s'est finalement décidé à prendre une année sabbatique.	**Karim finally decided to take a sabbatical.**

demander

Puis-je te demander une faveur?	**Can I ask you a favor?**
Le médecin a demandé au patient de lui faxer les résultats.	**The doctor asked the patient to fax him the results.**
J'ai demandé à être effacée de la liste.	**I asked to be taken off the list.**

jouer

Je vais jouer le jeu et on verra ce qui se passera.	I will play the game and we will see what happens.
Martha joue au tennis.	Martha plays tennis.
Ils jouent aux échecs.	They are playing chess.
Ne jouez pas au chat et à la souris!	Don't play cat and mouse!
Patrick joue de la guitare.	Patrick plays the guitar.
Véronique joue de la batterie.	Véronique plays drums.

parler

Valérie parle à son chirurgien dentiste.	Valérie is talking to her dental surgeon.
Vous désirez me parler?	Do you want to talk to me?
Ounissa parle de son engagement politique.	Ounissa is talking about her political commitment.
De quoi vas-tu parler ce soir?	What are you going to talk about tonight?

croire

Il la croit.	He believes her.
Tu le crois honnête?	Do you think he is honest?
La police croit sa version de l'histoire.	The police believe his version of the story.
Pierre croit à la magie.	Pierre believes in magic.
Il croit au progrès.	He believes in progress.
Crois-tu en Dieu?	Do you believe in God?
Je crois en l'humanité.	I have confidence in mankind.
Le médecin croit pouvoir aider son collègue.	The doctor thinks he can help his colleague.
Christina croit avoir raison.	Christina thinks she is right.

tenir

Je tiens beaucoup à lui.	I am very much attached to him.
Elle tenait à lui dire la vérité.	She was eager to tell him the truth.
Le bébé tient de sa mère.	The baby looks like her mother.
Jules tient de son père.	Jules takes after his father.

rêver

Elle rêve à une vie plus douce.	She dreams about a sweeter life.
Il a rêvé de Louisa la nuit dernière.	He dreamed about Louisa last night.

manquer

Le guitariste a manqué deux concerts.	**The guitar player missed two concerts.**
Boris a manqué le début du spectacle.	**Boris missed the beginning of the show.**
Les pâtes manquent de sel.	**The pasta lacks salt.**
Hubert manque de dextérité.	**Hubert lacks dexterity.**
Je ne manque de rien.	**I lack nothing.**
Vous avez manqué à votre promesse.	**You failed to keep your word.**
Claude a manqué à tous ses devoirs.	**Claude failed to do all of his duties.**
Tu me manques.	**I miss you.**
Lisa lui manque.	**He misses Lisa.**
Est-ce que la France te manque?	**Do you miss France?**
Est-ce que ton pays te manque?	**Do you miss your country?**

Exercise 9-21: *Where Have the Prepositions Gone?*

In the following text, all the prepositions after the verbs have disappeared. Write the text again, placing the right prepositions after the verbs.

Marie tient sa mère. Comme elle, elle rêve d'un meilleur monde. Elle vient finir ses études. Elle a décidé faire le tour du monde. Elle a parlé président d'une association humanitaire. Elle lui a demandé être volontaire dans cette association. Marie croit la bonté humaine. Elle tient ne pas rester dans l'inaction. Marie ne manque pas courage. Elle n'a pas fini nous étonner!

....

....

....

....

....

....

....

....

....

Verbs That Change Meaning

Six very common verbs change meaning when they are followed by a preposition and when they are not. Moreover, in the compound past tenses using *avoir* or *être*—the *passé composé* for example—the verb followed by a direct object will take *avoir* whereas the verb followed by a preposition and an indirect object will take *être*.

monter

Les déménageurs montent les cartons au quatrième étage.	The movers take the boxes up to the fourth floor.
Les touristes montent en haut de la Tour Eiffel.	The tourists go up the Eiffel Tower.
Le jeune homme a monté sa propre société.	The young man started his own company.
La vieille dame est montée jusqu'au dernier étage à pied.	The old woman walked up to the top floor.

descendre

Peux-tu descendre ton vélo à la cave?	Can you take your bicycle down to the cellar?
Nous descendrons la montagne par le téléphérique.	We will take the cable car down the mountain.
Ils ont descendu le fleuve en péniche.	They went down the river by barge.
Janine est descendue voir ce qui se passait.	Janine went down to see what was happening.

passer

Mes parents passent leurs vacances au Maroc.	My parents spend their vacation in Morocco.
Mireille passe devant la boulangerie tous les jours.	Mireille passes the bakery every day.
Vincent a passé son examen lundi.	Vincent took his exam on Monday.
Sur le chemin du retour, je suis passé en voiture par ma ville natale.	On my way back, I drove through my hometown.

rentrer

Nicolas va rentrer la voiture dans le garage.	Nicolas is going to put the car in the garage.
Je rentre dans trois jours.	I will come back in three days.

La fermière a rentré les vaches dans l'étable.	The farmer brought the cows into the barn.
L'homme a rentré les boîtes dans l'entrepôt.	The man put away the boxes in the storage room.
Nous sommes rentrés de ce voyage absolument ravis.	We came home from that trip absolutely delighted.

sortir

Le gardien sort les poubelles tous les soirs.	The superintendent takes the garbage out every evening.
Leur fille sort avec un garçon depuis quelques semaines.	Their daughter has been going out with a boy for a few weeks.
Madame Dubois a sorti ses plantes dans la cour.	Mrs. Dubois took her plants out in the courtyard.
Hélène est sortie de l'immeuble il y a deux minutes.	Hélène left the building two minutes ago.

retourner

Le cuisinier retourne la crêpe.	The cook flips the crepe.
Elle est retournée à Istanbul pour la troisième fois.	She went back to Istanbul for the third time.
Gérard a retourné le steak haché.	Gèrard flipped the hamburger.
Michelle est retournée voir sa tante la semaine dernière.	Michelle went to see her aunt again last week.

Exercise 9-22: *Putting Prepositions to Work*

Translate the following sentences using a preposition when necessary. Use the *tu* form and inversion.

1. Patricia spends her vacation in the countryside.

   ....

2. I missed you.

   ....

3. Jean-Louis is attached to his nephew Patrick.

   ....

4. Fabiola believes in reincarnation.

   ....

5. I am eager to go to that dinner party.

....

6. You should talk to them.

....

7. Do you want to play chess tonight?

....

8. Stop talking about your work all the time!

....

9. You look like your sister.

....

10. They think they saw her in the street.

....

Exercise 9-23: Beginning and End

Make an appropriate sentence by matching the phrase in the right-hand column with the phrase in the left-hand column.

1. *Les artistes ne manquent pas*   a. *à sa petite nièce.*
2. *Elles jouent*   b. *de créativité.*
3. *Bertrand croit*   c. *sa promesse d'augmentation.*
4. *Oncle René tient beaucoup*   d. *à la corde à sauter dans la rue.*
5. *Mon patron n'a pas tenu*   e. *à la bonne volonté de sa fille.*

Let's Recap

In the following section, you will review many of the different prepositions.

Exercise 9-24: Pick the Right Preposition

Write the whole sentence, using the right prepositive locution.

1. *Elle porte son gilet . . . la peau car il fait trop chaud.*

....

2. *. . . être en retard, je vais rester jusqu'à la fin de la séance.*

....

3. *Ce plat manque vraiment . . . épices.*

....

4. *Je ne t'ai pas appelé . . . te réveiller, je croyais que tu dormais.*

....

5. *La police a relâché le suspect . . . preuves.*

....

6. *Il a agi . . . de tout le monde, sans rien dire à personne.*

....

7. *Elle n'en peut plus, elle est . . . la crise de nerfs.*

....

8. *Merci Olivier, . . . toi, j'ai retrouvé le moral.*

....

9. *Denise est partie . . . Paris, elle avait besoin de prendre l'air.*

....

10. *Elle tient . . . l'armoire de la grand-mère. Elle ne te la donnera jamais.*

....

Exercise 9-25: Intruder Alert

In some sentences, the preposition is wrong. Identify the intruders and rewrite the sentences correctly.

1. *Aidez-le à trouver du travail.*

....

2. *Jean envisage à acheter un nouvel appartement.*

....

3. *Les pompiers ont cherché à entrer dans la maison en feu.*

....

4. *J'ai oublié à mettre le réveil.*

....

5. *Kim hésite à partir maintenant en vacances.*

....

6. *Le professeur s'est efforcé à ne pas mettre trop de mauvaises notes.*

....

7. *Je t'invite à lire ce livre passionnant.*

....

8. *La voisine m'a remercié de lui avoir apporté des biscuits.*

....

9. *Fais attention de ne pas prendre trop de coups de soleil!*

....

10. *Ils soupçonnent le gardien … être le voleur.*

....

Part 10

The Final Exam

Now let's review all the different grammar rules and vocabulary you have learned in this book. Are you ready?

Exercise 10-1: To Be Noted

Rewrite each sentence, putting the verbs in parentheses into the *présent* or the *passé composé*. Be sure the adverb is in the correct place.

1. *Je (manger, présent) rarement des légumes crus.*

   ....

2. *Ils (faire semblant, passé composé) souvent de ne pas me voir.*

   ....

3. *Il (prétendre, présent) toujours m'aimer.*

   ....

4. *Nous (habiter, passé composé) cette maison pendant des années.*

   ....

5. *Je (vouloir, présent) bien répondre à sa question.*

   ....

6. *Il (se tromper, passé composé) déjà.*

   ....

7. *Il (sembler, présent) très heureux en province.*

   ....

8. *Elle (ne jamais avouer, passé composé) son amour pour lui.*

   ....

9. *Je (profiter, présent) du beau temps pour faire du vélo.*

   ....

10. *Il (reconnaître, passé composé) ses erreurs.*

Exercise 10-2: What About?

Suggest an activity to a friend using the form *si + on + imparfait*

1. *partir en Asie*

   ....

2. *inviter Valérie à déjeuner*

   ....

3. *acheter un appartement*

....

4. *se marier*

....

5. *créer une entreprise*

....

6. *vendre la maison*

....

7. *aller à l'opéra*

....

8. *aller faire une promenade*

....

9. *fermer les volets*

....

10. *fêter ma promotion*

....

Exercise 10-3: Who Is in Charge?

Translate the correct pronoun for each sentence:

1. (I, he, they) .... *a organisé une réunion.*

2. (he, we, they) .... *avons pris des décisions.*

3. (she, you, we) .... *as décoré sa nouvelle maison.*

4. (he, you, they) .... *sont allés en Normandie ce week-end.*

5. (I, we, they) .... *ai visité Moscou l'été dernier.*

6. (you, we, they) .... *ont travaillé toute la nuit.*

7. (he, we, I) .... *a bien voulu recevoir les invités.*

8. (you, she, they) .... *est partie trop tôt.*

9. (she, you, we) .... *a voyagé dans le monde entier.*

10. (you, she, they) .... *as mal compris ce que j'ai dit.*

Exercise 10-4: Get Tense

Rewrite each sentence, putting the verb in the correct tense.

1. *Ils (donner, passé composé) de la nourriture aux animaux.*

   ....

2. *Nous (regarder, futur) l'émission à la télévision vendredi soir.*

   ....

3. *Tu (parler, imparfait) de prendre des vacances la semaine prochaine?*

   ....

4. *Elles (correspondre, présent) depuis plusieurs années.*

   ....

5. *Vous (comprendre, futur) plus tard ce que je vous dis.*

   ....

6. *Elle (étudier, présent) la philosophie à la Sorbonne.*

   ....

7. *Il (contredire, présent) sans arrêt mes arguments.*

   ....

8. *Nous (imaginer, imparfait) une grande maison avec un jardin.*

   ....

9. *Je (dire, passé composé) à Tim de passer nous voir.*

   ....

10. *Il (finir, futur antérieur) sa thèse dans un an.*

    ....

Exercise 10-5: Perfecting Your Imperfect

Rewrite each sentence, using the imperfect form of the verb in parentheses.

1. *Les acteurs (être) vraiment très bons.*

   ....

2. *Tous les matins, Martha (aller) faire le marché.*

   ....

3. *Le conducteur (s'énerver) au volant.*

   ....

4. *L'arbre (faire) de l'ombre dans le jardin.*

   ....

5. *Ma grand-mère (préparer) mon goûter tous les jours après l'école.*

   ....

6. *Le conservateur de musée (connaître) très bien sa collection.*

   ....

7. *La promenade quotidienne (durer) des heures.*

   ....

8. *La gardienne (interdire) aux enfants de jouer dans la cour de l'immeuble.*

   ....

9. *Valentin (offrir) des fleurs à sa mère toutes les semaines.*

   ....

10. *La neige ne (faire) que tomber.*

   ....

Exercise 10-6: Past Subtleties

Rewrite each sentence, using the *imparfait* or *passé composé* form of the verbs in parentheses. In deciding which tense to use, pay careful attention to whether the action is specific or continuous.

1. *Julien (cuisiner) quand Vincent (tomber) dans les escaliers.*

   ....

2. *Nous (faire les courses) quand il (téléphoner).*

   ....

3. *Les touristes (prendre) des photos quand il (se mettre) à neiger.*

   ....

4. *Patrick (être en réunion) quand sa secrétaire (rentrer dans son bureau).*

   ....

5. *Les comédiens (se préparer) dans leur loge quand le directeur du théâtre (decider) d'annuler le spectacle.*

   ....

6. *Boris (chanter) quand Madeleine (entrer) sur scène.*

   ....

7. *Le bus (être) à l'arrêt quand le piéton (tomber) du trottoir.*

....

8. *Je (regarder) les livres en vitrine quand le libraire (me proposer) ses conseils.*

....

9. *Tout le monde (dormir) quand la tempête (s'abattre) sur le village.*

....

10. *Je (s'ennuyer) dans mon travail lorsque je (recevoir) une nouvelle proposition d'emploi.*

....

Exercise 10-7: Perfect Future Ahead

Rewrite each sentence, using the *futur* and the *futur antérieur* forms of the verbs in parentheses.

1. *Elle (se marier) quand elle (trouver) quelqu'un qui lui plaît vraiment.*

....

2. *Je (partir) en voyage quand je (économiser) assez d'argent.*

....

3. *Le plombier (changer) le tuyau quand il en (trouver) un autre pour le remplacer.*

....

4. *Anna (se sentir) mieux quand elle (prendre) une décision.*

....

5. *Mon fils (s'installer) à Paris quand il (trouver) un travail.*

....

6. *Valentin (demander) Ariane en mariage quand elle (rentrer) de voyage.*

....

7. *Il (être) de bonne humeur quand il (dormir) assez.*

....

8. *Mon appartement (être) moins bruyant quand on y (installer) des doubles vitrages.*

....

9. *Ma colocataire (ne pas être) contente quand elle (voir) que sa télévision ne marche plus.*

....

10. *Nous (rendre visite) à tes parents dès que nous (terminer) les travaux dans la maison.*

....

Exercise 10-8: The Right Time and the Right Place

Translate the following sentences using the right expressions of location and time. Use the *vous* form.

1. Tomorrow I have to go to work early.

....

2. I have been living here since I was born.

....

3. He always comes home late.

....

4. Her house is over there.

....

5. I need to spend a few days by the sea.

....

6. She lives far away, but she will be here in less than an hour.

....

7. The children are playing outside.

....

8. They work in town but they live hours away.

....

9. Look under the bed to see if the cat is there.

....

10. I went to the new bakery the day before yesterday.

....

Exercise 10-9: It's All Conditional!

Rewrite each sentence, putting the first verb into the present conditional and the second verb into the imperfect. Then rewrite each sentence a second time, changing the present conditional into past conditional and the imperfect into the pluperfect.

Je (travailler) moins si je (gagner) plus d'argent.
Je travaillerais moins si je gagnais plus d'argent.
J'aurais moins travaillé si j'avais gagné plus d'argent

1. *Elle (être) en colère si tu la (réveiller).*

   ....

   ....

2. *Je (prendre) ma décision tout de suite si j'(avoir) tous les éléments en main.*

   ....

   ....

3. *Les enfants (dormir) plus longtemps s'il y (avoir) moins de bruit dans la chambre.*

   ....

   ....

4. *Les éditeurs (publier) plus de livres d'art si le public en (acheter) plus.*

   ....

   ....

5. *Les musiciens (jouer) plus fort si le patron de la salle de concert le leur (autoriser).*

   ....

   ....

6. *Mon frère (sortir) tous les soirs si ma mère le (laisser) faire.*

   ....

   ....

7. *Cette plante verte (s'épanouir) si elle (laisser) au soleil.*

   ....

   ....

8. *Il lui (téléphoner) s'il (être) sûr de ne pas la déranger.*

....

....

9. *Je (venir) à Barcelone ce week-end si je (trouver) un billet d'avion bon marché.*

....

....

10. *(Accepter)-tu de venir nous présenter ton travail si nous te (payer) les frais de déplacement?*

....

....

Exercise 10-10: News Stories

Translate the following sentences using the present or past journalistic conditional.

1. The mayor reportedly refused to shake the President's hand.

....

2. The winner reportedly gave all the money to a church.

....

3. Five people were reportedly injured.

....

4. The tornado has reportedly destroyed two villages.

....

5. Natural disasters are reportedly going to increase in the years to come.

....

6. A Van Gogh painting was reportedly sold for a million dollars.

....

7. The director reportedly signed his resignation.

....

8. The captain is allegedly responsible for the accident.

....

9. The students reportedly started striking last week.

....

10. The musicians reportedly played very well.

....

Exercise 10-11: Who Does It?

Rewrite each sentence, changing to the causative form and the *passé composé*.

Je nettoie la maison de ma tante. ⟶ *J'ai fait nettoyer la maison de ma tante.*

1. *Vous faites les courses.*

....

2. *Je prépare ma valise.*

....

3. *Elle répare la machine à laver.*

....

4. *Il expédie le colis aux États-Unis.*

....

5. *Nous appelons le directeur tout de suite.*

....

6. *Vous apportez le repas à la chambre.*

....

7. *Il écrit au juge d'instruction.*

....

8. *Ils interdisent l'entrée du bâtiment.*

....

9. *L'artiste explique son oeuvre au journaliste.*

....

10. *Le directeur du musée assure le tableau.*

....

Exercise 10-12: Grammar Rule and Order

Write sentences with the following elements in the correct order using the present tense. Watch out for the agreements.

1. *Valérie / adorer / les peintres / cubiste.*

   ....

2. *Boris / jouer / à des jeux de hasard / stupide.*

   ....

3. *Le directeur / bien / vouloir / augmenter / les salariés.*

   ....

4. *Carine / peu / voir / sa soeur / aîné.*

   ....

5. *Le musicien / donner / un concert / gratuit.*

   ....

6. *Tu / trop / travailler.*

   ....

7. *La Tour Eiffel / tous les soirs / scintiller.*

   ....

8. *Je / ne pas aimer / la cuisine / chinois.*

   ....

9. *Ce chanteur / bien / interpréter / cette ballade.*

   ....

10. *Eléonore / ne pas comprendre / sa soeur / petit.*

    ....

Exercise 10-13: In What Order?

Write sentences with the following elements using the present tense of *être*. Put the words in the correct order and make sure the adjectives agree in number and gender.

1. *Mes voisins du dessus / bruyant / mes voisins du dessous / moins.*

   ....

2. *Le violoniste / musicien / le guitariste / meilleur.*

....

3. *Paul / son frère / généreux / aussi.*

....

4. *Cette jupe-ci / celle-là / joli / moins.*

....

5. *Les vacances à Marseille / les vacances à la campagne / fatigant / plus.*

....

6. *Nager le crawl / nager la brasse / difficile / beaucoup plus.*

....

7. *Aimer / être aimé / facile / plus.*

....

8. *Lucas / gentil / son colocataire / moins.*

....

9. *Ma fille / élève / mon fils / meilleur.*

....

10. *Je / enthousiaste / toi / moins.*

....

Exercise 10-14: From Time to Time . . .

TRACK 34

Listen to the audio track and repeat. Then listen again and write down each sentence.

1. ....

2. ....

3. ....

4. ....

5. ....

6. ....

7. ....

8. ....

9. ....

10. ....

Exercise 10-15: Match the Phrases

Make an appropriate sentence by matching the phrase in the right-hand column with the phrase in the left-hand column.

1. *Ce disque est de grande qualité:*   a. *j'y vais tous les jours avec plaisir.*
2. *Le son est trop fort:*   b. *elle sourit tout le temps.*
3. *La concierge est très gentille:*   c. *je l'écoute tous les jours.*
4. *Mon travail est très intéressant:*   d. *je ne peux pas la boire.*
5. *Cette boisson est trop sucrée:*   e. *je n'arrive pas à me concentrer.*

Exercise 10-16: Let's See If We Have Our Genders Together

Place the proper indefinite article before the noun and make sure the adjective agrees.

1. .... *vérité n'est pas toujours (bon)* .... *à savoir.*

2. .... *brasserie est (ouvert)* .... *le dimanche.*

3. .... *journalistes sont (courageux)* ....

4. .... *chambre à coucher est (peint)* .... *en rose.*

5. .... *éditeur est (fidèle)* .... *à son auteur.*

6. .... *jeunes filles sont (content)* .... *de partir ensemble*

   en vacances.

7. .... *élections (municipale)* .... *ont lieu en*

   mars cette année.

8. .... *bureau du patron est très (lumineux)* ....

9. .... *plante (vert)* .... *a soif.*

10. .... *fête de Pierre et Catherine était (fabuleux)* ....

Exercise 10-17: What Does It All Mean?

Translate the following sentences into English.

1. *La librairie est ouverte tous les jours.*

   ....

2. *Il est étudiant en art.*

   ....

3. *Je viendrai éventuellement avec ma tante.*

   ....

4. *Il achèvera sa thèse fin mai.*

   ....

5. *Achète une autre éponge!*

   ....

6. *J'ai rencontré mon nouveau patron.*

   ....

7. *Le boulanger est très sympathique.*

   ....

8. *Actuellement, je gagne 2000 euros par mois.*

   ....

9. *J'adore les nouvelles de cet auteur!*

   ....

10. *Il y a beaucoup d'artistes étrangers ici.*

    ....

Exercise 10-18: Famille et Compagnie . . .

TRACK 35

Listen to the audio track and repeat Nora's response to an interviewer, who is asking her for biographical details. Then listen again and write down each sentence.

1. ....

2. ....

3. ....

4. ....

5. ....

6. ....

7. ....

8. ....

9. ....

10. ....

Exercise 10-19: Build Your Own Sentence

Write sentences following the model, using the present tense of the verb, the appropriate indefinite relative pronoun, and the right article.

aimer/cuisine italienne (il) ⟶ *Ce qu'il aime, c'est la cuisine italienne.*

1. *envisager / vente de notre appartement (nous)*

....

2. *vous souhaiter / une bonne nuit de sommeil (nous)*

....

3. *ne pas comprendre / comment c'est arrivé (il)*

....

4. *manigancer / renvoi de leur collègue (elles)*

....

5. *appréhender / réaction de sa belle-soeur (il)*

....

6. *avoir peur de / ne pas trouver le chemin (nous)*

....

7. *espérer / fin de la guerre (ils)*

....

8. *se demander / combien ça côte (tu)*

....

9. *voir / fleurs du jardin (il)*

....

10. *vouloir / la vérité (je)*

....

Exercise 10-20: Who? What?

Complete each sentence using *qui*, *que*, *dont*, or *auquel*.

1. *Elle a acheté le livre* .... *tu lui avais conseillé.*

2. *Il a écrit à l'avocat* .... *vous lui aviez donné les coordonnées.*

3. *Nous ne savons pas* .... *est cet homme étrange.*

4. *Je suis allée voir le film* .... *tu faisais allusion l'autre jour.*

5. *Nous habitons l'immeuble* .... *donne sur la rivière.*

6. *J'ai enfin trouvé le métier* .... *j'ai toujours rêvé.*

7. *Elles se demandent* .... *peut bien sonner à la porte à une heure aussi tardive.*

8. *C'est la personne* .... *je t'ai parlé la semaine dernière.*

9. *Voici la maison* .... *est à vendre.*

10. *Montrez-moi le tableau* .... *vous souhaitez acheter.*

Exercise 10-21: Multiple Pronouns

Rewrite each sentence, replacing the words in parentheses with the appropriate pronouns. Pay careful attention to the placement of the pronouns in the sentence.

1. *Je ne parlerai pas (de tes problèmes au patron).*

....

2. *Il a donné (des vêtements à Jean).*

....

3. *Cet hôtel aurait besoin (d'un petit coup de peinture).*

....

4. *Fabienne raconte (ses vacances à sa meilleure amie).*

....

5. *Le peintre envoie (son dernier tableau au marchand).*

....

6. *Le policier a demandé (des renseignements aux pompiers).*

....

7. *Vous m'emmènerez (à Paris).*

....

8. *Sylvie a besoin (de vacances au calme).*

....

9. *Mon père a donné (toutes les instructions au notaire).*

....

10. *Je vous déconseille (de vous promener seul la nuit).*

....

Exercise 10-22: En or Y?

Rewrite each sentence, replacing the words in parentheses with the pronoun *en* or *y*.

1. *Je les ai rapportés (à la maison).*

....

2. *Il ne prête aucune attention (à mes remarques).*

....

3. *Nous aurions bien besoin (d'un peu de repos).*

....

4. *Il s'éloigne (de la fenêtre).*

....

5. *Tu devrais renoncer (à cette idée folle).*

....

6. *Elle a peur (de ne pas réussir).*

....

7. *Elles sont conscientes (des risques).*

....

8. *Nous nous rendrons (au restaurant).*

....

9. *J'ai envie (de partir loin).*

....

10. *Tu seras responsable (de l'ensemble de la chaîne de production).*

....

Exercise 10-23: On Your Mark . . .

Translate the following sentences, using the pronoun *on*.

1. One should be aware of the danger.

   ....

2. We are not stupid!

   ....

3. Chinese is spoken here.

   ....

4. One is never a hundred percent sure.

   ....

5. Dollars are accepted here.

   ....

6. In Canada, one is used to the snow.

   ....

7. In France, one eats lots of cheese.

   ....

8. Elena and I, we are going to Asia this summer.

   ....

9. Shall we take a nap?

   ....

10. So, you are watching a movie tonight?

   ....

Exercise 10-24: How Do You Say?

Translate the following sentences using the *tu* form.

1. At the moment, they are on vacation in Europe.

   ....

2. Remind me to call her after work!

   ....

3. She drove to the country last weekend.

   ....

4. She is French.

....

5. She does not like to talk in public.

....

6. Last week, I saw Julie at the supermarket.

....

7. My impression is that you would leave now if you could.

....

8. They have been waiting at the bus station for twenty minutes.

....

9. They speak Italian.

....

10. We are hungry.

....

Exercise 10-25: Say It Your Way

Translate the following sentences using the *vous* form when necessary.

1. I will stay here until you ask me to leave.

....

2. Wherever you go, I will follow you.

....

3. Valérie will call you as soon as she can.

....

4. She will print her essay for her teacher.

....

5. What is the price of this beautiful lamp?

....

6. In spite of her lack of competence, I like working with her.

....

7. Instead of staying here, go to Paris!

....

8. Whatever you think, I am sure he is wrong.

....

9. I am surprised he didn't arrive earlier.

....

10. Thanks to my uncle, I found a large apartment in a very short time.

....

Exercise 10-26: Which One Is the Right Preposition?

Complete each sentence with the right preposition.

1. *J'ai réussi* .... *convaincre Mireille de partir à la mer avec moi.*

2. *Marine m'a demandé* .... *chercher des billets d'avion pour la Grèce.*

3. *Evelyne refuse* .... *laisser tomber ce projet.*

4. *Pascal tient* .... *se lever de bonne heure demain.*

5. *Les piétons hésitent* .... *traverser la route au feu vert.*

6. *Ne nous empêche pas* .... *aller à ce concert!*

7. *Pense* .... *prévenir ta collègue de ton absence.*

8. *Je te remercie* .... *avoir pensé à moi.*

9. *Fais attention* .... *coups de soleil!*

10. *Elle lui interdit* .... *prendre la voiture la nuit.*

ercise 10-27: Balzac à sa Comtesse

TRACK 36

Listen to the audio track of one of Honoré de Balzac's love letters to a countess in Ukraine. Listen again and identify the ten adjectives in the letter.

1. ....   6. ....

2. ....   7. ....

3. ....   8. ....

4. ....   9. ....

5. ....   10. ....

Appendix A
Verb Conjugation Tables

-er Verbs

Parler (to speak); past participle, parlé

Subject	Present	Imperfect	Future	Conditional	Subjunctive
je	parle	parlais	parlerai	parlerais	parle
tu	parles	parlais	parleras	parlerais	parles
il	parle	parlait	parlera	parlerait	parle
nous	parlons	parlions	parlerons	parlerions	parlions
vous	parlez	parliez	parlerez	parleriez	parliez
ils	parlent	parlaient	parleront	parleraient	parlent

-ir Verbs

Finir (to finish); past participle, fini

Subject	Present	Imperfect	Future	Conditional	Subjunctive
je	finis	finissais	finirai	finirais	finisse
tu	finis	finissais	finiras	finirais	finisses
il	finit	finissait	finira	finirait	finisse
nous	finissons	finissions	finirons	finirions	finissions
vous	finissez	finissiez	finirez	finiriez	finissiez
ils	finissent	finissaient	finiront	finiraient	finissent

-re Verbs

Attendre (to wait for); past participle, attendu

Subject	Present	Imperfect	Future	Conditional	Subjunctive
j'	attends	attendais	attendrai	attendrais	attende
tu	attends	attendais	attendras	attendrais	attendes
il	attend	attendait	attendra	attendrait	attende

nous	attendons	attendions	attendrons	attendrions	attendions
vous	attendez	attendiez	attendrez	attendriez	attendiez
ils	attendent	attendaient	attendront	attendraient	attendent

Irregular Verbs

Aller (to go); past participle, allé

SUBJECT	PRESENT	IMPERFECT	FUTURE	CONDITIONAL	SUBJUNCTIVE
je (j')	vais	allais	irai	irais	aille
tu	vas	allais	iras	irais	ailles
il	va	allait	ira	irait	aille
nous	allons	allions	irons	irions	allions
vous	allez	alliez	irez	iriez	alliez
ils	vont	allaient	iront	iraient	aillent

Avoir (to have); past participle, eu

SUBJECT	PRESENT	IMPERFECT	FUTURE	CONDITIONAL	SUBJUNCTIVE
j'	ai	avais	aurai	aurais	aie
tu	as	avais	auras	aurais	aies
il	a	avait	aura	aurait	ait
nous	avons	avions	aurons	aurions	ayons
vous	avez	aviez	aurez	auriez	ayez
ils	ont	avaient	auront	auraient	aient

Devoir (to have to); past participle, dû

SUBJECT	PRESENT	IMPERFECT	FUTURE	CONDITIONAL	SUBJUNCTIVE
je	dois	devais	devrai	devrais	doive
tu	dois	devais	devras	devrais	doives
il	doit	devait	devra	devrait	doive

nous	devons	devions	devrons	devrions	devions
vous	devez	deviez	devrez	devriez	deviez
ils	doivent	devaient	devront	devraient	doivent

Dire (to say, tell); past participle, dit

SUBJECT	PRESENT	IMPERFECT	FUTURE	CONDITIONAL	SUBJUNCTIVE
je	dis	disais	dirai	dirais	dise
tu	dis	disais	diras	dirais	dises
il	dit	disait	dira	dirait	dise
nous	disons	disions	dirons	dirions	disions
vous	dites	disiez	direz	diriez	disiez
ils	disent	disaient	diront	diraient	disent

Être (to be); past participle, été

SUBJECT	PRESENT	IMPERFECT	FUTURE	CONDITIONAL	SUBJUNCTIVE
je (j')	suis	étais	serai	serais	sois
tu	es	étais	seras	serais	sois
il	est	était	sera	serait	soit
nous	sommes	étions	serons	serions	soyons
vous	êtes	étiez	serez	seriez	soyez
ils	sont	étaient	seront	seraient	soient

Faire (to make, do); past participle, fait

SUBJECT	PRESENT	IMPERFECT	FUTURE	CONDITIONAL	SUBJUNCTIVE
je	fais	faisais	ferai	ferais	fasse
tu	fais	faisais	feras	ferais	fasses
il	fait	faisait	fera	ferait	fasse
nous	faisons	faisions	ferons	ferions	fassions

vous	faites	faisiez	ferez	feriez	fassiez
ils	font	faisaient	feront	feraient	fassent

Mettre (to put); past participle, *mis*

SUBJECT	PRESENT	IMPERFECT	FUTURE	CONDITIONAL	SUBJUNCTIVE
je	mets	mettais	mettrai	mettrais	mette
tu	mets	mettais	mettras	mettrais	mettes
il	met	mettait	mettra	mettrait	mette
nous	mettons	mettions	mettrons	mettrions	mettions
vous	mettez	mettiez	mettrez	mettriez	mettiez
ils	mettent	mettaient	mettront	mettraient	mettent

Pouvoir (to be able to, can); past participle, *pu*

SUBJECT	PRESENT	IMPERFECT	FUTURE	CONDITIONAL	SUBJUNCTIVE
je	peux	pouvais	pourrai	pourrais	puisse
tu	peux	pouvais	pourras	pourrais	puisses
il	peut	pouvait	pourra	pourrait	puisse
nous	pouvons	pouvions	pourrons	pourrions	puissions
vous	pouvez	pouviez	pourrez	pourriez	puissiez
ils	peuvent	pouvaient	pourront	pourraient	puissent

Recevoir (to receive); past participle, *reçu*

SUBJECT	PRESENT	IMPERFECT	FUTURE	CONDITIONAL	SUBJUNCTIVE
je	reçois	recevais	recevrai	recevrais	reçoive
tu	reçois	recevais	recevras	recevrais	reçoives
il	reçoit	recevait	recevra	recevrait	reçoive

nous	recevons	recevions	recevrons	recevrions	recevions
vous	recevez	receviez	recevrez	recevriez	receviez
ils	reçoivent	recevaient	recevront	recevraient	reçoivent

Savoir (to know); past participle, *su*

SUBJECT	PRESENT	IMPERFECT	FUTURE	CONDITIONAL	SUBJUNCTIVE
je	sais	savais	saurai	saurais	sache
tu	sais	savais	sauras	saurais	saches
il	sait	savait	saura	saurait	sache
nous	savons	savions	saurons	saurions	sachions
vous	savez	saviez	saurez	sauriez	sachiez
ils	savent	savaient	sauront	sauraient	sachent

Vouloir (to want); past participle, *voulu*

SUBJECT	PRESENT	IMPERFECT	FUTURE	CONDITIONAL	SUBJUNCTIVE
je	veux	voulais	voudrai	voudrais	veuille
tu	veux	voulais	voudras	voudrais	veuilles
il	veut	voulait	voudra	voudrait	veuille
nous	voulons	voulions	voudrons	voudrions	voulions
vous	voulez	vouliez	voudrez	voudriez	vouliez
ils	veulent	voulaient	voudront	voudraient	veuillent

Appendix B
French-to-English Dictionary

A	
FRENCH	**ENGLISH**
à cause de	because of
à l'étranger	abroad
à l'heure	on time
à l'instar de	following the example of
à l'insu de	without somebody's knowing
à même	straight from
à même de	in a position to
à peine	hardly
à temps	in time
abolir	to abolish
abonner (s')	to subscribe
accomplir	to accomplish
accord (m)	agreement
accrocher (s')	to hang
accueillir	to accommodate, to have room for
achat (m)	purchase
acheter	to buy
achever	to finish, to complete
acquérir	to acquire
acteur (m)	actor
actuel	present
actuellement	presently
addition (f)	bill
adresse (f)	address
aéroport (m)	airport
affiche (f)	poster
afin que	so that, in order to
âge (m)	age
agence (f)	agency
agir	to act
agrandir	to enlarge
aider	to help
ail (m)	garlic
ailleurs	elsewhere
aimer	to like
ainsi	thus
aller	to go
allumer	to turn on
améliorer	to improve
amer	bitter
ami (m)	friend
amitié(f)	friendship
amour (m)	love
amoureux	in love
an(m)	year

ananas (m)	pineapple
anglais	English
année(f)	year
anniversaire(m)	birthday
annoncer	to announce
annuler	to cancel
août	August
apercevoir	to see, to perceive
appartement (m)	apartment
appartenir	to belong
appeler	to call, to name
applaudir	to applaud
apporter	to bring
apprendre	to learn
après-demain	the day after tomorrow
araignée (f)	spider
arbre (m)	tree
argent (m)	money
arrêter	to stop
arrivée (f)	arrival
arriver	to arrive
arroser	to water, to spray
article (m)	article
ascenseur (m)	elevator
asseoir (s')	to sit
assiette (f)	plate
assister	to attend
atelier(m)	workshop
atteindre	to reach
attendre	to wait (for)
attendre (s')	to expect
au bord de	on the verge of, on the brink of
au cas où	in case
au-delà de	beyond
au hasard	randomly, at random
au lieu de	instead of
au milieu de	in the middle of
aube (f)	dawn
auberge (f)	inn, hostel
augmentation (f)	increase
augmenter	to increase
aujourd'hui	today
aussitôt que	as soon as
autobus(m)	bus
autour	around
autre	another
autrefois	formerly
autrement	otherwise

aux dépens de	at the expense of
avaler	to swallow
avant-hier	the day before yesterday
avec	with
avenir (m)	future
aventure (f)	adventure
avenue (f)	avenue
avion (m)	plane
avis (m)	opinion, notice
avocat (m)	lawyer, avocado
avoir	to have
avoir besoin de	to need
avoir envie de	to feel like
avril	April

B

FRENCH	ENGLISH
bague (f)	ring
bain (m)	bath
baisser	to lower
banlieue (f)	suburb
barbe (f)	beard
bas	low
bateau (m)	boat
bâtiment (m)	building
bâtir	to build
battre	to beat
bavarder	to chat
beau	beautiful, handsome
beau-frère (m)	brother-in-law
beau-père (m)	father-in-law, stepfather
beauté (f)	beauty
belle-fille (f)	daughter-in-law
belle-mère (f)	mother-in-law, stepmother
belle-sœur(f)	sister-in-law
bénéfice (m)	profit
beurre (m)	butter
bicyclette (f)	bicycle
bien	good, well
bien que	although
bientôt	quickly, soon
bienvenue	welcome
bijou (m)	jewel
billet (m)	ticket
blanc	white
blesser	to hurt
blessure (f)	lesion
bleu	blue
boire	to drink
boîte (f)	box
boîte vocale (f)	voice mail
bon marché	cheap
bondé	crowded
bonheur (m)	happiness
bonjour	good morning, good afternoon
botte (f)	boot
bouche (f)	mouth

bouchon (m)	cap, cork
boue (f)	dirt, mud
boulangerie (f)	bakery
bouteille (f)	bottle
brancher	to plug in
bras (m)	arm
briller	to shine
brosse (f)	brush
brosser	to brush
bruit (m)	noise
brûler	to burn
bruyant	noisy, loud
bureau (m)	desk, office

C

FRENCH	ENGLISH
cacher	to hide
café (m)	coffee, café
camion (m)	truck
campagne (f)	countryside, campaign
canard (m)	duck
carré (m)	square
carte (f)	card, map
carte postale (f)	postcard
casser	to break
célèbre	famous
célibataire	single
cerise (f)	cherry
chaise (f)	chair
chaleur (f)	heat
chambre (f)	room
champignon (m)	mushroom
chance (f)	chance, luck
chanson (f)	song
chanter	to sing
chapeau (m)	hat
chapitre (m)	chapter
charger	to load
charmant	charming, delightful
chat (m)	cat
château (m)	castle
chauffage (m)	heating
chaussette (f)	sock
chaussure (f)	shoe
chef-d'œuvre (m)	masterpiece
chemin (m)	way, path
chemise (f)	shirt
chercher	to look for
cheval (m)	horse
chez	at, with, at the home of
chien (m)	dog
chinois	Chinese
chocolat (m)	chocolate
choisir	to choose
chômage (m)	unemployment
chou (m)	cabbage
circulation (f)	traffic, circulation

clé (f)	key
client (m)	customer
climatisation (f)	air conditioning
climatiseur (m)	air conditioner
clinique (f)	clinic
cœur (m)	heart
coiffeur(m)	hairdresser
coin (m)	corner
colère (f)	anger
colis (m)	parcel
collier (m)	necklace
colline (f)	hill
combattre	to fight
combien	how much
commander	to order
comme	like, as
commun	common
comptable	bookkeeper
compter	to count
comptoir (m)	counter
conclure	to conclude
conduire	to drive
confiture (f)	jam
confortable	comfortable
conjuguer	to conjugate
connaissance (f)	knowledge
connaître	to know
conseiller (m)	advisor
construire	to build
contacter	to contact
content	happy, pleased
conteur (m)	storyteller
contre	against
convaincre de	to convince
copain (m)	friend
corde (f)	rope
corps (m)	body
coucher de soleil (m)	sundown, sunset
couleur (f)	color
couloir (m)	hallway, corridor
coup de fil (m)	phone call
coupable	guilty
couper	to cut
courir	to run
courriel (m)	email
courrier (m)	mail
cours (m)	course
court	short
coussin (m)	cushion
coûter	to cost
couvrir	to cover
cracher	to spit
craindre	to fear
cravate (f)	tie
créer	to create
crème (f)	cream
crier	to scream, to yell
crime (m)	crime

crise (f)	crisis
croire	to believe
cueillir	to pick
cuillère (f)	spoon
cuir (m)	leather
culpabilité (f)	guilt
culture (f)	culture, civilization, cultivation

D

FRENCH	ENGLISH
d'habitude	usually
dans quelle mesure	to what extent
danser	to dance
danseur(m)	dancer
de peur que	for fear that
débarrasser (se) de	to get rid of, to discard
décembre	December
décevoir	to disappoint
décrire	to describe
défendre	to defend
défi (m)	challenge
déjà	already
déjeuner	to have lunch
demain	tomorrow
demander	to ask
déménager	to move
démissionner	to quit, to resign
dent (f)	tooth
dépêcher (se) de	to hurry
dépendre	to depend on
dépenser	to spend
déprimé	depressed
depuis	since, from
déranger	to disturb
derrière	behind
dès que	as soon as
descendre	to go down
désirer	to desire, to wish
désolé	afraid, sorry
dessert (m)	dessert
dessin (m)	drawing
destination (f)	destination
devant	in front of
devenir	to become
devoir	to have to, must, should
dictionnaire (m)	dictionary
différence (f)	difference
différent	different, otherwise
dimanche	Sunday
dinde (f)	turkey
dîner (m)	dinner, supper
dire	to say
discours (m)	speech
discuter	to discuss
disponible	available
divertissant	fun, enjoyable, entertaining
diviser	to divide, to separate

French	English
doigt (m)	finger
donner	to give
dormir	to sleep
douche (f)	shower
doux	soft, gentle, sweet
drapeau (m)	flag
drôle	strange, weird, funny
dur	hard

E

French	English
eau (f)	water
échapper	to escape
écharpe (f)	scarf
échouer	to fail
école(f)	school
écouter	to listen to
écran (m)	screen
écrire	to write
écriture (f)	writing
écrivain (m)	writer
effacer	to erase
efficace	efficient
efforcer (s') de	to try hard
égal	equal
église (f)	church
élire	to elect
emballer	to wrap
embrasser	to kiss
emmener	to take along
empêcher de	to prevent
empêcher (s') de	to refrain from
emploi (m)	job
emprunter	to borrow
en retard	late
enchanté	delighted
encore	again
encre (f)	ink
endroit (m)	place
énergie (f)	energy, power
enfance (f)	childhood
enfant (m)	kid, child
enfin	finally, at last
enfoncer	to push in
enjeu (m)	stake
enlever	to remove
ennuyeux	annoying
enregistrer	to record
enseigner	to teach
ensemble	together
entendre	to hear
entendre (s')	to get along
entre	between
entrée (f)	entrance
entrer	to enter
entretien (m)	interview, discussion
envers	toward

French	English
envisager de	to contemplate, to plan
épeler	to spell
épice (f)	spice
épinards (m pl)	spinach
éplucher	to peel
éponge (f)	sponge
équipe (f)	team
erreur (f)	mistake
espèce (f)	species, kind
espérer	to hope
espion (m)	spy
essayer	to try
et	and
établir	to establish
étage (m)	floor
étalage (m)	display
état (m)	state
étiquette (f)	label
étonnant	astonishing, surprising
étonner	to surprise, to amaze
étouffer	to choke
étrange	strange, weird, funny
étranger (m)	stranger, foreigner
être	to be
être au courant	to be informed
étude (f)	study
étudiant (m)	student
étudier	to study
euro (m)	euro
évanouir (s')	to faint
événement (m)	event
éventuellement	possibly
évidemment	of course, obviously
évident	obvious
excuser (s')	to apologize
exemple (m)	example
exiger	to require, to demand
exister	to exist
explication (f)	explanation
exposition (f)	exhibit, exhibition, show
exprès	on purpose
exprimer	to express

F

French	English
facile	easy
faible	weak
faire	to do, to make
faire la queue	to stand in line
faire les courses	to shop
faire semblant de	to pretend
fait (m)	fact
falloir	to have to
famille (f)	family
farine (f)	flour
fasciner	to fascinate
fatigué	tired

faux	false
fée (f)	fairy
féliciter	to congratulate
femme (f)	woman
fenêtre (f)	window
fermeture (f)	closing
feu (m)	fire
février	February
ficeler	to tie
fichier (m)	file
fier	proud
fille (f)	daughter, girl
fils (m)	son
finalement	finally
finir	to end up, to finish
fleur (f)	flower
fleuriste	florist
foie (m)	liver
fois (f)	time
follement	madly
fou	crazy, insane
foulard (m)	scarf
four (m)	oven
fourchette (f)	fork
frais	fresh
framboise (f)	raspberry
français	French
frémir	to shiver
frère (m)	brother
froid (m)	cold
fromage (m)	cheese
frontière (f)	border
fuir	to flee from, to avoid
fuite (f)	evasion, escape
fumer	to smoke

G

FRENCH	ENGLISH
gagner	to win, to earn, to obtain
gant (m)	glove
garage (m)	garage
garder	to keep
gare (f)	station
garer	to park
gaspiller	to waste
gâteau (m)	cake
gauche	left
gémir	to moan
gendre (m)	son-in-law
généreux	generous
génie (m)	genius
gens (m pl)	people
gérer	to manage
glace (f)	ice, ice-cream
goûter	to taste
gouvernement (m)	government
grand	large

grandir	to grow
grand-mère (f)	grandmother
grand-père (m)	grandfather
grenier (m)	attic
grenouille (f)	frog
grimper	to climb
grippe (f)	flu
gris	grey
grossir	to put on weight
guérir	to heal
guerre (f)	war

H

FRENCH	ENGLISH
habiter	to live
haricot (m)	bean
haut	high
hauteur (f)	height
hebdomadaire	weekly
heure (f)	time, hour
heureux	happy
hier	yesterday
histoire (l') (f)	story, history
hiver (l') (m)	winter
homme (l') (m)	man
honte (f)	shame
hôpital (l') (m)	hospital
horaire (l') (m)	schedule, timetable
hôtel (l') (m)	hotel
huile (l') (f)	oil
humeur (l') (f)	mood

I

FRENCH	ENGLISH
idéalisme (m)	idealism
île (f)	island
imprimante (f)	printer
imprimer	to print
inclure	to include, to carry
inconnu	unknown
incroyable	incredible, extraordinary
influencer	to influence, to induce
inquiet	worried
interdire de	to forbid
intéressant	interesting
investir	to invest
italien	Italian

J

FRENCH	ENGLISH
jadis	once, a long time ago
jamais	never
jambe (f)	leg
janvier	January
japonais	Japanese

French	English
jardin (m)	garden
jaune	yellow
jeter	to throw, to toss
jeudi	Thursday
jeune	young
joie (f)	joy
joindre	to join
jouer	to play
jouet (m)	toy
jour (m)	day
journal (m)	diary, newspaper
juste	just, only, fair
juillet	July
juin	June

L

French	English
là	there
laid	ugly, unattractive
laine (f)	wool
laisser	to leave, to let
lait (m)	milk
lampe (f)	lamp
langue (f)	language, tongue
lapin (m)	rabbit
laver	to wash
leçon (f)	lesson
lecture (f)	reading
léger	light
lent	slow
lettre (f)	letter
lèvre (f)	lip
liberté (f)	liberty, freedom
librairie (f)	bookstore
libre	free
lien (m)	link
ligne (f)	line
lire	to read
lit (m)	bed
livre (m)	book
locataire (f or m)	tenant
loin	far
lorsque	when
loyer (m)	rent
lumière (f)	light
lunettes (f pl)	glasses
lunettes de soleil (f pl)	sunglasses
lundi	Monday

M

French	English
machine à coudre (f)	sewing machine
machine à écrire (f)	typewriter
machine à laver (f)	washing machine
magasin (m)	store
magazine (m)	magazine, review
magie (f)	magic

French	English
mai	May
maigrir	to lose weight
main (f)	hand
mais	but
maison (f)	house
maîtriser	to master, to control
mal	bad, badly
malade	sick
malgré	in spite of
malheureusement	unfortunately
manger	to eat
manquer	to miss
manteau (m)	coat
marbre (m)	marble
marché (m)	market
marcher	to walk
mardi	Tuesday
mari (m)	husband
marron	brown
matelas (m)	mattress
matin (m)	morning
méchant	nasty, mean
mars	March
médecin (m)	doctor
mélanger	to mix
melon (m)	melon
mémoire (f)	memory
menacer de	to threaten
mériter de	to deserve
mendier	to beg
mensonge (m)	lie
mentir	to lie
menu (m)	menu
mer (f)	sea
merci	thank you
mercredi	Wednesday
mère (f)	mother
merveilleux	marvelous, terrific
météo (f)	weather forecast
mettre	to put
midi	midday, noon
mieux	better
mignon	cute
mince	slim
miroir (m)	mirror
moins	less
mois (m)	month
moitié (f)	half
moment (m)	moment
monde (m)	world
montagne (f)	mountain
monter	to go up
montre (f)	watch
montrer	to show, to indicate
morceau (m)	piece
mordre	to bite
mosquée (f)	mosque
mot (m)	word
mot de passe (m)	password

French	English
mouillé	wet
moulin à café (m)	coffee mill
moulin à poivre (m)	pepper mill
moulin à vent (m)	windmill
mourir	to die
moustache (f)	moustache
mouton (m)	sheep
mur (m)	wall
musée (m)	museum
musicien (m)	musician
musique (f)	music

N

French	English
n'importe où	anywhere
n'importe quoi	anything
nager	to swim
naissance (f)	birth
naître	to be born
nappe (f)	tablecloth
nature (f)	nature
néanmoins	nevertheless
neiger	to snow
nettoyer	to clean
neuf	new, nine
neveu (m)	nephew
nez (m)	nose
nièce (f)	niece
nier	to deny
niveau (m)	level
noir	black
noisette (f)	hazelnut
nom (m)	noun, name
nouveau	new
novembre	November
nuage (m)	cloud
nuit (f)	night
numérique	digital

O

French	English
obéir	to obey
objet (m)	object
obtenir	to obtain
octobre	October
œuf (m)	egg
offre (f)	offer
offrir	to offer
oiseau (m)	bird
olive (f)	olive
oncle (m)	uncle
opinion (f)	opinion, view
or	although, yet, but
or (m)	gold

French	English
ordinateur (m)	computer
ordonnance (f)	prescription
oreiller (m)	pillow
oser	to dare
où	where
oublier de	to forget
outil (m)	tool
ouverture (f)	opening
ouvrir	to open

P

French	English
page (f)	page
pair	even
paire (f)	pair, couple
panier (m)	basket
pantalon (m)	pants
papillon (m)	butterfly
paquet (m)	package, bag
par	by, through
par cœur	by heart
paraître	to appear
parapluie (m)	umbrella
paresseux	lazy
parfois	sometimes
parfum (m)	perfume
parisien	Parisian
parler	to speak, to talk
parmi	among
partir	to leave
partout	everywhere
passeport (m)	passport
passer	to pass by, to spend
passer (se) de	to do without
passionnant	fascinating
pâtisserie (f)	pastry shop, pastry
patron (m)	boss
pauvre	poor
payer	to pay
pays (m)	country, nation
paysage (m)	landscape
peau (f)	skin
peindre	to paint
peintre (m)	painter
peinture (f)	painting
pellicule (f)	roll of film
pelouse (f)	lawn
pendant	during
pensée (f)	thought
penser	to think
père (m)	father
permettre de	to allow, to permit
permis	allowed
permis de conduire (m)	driver's license
personne (f)	person
peser	to weigh
petit	little, small

French	English
petit-déjeuner (m)	breakfast
peu (m)	bit, few
peur (f)	fear
peut-être	maybe, perhaps
phrase (f)	sentence
pièce (f)	coin, room
pied (m)	foot
pire	worse
piscine (f)	swimming pool
placard (m)	cupboard
place (f)	place
plage (f)	beach
plaindre (se)	to complain
plaire	to please
plaisanter	to joke
plan (m)	map, plan
planète (f)	planet
plat (m)	dish, meal
plateau (m)	tray
plein	full
pleurer	to cry
pleuvoir	to rain
plonger	to dive
plume (f)	feather
plutôt	rather
pneu (m)	tire
poète (m)	poet
poire (f)	pear
poisson (m)	fish
poivre (m)	pepper
poli	polite
politique (f)	politics
pomme (f)	apple
pomme de terre (f)	potato
pont (m)	bridge
porte (f)	door
portefeuille (m)	wallet
porter	to carry, to wear
posséder	to own
poste (m)	position, place
poste (f)	post office
poubelle (f)	trash can, bin
poulet (m)	chicken
pour	for
pour que	so that, in order to
pourquoi	why
pourri	rotten
pourvu que	provided that
pouvoir	can, to be able to
premier	first
prendre	to take
prénom (m)	first name
près	near, close
présenter	to introduce
presque	almost
prévoir	to foresee
prier	to pray
privé	private

French	English
prix (m)	price
prochain	next
produit (m)	product
projet (m)	project
projeter de	to plan
promettre	to promise
proposer	to suggest
protéger	to protect
prudent	cautious
publicité (f)	promotion, advertising, commercial
pur	pure

Q

French	English
qualité (f)	quality
quand	when
quartier (m)	neighborhood
quelque chose	something
quelquefois	sometimes
queue (f)	queue, lineup, tail
qui	who, whom
quoi	what
quoique	although

R

French	English
raisin (m)	grape
raison (f)	reason
randonnée (f)	hike, long walk
rang (m)	row, rank
ranger	to put away
rapide	fast
rapport (m)	report
raser (se)	to shave
rater	to fail
ravi	delighted
recette (f)	recipe, receipts
recevoir	to receive
recommander	to recommend
récompenser	to reward
reçu (m)	receipt
recueillir	to gather, to collect
rédacteur (m)	editor
réduire	to cut down, to reduce
réfléchir	to reflect
réforme (f)	reform
refuser	to refuse
regarder	to look at
région (f)	region, area
rembourser	to reimburse
remercier de	to thank
remplir	to fill
rencontrer	to meet
renouveler	to renew
renseignement (m)	information
répandre	to spread

French	English
repas (m)	meal
répéter	to repeat
répétition (f)	rehearsal
répondre	to answer, to reply
repos (m)	rest
réseau (m)	network
réserver	to reserve, to book
résigner (se) à	to resign oneself
résoudre	to resolve
rester	to stay
retard	delay
retourner	to return
réunion (f)	meeting
réussir	to succeed
révéler	to reveal
revenir	to return, to come back
rêver	to dream
rez-de-chaussée (m)	main floor, first floor
riche	rich, wealthy
rideau (m)	curtain
rien	nothing
rire	to laugh
rire (m)	laughter
riz (m)	rice
robe (f)	dress
roi (m)	king
romancier (m)	novelist
roue (f)	wheel
rouge	red
route (f)	road
royal	majestic, royal
rue (f)	street
russe	Russian

S

French	English
s'il vous plaît	please
sable (m)	sand
sac (m)	bag
sac à dos (m)	backpack
sacré	sacred
sage	wise
sain	healthy
salade (f)	salad
sale	filthy, dirty
salle (f)	hall, room
salle à manger (f)	dining room
salon (m)	living room
samedi	Saturday
sandale (f)	sandal
sans	without
sauf	except
sauter	to jump
sauver	to save
savoir	to know
savon (m)	soap
selon	according to

French	English
se souvenir	to remember
secret (m)	secret
séduire	to seduce
sel (m)	salt
semaine (f)	week
sensible	sensitive
sentiment (m)	feeling, sense
sentir	to feel
senti	well-chosen, felt
septembre	September
sérieux	serious
serveur (m)	waiter
servir	to serve
servir (se) de	to use
seul	alone
seulement	only
siècle (m)	century
siège (m)	siege, seat
sieste (f)	nap
signer	to sign, to subscribe
silence (m)	silence
sœur (f)	sister
soie (f)	silk
soif (f)	thirst
soin (m)	care
soirée (f)	night, evening
soleil (m)	sun
sombre	dark
sommeil (m)	sleep
sonner	to ring
sortie (f)	exit
souffrir	to suffer
souhaiter	to hope for, to wish
soulever	to lift
soupçonner de	to suspect
souple	supple
sourire	to smile
sourire (m)	smile
souris (f)	mouse
sous	under
sous-sol (m)	basement
sous-titre (m)	subtitle
soutenir	to stick by, to stand by
souvenir (m)	memory, souvenir
spécial	special
spectacle (m)	show
stage (m)	internship
stagiaire (m)	intern
stylo (m)	pen
suivre	to follow
sucre (m)	sugar
suivant	according to
supermarché (m)	supermarket
sur	on
sûr	sure
survivre à	to live through, to survive
sympathique	nice, friendly

T

FRENCH	ENGLISH
table (f)	table
tableau (m)	picture, scene, blackboard
tache (f)	stain
tâche (f)	task
taille (f)	size, waist
tambour (m)	drum
tant de	so many
tant que	as long as
tante (f)	aunt
tard	late
tasse (f)	cup
teindre	to dye
télécharger	to download
télévision (f)	television
temps (m)	time
tendance (f)	tendency, trend
tendrement	tenderly, lovingly
tenir	to hold
tenir à	to insist, to be eager
terrasse (f)	patio, terrace
testament (m)	will
tête (f)	head
têtu	stubborn
thé (m)	tea
théière (f)	teapot
thon (m)	tuna fish
timbre (m)	stamp
tissu (m)	fabric
toit (m)	roof
tomber	to fall
tomber en panne	to break down (car)
tôt	early
toujours	always
tourner	to turn around
tousser	to cough
tout	all
tout de suite	right away
traduire	to translate
trahir	to betray
train (m)	train
traité (m)	treaty
tranquille	calm, quiet
transmettre	to hand on
travailler	to work
traverser	to cross
tremblement de terre (m)	earthquake
très	very
trésor (m)	treasure
tricoter	to knit
triste	sad
tristesse (f)	sadness
trop	too, too much
trouver	to find, to get

U

FRENCH	ENGLISH
unir	to blend, to mix
usine (f)	factory
utile	helpful, useful

V

FRENCH	ENGLISH
vacances (f pl)	holidays, vacation
vache (f)	cow
vague (f)	wave
vaisselle (f)	dishes
valise (f)	suitcase
valoir	to be worth
vanille (f)	vanilla
varier	to vary, to differ
veille (f)	the day before
vélo (m)	bicycle
vendre	to sell
vent (m)	wind
verbe (m)	verb
vérité (f)	truth
verre (m)	glass
vers	toward
vert	green
vendredi	Friday
veste (f)	jacket
vêtement (m)	clothing
viande (f)	meat
vie (f)	life
vieillir	to grow old
vietnamien	Vietnamese
vieux	old
village (m)	village
ville (f)	city, town
vin (m)	wine
vinaigre (m)	vinegar
virgule (f)	comma
visage (m)	face
visiter	to visit
vivre	to live
voir	to see
voisin (m)	neighbor
voiture (f)	car
voix (f)	voice
vol (m)	flight, robbery
voler	to fly, to steal
volontiers	with pleasure
voyage (m)	trip, travel, journey
voyager	to travel

Z

FRENCH	ENGLISH
zéro	zero

Appendix C
English-to-French Dictionary

A

ENGLISH	FRENCH
abolish (to)	abolir
abroad	à l'étranger
accomplish (to)	accomplir
according to	selon
acquire (to)	acquérir
act (to)	agir
actor	acteur (m)
address	adresse (f)
adventure	aventure (f)
advisor	conseiller (m)
afraid (to be)	avoir peur de
again	encore
against	contre
age	âge (m)
agency	agence (f)
agreement	accord (m)
air conditioner	climatiseur (m)
air conditioning	climatisation (f)
airport	aéroport (m)
all	tout
allow (to)	permettre de
allowable	admissible, légitime
almost	presque
alone	seul
already	déjà
although	bien que, quoique
always	toujours
amaze (to)	étonner
among	parmi
amusing	drôle
and	et
anger	colère (f)
annoying	ennuyant
announce (to)	annoncer
answer (to)	répondre
anything	n'importe quoi
anywhere	n'importe où
apartment	appartement (m)
apologize (to)	excuser (s')
appear (to)	paraître
applaud (to)	applaudir
apple	pomme (f)
appear (to)	paraître
April	avril
around	autour
arrival	arrivée(f)
arrive (to)	arriver
article	article(m)

as long as	tant que
as soon as	dès que, aussitôt que
ask (to)	demander
astonishing	étonnant
at, with	chez
at random	au hazard
at the expense of	aux dépens de
attend (to)	assister à
attic	grenier (m)
August	août
aunt	tante (f)
available	disponible
avenue	avenue (f)
avoid (to)	éviter

B

ENGLISH	FRENCH
backpack	sac à dos (m)
badly	mal
bag	sac (m)
bakery	boulangerie (f)
basement	sous-sol (m)
basket	panier (m)
bath	bain (m)
be (to)	être
beach	plage (f)
bean	haricot (m)
beard	barbe (f)
beauty	beauté (f)
beat (to)	battre
because of	à cause de
become (to)	devenir
bed	lit (m)
behind	derrière
believe (to)	croire
belong (to)	appartenir
better	mieux
betray (to)	trahir
between	entre
beyond	au-delà de
bicycle	bicyclette (f), vélo (m)
bird	oiseau (m)
birth	naissance (f)
birthday	anniversaire (m)
bite (to)	mordre
bitter	amer
black	noir
blackboard	tableau (m)
blend (to)	mélanger
blue	bleu

boat	*bateau (m)*	cheese	*fromage (m)*
body	*corps (m)*	cherry	*cerise (f)*
book	*livre (m)*	chicken	*poulet (m)*
book (to)	*réserver*	child	*enfant (m)*
bookkeeper	*comptable*	childhood	*enfance (f)*
boot	*botte (f)*	Chinese	*chinois*
border	*frontière (f)*	chocolate	*chocolat (m)*
born (to be)	*naître*	choke (to)	*étouffer*
borrow (to)	*emprunter*	choose (to)	*choisir*
boss	*patron (m)*	church	*église (f)*
bottle	*bouteille (f)*	city	*ville (f)*
box	*boîte (f)*	clean (to)	*nettoyer*
break (to)	*casser*	climb (to)	*grimper*
break down (to)	*tomber en panne*	clock	*horloge (f)*
breakfast	*petit-déjeuner (m)*	closing	*fermeture (f)*
bridge	*pont (m)*	cloud	*nuage (m)*
bring (to)	*apporter*	coat	*manteau (m)*
brother	*frère (m)*	coffee	*café (m)*
brother-in-law	*beau-frère (m)*	coffee mill	*moulin à café (m)*
brown	*marron*	coin	*pièce (f)*
brush	*brosse (f)*	cold	*froid (m)*
brush (to)	*brosser*	color	*couleur (f)*
build (to)	*bâtir*	comfortable	*confortable*
building	*bâtiment (m)*	comma	*virgule (f)*
burn (to)	*brûler*	common	*commun*
bus	*autobus (m), bus (m)*	complain (to)	*plaindre (se)*
but	*mais*	computer	*ordinateur (m)*
butter	*beurre (m)*	congratulate (to)	*féliciter*
butterfly	*papillon (m)*	conjugate (to)	*conjuguer*
buy (to)	*acheter*	construct (to)	*construire*
by	*par*	contact (to)	*contacter*
by heart	*par cœur*	contemplate (to)	*envisager de*
		convince (to)	*convaincre*
		cork	*bouchon (m)*

C

ENGLISH	FRENCH	corner	*coin (m)*
		cost (to)	*coûter*
cabbage	*chou (m)*	cough (to)	*tousser*
cake	*gâteau (m)*	count (to)	*compter*
call (to)	*appeler*	counter	*comptoir (m)*
calm	*calme, tranquille*	country	*pays (m)*
can	*pouvoir*	countryside	*campagne (f)*
cancel (to)	*annuler*	course	*cours (m)*
car	*voiture (f)*	cover (to)	*couvrir*
card	*carte (f)*	cow	*vache (f)*
care	*soin (m)*	crazy	*fou*
carry (to)	*porter*	cream	*crème (f)*
castle	*château (m)*	create (to)	*créer*
cat	*chat (m)*	crime	*crime (m)*
cautious	*prudent*	cross (to)	*traverser*
century	*siècle (m)*	crowded	*bondé*
chair	*chaise (f)*	cry (to)	*pleurer*
challenge	*défi (m)*	cup	*tasse (f)*
chance	*chance (f)*	cupboard	*placard (m)*
change	*changement (m)*	curtain	*rideau (m)*
chapter	*chapitre (m)*	cushion	*coussin (m)*
charming	*charmant*	customer	*client (m)*
chat (to)	*bavarder*	cut (to)	*couper*
cheap	*bon marché*	cute	*mignon*

D

ENGLISH	FRENCH
dance (to)	danser
dancer	danseur(m)
dare (to)	oser
dark	sombre
daughter	fille (f)
daughter-in-law	belle-fille (f)
dawn	aube (f)
day	jour (m)
day after (the)	lendemain
day after tomorrow (the)	après-demain
day before (the)	veille (f)
day before yesterday (the)	avant-hier
December	décembre
defend (to)	défendre
delighted	enchanté, ravi
deny (to)	nier
depend (to)	dépendre
depressed	déprimé
describe (to)	décrire
deserve (to)	mériter
desire (to)	désirer
desk	bureau (m)
dessert	dessert (m)
destination	destination (f)
diary	journal intime (m)
dictionary	dictionnaire (m)
die (to)	mourir
difference	différence (f)
different	différent
digital	numérique
dining room	salle à manger (f)
dinner	dîner (m)
dirt	boue (f), saleté (f)
dirty	sale
disappoint (to)	décevoir
discuss (to)	discuter
dish	plat (m)
display	étalage (m)
display (to)	étaler, presenter
disturb (to)	déranger
dive (to)	plonger
divide (to)	diviser
do (to)	faire
do without (to)	passer (se) de
doctor	médecin (m)
dog	chien (m)
door	porte (f)
download (to)	télécharger
drawing	dessin (m)
dream (to)	rêver
dress	robe (f)
drink (to)	boire
drive (to)	conduire
drum	tambour (m)
duck	canard (m)

during	pendant, lors de
dye (to)	teindre

E

ENGLISH	FRENCH
eager (to be)	tenir à
eat (to)	manger
early	tôt
earn (to)	gagner
earthquake	tremblement de terre (m), séisme (m)
easy	facile
editor	rédacteur (m)
efficient	efficace
egg	œuf (m)
elect (to)	élire
elevator	ascenseur (m)
elsewhere	ailleurs
email	courrier électronique (m), courriel (m), mel (m)
end (to)	finir, terminer
energy	énergie (f)
English	anglais
enlarge (to)	agrandir
enter (to)	entrer
equal	égal
erase (to)	effacer
escape (to)	échapper
establish (to)	établir
euro	euro (m)
even	même
event	événement (m)
everywhere	partout
example	exemple (m)
except	sauf
exhibit	exposition (f)
exit	sortie (f)
expect (to)	attendre (s') à
explanation	explication (f)
express (to)	exprimer

F

ENGLISH	FRENCH
fabric	tissu (m)
face	visage (m)
fact	fait (m)
factory	usine (f)
fail (to)	échouer, rater
faint (to)	évanouir (s')
fairy	fée (f)
fall (to)	tomber
family	famille (f)
famous	célèbre
far	loin
fascinate (to)	fasciner
fascinating	fascinant, passionnant
fast	rapide

father	père (m)
father-in-law	beau-père (m)
fear	peur (f)
fear (to)	craindre
feather	plume (f)
February	février
feel (to)	sentir
feel like (to)	avoir envie de
feeling	sentiment (m)
fight (to)	combattre
file	fichier (m)
fill (to)	remplir
find (to)	trouver
finally	enfin, finalement
finger	doigt (m)
finish (to)	finir, terminer
fire	feu (m)
first	premier (m)
first name	prénom (m)
fish	poisson (m)
flag	drapeau (m)
floor	étage (m), plancher (m), sol (m)
florist	fleuriste (m)
flour	farine (f)
flower	fleur (f)
flu	grippe (f)
following the example of	à l'instar de
foot	pied (m)
follow (to)	suivre
for	pour
for fear that	de peur que
forbid (to)	interdire de
forget (to)	oublier
fork	fourchette (f)
formerly	autrefois
foresee (to)	prévoir
free	libre
French	français
fresh	frais
Friday	vendredi
friend	ami (m), copain (m)
friendship	amitié(f)
frog	grenouille (f)
full	plein
fun, funny	amusant, divertissant, drôle
future	avenir (m)

G

ENGLISH	FRENCH
garage	garage (m)
garden	jardin (m)
garlic	ail (m)
gather (to)	rassembler, recueillir
generous	généreux
genius	génie (m)
get along (to)	entendre (s')
get rid of (to)	débarrasser (se) de

give (to)	donner
glass	verre (m)
glasses	lunettes (f pl)
glove	gant (m)
go (to)	aller
go down (to)	descendre
good-looking	beau
good morning	bonjour
go up (to)	monter
government	gouvernement (m)
grandfather	grand-père (m)
grandmother	grand-mère (f)
grape	raisin (m)
green	vert
grey	gris
grow (to)	grandir
grow old (to)	vieillir
guilt	culpabilité (f)
guilty	coupable

H

ENGLISH	FRENCH
hairdresser	coiffeur (m)
half	moitié (f)
hall, room	salle (f)
hallway	couloir (m)
hand	main (f)
hand on (to)	transmettre
hang (to)	accrocher, accrocher (s')
happiness	bonheur (m)
happy	heureux
hard	dur
hardly	à peine
hat	chapeau (m)
have (to)	avoir
have lunch (to)	déjeuner
have to (to)	falloir, devoir
hazelnut	noisette (f)
head	tête (f)
heal (to)	guérir
healthy	sain
heart	cœur (m)
heat	chaleur (f)
heating	chauffage (m)
hear (to)	entendre
heavy	lourd
height	hauteur (f)
help (to)	aider
helpful, useful	utile
hide (to)	cacher
hill	colline (f)
hold (to)	tenir
holidays, vacation	vacances (f pl)
hope (to)	espérer
hope for (to), wish (to)	souhaiter
horse	cheval (m)
horses	chevaux (m pl)

hospital	*hôpital (m)*
hotel	*hôtel (m)*
hostel, inn	*auberge (f)*
house	*maison (f)*
how much	*combien*
hurry (to)	*dépêcher (se) de*
hurt (to)	*blesser*
husband	*mari (m)*

I

ENGLISH	FRENCH
ice	*glace (f)*
idealism	*idéalisme (m)*
implore (to)	*mendier, implorer*
improve (to)	*améliorer*
in a position to	*à même de*
in case	*au cas où*
in front of	*devant*
in love	*amoureux*
in spite of	*malgré*
in the middle of	*au milieu de*
in time	*à temps*
include (to), carry (to)	*inclure*
increase (to)	*augmenter*
increase	*augmentation (f)*
incredible, extraordinary	*incroyable*
induce (to)	*influencer*
information	*renseignement (m), information (f)*
informed (to be)	*être au courant, être mis au courant*
influence (to)	*influencer*
ink	*encre (f)*
inn	*auberge (f)*
insincere	*faux*
insist (to)	*insister, tenir à*
instead of	*au lieu de*
interesting	*intéressant*
intern	*stagiaire*
internship	*stage (m)*
interview	*entretien (m)*
introduce (to)	*présenter*
invest (to)	*investir*
island	*île (f)*
Italian	*italien*

J

ENGLISH	FRENCH
jacket	*veste (f)*
jam	*confiture (f)*
January	*janvier*
Japanese	*japonais*
jewel	*bijou (m)*
job	*emploi (m)*
join (to)	*joindre*
joke	*plaisanterie, blague*

joke (to)	*plaisanter*
joy	*joie (f)*
July	*juillet*
jump (to)	*sauter*
June	*juin*
just	*juste, uniquement*

K

ENGLISH	FRENCH
keep (to)	*garder*
key	*clé (f)*
kid	*enfant (m)*
king	*roi (m)*
kiss	*baiser (m)*
kiss (to)	*embrasser*
knit (to)	*tricoter*
know (to)	*connaître, savoir*
knowledge	*connaissance (f)*

L

ENGLISH	FRENCH
label	*étiquette (f)*
lamp	*lampe (f)*
landscape	*paysage (m)*
language	*langue (f), langage (m)*
large	*grand*
late	*tard, en retard*
laugh (to)	*rire*
laughter	*rire (m)*
lawn	*pelouse (f)*
lawyer	*avocat (m)*
lazy	*paresseux*
learn (to)	*apprendre*
leather	*cuir (m)*
leave (to)	*partir, laisser*
left	*gauche*
leg	*jambe (f)*
lesion	*blessure (f)*
less	*moins*
lesson	*leçon (f)*
letter	*lettre (f)*
level	*niveau (m)*
liberty	*liberté (f)*
librarian	*bibliothécaire (f or m)*
library	*bibliothèque (f)*
lie	*mensonge (m)*
lie (to)	*mentir*
life	*vie (f)*
lift (to)	*soulever*
light	*lumière (f)*
light	*léger*
like	*comme*
like (to)	*aimer*
line	*ligne (f)*
lineup	*queue (f), file d'attente (f)*
link	*lien (m)*

English	French
lip	*lèvre (f)*
listen (to)	*écouter*
little	*petit*
live (to)	*vivre, habiter*
live through (to)	*survivre à*
liver	*foie (m)*
living room	*salon (m)*
load (to)	*charger*
long walk	*randonnée (f)*
look at (to)	*regarder*
look for (to)	*chercher*
lose weight (to)	*maigrir*
loud	*bruyant*
love	*amour (m)*
love (to)	*aimer*
low	*bas*
lower (to)	*baisser*

M

English	French
madly	*follement*
magazine	*magazine (m)*
magic	*magie (f)*
main floor	*rez-de-chaussée (m)*
majestic	*royal, majestueux, fier*
man	*homme (m)*
manage (to)	*gérer, débrouiller (se)*
map	*plan (m)*
marble	*marbre (m)*
March	*mars*
market	*marché (m)*
master (to)	*maîtriser*
masterpiece	*chef-d'œuvre (m)*
mattress	*matelas (m)*
May	*mai*
maybe	*peut-être*
meal	*repas (m)*
mean	*méchant*
meat	*viande (f)*
meet (to)	*rencontrer*
meeting	*réunion (f)*
melon	*melon (m)*
memory	*mémoire (f), souvenir (m)*
menu	*menu (m)*
midday, noon	*midi*
milk	*lait (m)*
mirror	*miroir (m)*
miss (to)	*manquer*
mistake	*erreur (f)*
mix (to)	*mélanger*
moan (to)	*gémir*
moment	*moment (m)*
Monday	*lundi*
money	*argent (m)*
month	*mois (m)*
mood	*humeur (f)*
morning	*matin (m)*

mosque	*mosquée (f)*
mother	*mère (f)*
mother-in-law	*belle-mère (f)*
mountain	*montagne (f)*
mouse	*souris (f)*
moustache	*moustache (f)*
mouth	*bouche (f)*
move (to)	*déménager*
museum	*musée (m)*
mushroom	*champignon (m)*
music	*musique (f)*
musician	*musicien (m)*
must, should	*devoir*

N

English	French
name	*nom (m)*
nap	*sieste (f)*
nature	*nature (f)*
near	*près*
necklace	*collier (m)*
need (to)	*avoir besoin de*
neighbor	*voisin (m)*
neighborhood	*quartier (m)*
nephew	*neveu (m)*
network	*réseau (m)*
never	*jamais*
nevertheless	*néanmoins*
newspaper	*journal (m)*
next	*prochain*
nice	*sympathique*
niece	*nièce (f)*
night	*nuit (f)*
night, evening	*soirée (f)*
noise	*bruit (m)*
noisy, loud	*bruyant*
noon	*midi*
nose	*nez (m)*
nothing	*rien*
novelist	*romancier*
November	*novembre*

O

English	French
obey (to)	*obéir*
object	*objet (m)*
obtain (to)	*gagner, obtenir*
October	*octobre*
of course, evidently	*évidemment*
offer	*offre(f)*
offer (to)	*offrir*
oil	*huile (f)*
old	*vieux*
olive	*olive (f)*
on	*sur*
on purpose	*exprès*

English	French
on the verge of, on the brink of	au bord de
on time	à l'heure
once	jadis
only	seulement
open (to)	ouvrir
opening	ouverture (f), vernissage (m)
opinion	avis (m), opinion (f)
order (to)	commander
otherwise	autrement
oven	four (m)
own (to)	posséder

P

English	French
pack	paquet (m)
pack (to)	faire ses bagages
page	page (f)
paint (to)	peindre
painter	peintre (m)
painting	peinture (f)
pants	pantalon (m)
parcel	colis (m)
Parisian	parisien
park (to)	garer
pass (to)	passer, réussir
passport	passeport (m)
password	mot de passe (m)
pastry	pâtisserie (f)
pastry shop	pâtisserie (f)
path	chemin (m), sentier (m)
patio, terrace	terrasse (f)
pay (to)	payer
pear	poire (f)
peel (to)	éplucher
pen	stylo (m)
people	gens (m pl)
pepper mill	moulin à poivre (m)
perceive (to)	apercevoir
perfume	parfum (m)
person	personne (f)
pepper	poivre (m)
phone call	coup de fil (m), appel (m)
pick (to)	cueillir
picture	image (f), tableau (m)
pillow	oreiller (m)
pineapple	ananas (m)
place	endroit (m), la place (f)
plan (to)	projeter de
plane	avion (m)
planet	planète (f)
plate	assiette (f)
play (to)	jouer
please	s'il vous plaît
please (to)	plaire
pleased	content
plug in (to)	brancher

English	French
poet	poète (m)
polite	poli
politics	politique (f)
poor	pauvre
position	position (f), poste (m)
possibly	éventuellement
post office	poste (f)
postcard	carte postale (f)
poster	affiche (f)
potato	pomme de terre (f)
pray (to)	prier
prescription	ordonnance (f)
present	présent (m)
present	présent, actuel
presently	actuellement
pretend (to)	faire semblant de
prevent (to)	empêcher de
price	prix (m)
print (to)	imprimer
printer	imprimante (f)
private	privé
product	produit (m)
profit	profit (m), bénéfice (m)
project	projet (m)
promise (to)	promettre
promotion	promotion (f), publicité (f)
protect (to)	protéger
proud	fier
provided that	pourvu que, à condition que
purchase	achat (m)
pure	pur
push in (to)	enfoncer
put (to)	mettre
put away (to)	ranger
put on weight (to)	grossir

Q

English	French
quality	qualité (f)
quickly	bientôt, rapidemment
quit (to), resign (to)	démissionner

R

English	French
rabbit	lapin (m)
reach (to)	atteindre
read (to)	lire
rage	crise (f), colère (f)
rain (to)	pleuvoir
raspberry	framboise (f)
rather	plutôt
reading	lecture (f)
reason	raison (f)
receipt	reçu (m)
receipts	recette (f), recettes (f pl)
receive (to)	recevoir

English	French
recipe	recette (f)
recommend (to)	recommander
record (to)	enregistrer
red	rouge
reduce (to)	réduire
reflect (to)	réfléchir
refrain from (to)	empêcher (s') de
refuse (to)	refuser
region	région (f)
rehearsal	répétition (f)
reimburse (to)	rembourser
rely (to)	dépendre de, se fier à, compter sur
remember (to)	se souvenir
remove (to)	enlever
renew (to)	renouveler
rent	loyer (m)
repeat (to)	répéter
report	rapport (m)
require (to)	exiger
resign (to)	démissionner
resign oneself (to)	résigner à (se)
resolve (to)	résoudre
rest	repos (m)
return (to)	revenir
reveal (to)	révéler
revenue	recette (f), revenu (m)
reward (to)	récompenser
rice	riz (m)
rich	riche
right	droite (f)
right	droit, juste, vrai, exact
right away	tout de suite
ring	bague (f)
ring (to)	sonner
rip-off, robbery	vol (m)
road	route (f)
roll of film	pellicule (f)
roof	toit (m)
room	chambre (f), pièce (f)
rope	corde (f)
rotten	pourri
row	rang (m)
run (to)	courir
Russian	russe

S

ENGLISH	FRENCH
sacred	sacré
sad	triste
sadness	tristesse (f)
sagely	sagement, prudemment
salad	salade (f)
salt	sel (m)
sand	sable (m)
sandal	sandale (f)
Saturday	samedi
save (to)	sauver

English	French
say (to)	dire
scarf	foulard (m), écharpe (l') (f)
schedule	horaire (m), emploi du temps (m)
school	école (f)
scream (to), yell (to)	crier
screen	écran (m)
sea	mer (f)
secret	secret (m)
seduce (to)	séduire
see (to)	voir
sell (to)	vendre
sensitive	sensible
sentence	phrase (f)
September	septembre
serious	sérieux
serve (to)	servir
sewing machine	machine à coudre (f)
shame	honte (f)
shave off (to)	raser (se)
sheep	mouton (m)
shirt	chemise (f)
shiver (to)	frémir
shoe	chaussure (f)
short	court
show	spectacle (m), exposition (f)
show (to)	montrer
shower	douche (f)
sick	malade
siege	siège (m)
sign (to)	signer
silence	silence (m)
silk	soie (f)
since	depuis
sing (to)	chanter
single	célibataire
sister	sœur (f)
sister-in-law	belle-sœur (f)
sit (to)	asseoir (s')
size, waist	taille (f)
skin	peau (f)
sleep (to)	dormir
slim	mince
sleep	sommeil (m)
slow	lent
small	petit
smile	sourire (m)
smile (to)	sourire
smoke (to)	fumer
snow (to)	neiger
so	si, tellement, tant
so many	tant de
so that	afin que, pour que
soap	savon (m)
sock	chaussette (f)
soft, gentle	doux
something	quelque chose
sometimes	parfois, quelquefois
son	fils (m)

song	chanson (f)
son-in-law	gendre (m)
sort	espèce (f), sorte (f)
speak (to)	parler
special	spécial
speech	discours (m)
spell (to)	épeler
spend (to)	dépenser
spice	épice (f)
spider	araignée (f)
spinach	épinards (m pl)
spit (to)	cracher
sponge	éponge (f)
spoon	cuillère (f)
spread (to)	répandre
spy	espion (m)
square	carré (m)
stain	tache (f)
stake	enjeu (m)
stay (to)	rester
steal (to)	voler
stamp	timbre (m)
state	état (m)
station	gare (f)
stepmother	belle-mère (f)
stick by (to), stand by (to)	soutenir
store	magasin (m)
story	histoire (f)
storyteller	conteur (m)
stop (to)	arrêter
straight from	à même
strange, weird	étrange, drôle
stranger, foreigner	étranger
street	rue (f)
string	ficelle (f), corde (f)
stubborn	têtu
student	étudiant (m)
study	étude (f)
study (to)	étudier
subscribe (to)	abonner (s') à
subtitle	sous-titre (m)
suburb	banlieue (f)
succeed (to)	réussir
suffer (to)	souffrir
sugar	sucre (m)
suggest (to)	suggérer, proposer
suitcase	valise (f)
sun	soleil (m)
Sunday	dimanche
sundown, sunset	coucher de soleil (m)
sunglasses	lunettes de soleil (f pl)
supermarket	supermarché (m)
supple	souple
sure	sûr
suspect (to)	soupçonner de
swallow (to)	avaler
sweet	sucré, doux, gentil
swim (to)	nager
swimming pool	piscine (f)

T

ENGLISH	FRENCH
table	table (f)
tablecloth	nappe (f)
take (to)	prendre
take along (to)	emmener
task	tâche (f)
taste (to)	goûter
tea	thé (m)
teach (to)	enseigner
team	équipe (f)
teapot	théière (f)
television	télévision (f)
tenant	locataire (m)
tendancy	tendance (f)
tenderly, lovingly	tendrement
terrific	merveilleux
thank (to)	remercier
thank you	merci
that way	ainsi
there	là
think (to)	penser
thirst	soif (f)
thought	pensée (f)
threaten (to)	menacer de
thrill (to)	emballer
throw (to)	jeter
Thursday	jeudi
ticket	billet (m)
tie	cravate (f)
tie (to)	ficeler
time	temps (m), heure (f), fois (f)
tire	pneu (m)
tired	fatigué
to what extent	dans quelle mesure
today	aujourd'hui
together	ensemble
tomorrow	demain
too much	trop
tool	outil (m)
tooth	dent (f)
toward	vers, envers
toy	jouet (m)
traffic	circulation (f)
train	train (m)
translate (to)	traduire
trash can	poubelle (f)
travel (to)	voyager
tray	plateau (m)
treasure	trésor (m)
treaty	traité (m)
tree	arbre (m)
trip	voyage (m)
truck	camion (m)
truth	vérité (f)
try (to)	essayer
try hard (to)	efforcer (s') de
Tuesday	mardi

tuna fish	thon (m)
turkey	dinde (f)
turn around (to)	tourner
turn down (to)	retourner, refuser
turn on (to)	allumer
typewriter	machine à écrire (f)

U

ENGLISH	FRENCH
ugly	laid
umbrella	parapluie (m)
uncle	oncle (m)
under	sous
unemployment	chômage (m)
unfortunately	malheureusement
unknown	inconnu
use (to)	servir (se) de
useful	utile
usually	d'habitude, habituellement

V

ENGLISH	FRENCH
vanilla	vanille (f)
vary (to), differ (to)	varier
verb	verbe (m)
very	très
Vietnamese	vietnamien
vinegar	vinaigre (m)
visible	visible, évident
visit (to)	visiter
voice	voix (f)
voice mail	boîte vocale (f), messagerie (f)

W

ENGLISH	FRENCH
waist	taille (f)
wait for (to)	attendre
waiter	serveur (m)
walk (to)	marcher
wall	mur (m)
wallet	portefeuille (m)
war	guerre (f)
wash (to)	laver
washing machine	machine à laver (f)
waste (to)	gaspiller
watch	montre (f)
watch (to)	regarder
water	eau (f)
water (to)	arroser
wave	vague (f)
way, path	chemin (m)
weak	faible
weather forecast	météo (f)
Wednesday	mercredi
week	semaine (f)

weekly	hebdomadaire
weigh (to)	peser
welcome	bienvenue
well, good	bien
well-chosen	senti, bien choisi
wet	mouillé
wheel	roue (f)
when	quand, lorsque
where	où
white	blanc
who, whom	qui
why	pourquoi
will	testament (m)
wind	vent (m)
windmill	moulin à vent (m)
window	fenêtre (f)
wine	vin (m)
winter	hiver (m)
wise	sage
wish (to)	souhaiter
with	avec
with pleasure	avec plaisir, volontiers
without	sans
without somebody's knowing	à l'insu de
woman	femme (f)
wool	laine (f)
word	mot (m)
work	travail (m)
work (to)	travailler
workshop	atelier (m)
world	monde (m)
worried	inquiet
worse	pire
wrap (to)	emballer
write (to)	écrire
writer	écrivain (m)
writing	écriture (f)

Y

ENGLISH	FRENCH
year	an (m), année (f)
yell (to)	crier, hurler
yellow	jaune
yesterday	hier
young	jeune

Z

ENGLISH	FRENCH
zero	zéro

Appendix D
Answer Key

Part 1: Articles and Nouns

Exercise 1-1: Masculine or Feminine?

1.	M	6.	F
2.	F	7.	F
3.	M	8.	M
4.	F	9.	M
5.	F	10.	M

Exercise 1-2: Indefinitely Yours

1.	*une*	5.	*un*
2.	*un*	6.	*des*
3.	*des*	7.	*une*
4.	*une*	8.	*un*

Exercise 1-4: Definitely Yours

1.	*le*	6.	*les*
2.	*le*	7.	*la*
3.	*le*	8.	*les*
4.	*la*	9.	*le*
5.	*le*	10.	*les*

Exercise 1-5: Where Is the Noun?

1.	*train, gare*	6.	*tableaux, salle*
2.	*terrasse*	7.	*question*
3.	*fromages*	8.	*ordinateur, imprimante*
4.	*agences*	9.	*château, siècle*
5.	*devoirs*	10.	*gants, écharpe*

Exercise 1-6: Let's Figure Out the Gender

1. *Il pose la fourchette et le couteau sur la table.*
2. *Il adore le pain, le fromage, et la ratatouille.*
3. *Le bâtiment sur votre gauche date du dix-neuvième siècle.*
4. *Le gouvernement a proposé des réformes.*
5. *La boulangerie ouvre à sept heures.*
6. *La gare est à dix kilomètres d'ici.*
7. *Les enfants sont à la plage.*
8. *J'ai lu ça dans le journal.*
9. *L'avion part à dix heures.*
10. *Le comité annoncera la décision à midi.*

Exercise 1-7: What's Your Job?

1. *Cette musicienne est italienne.*
2. *Le cabinet de leur avocate est fermé en août.*
3. *Cette actrice est vietnamienne.*
4. *Sa coiffeuse est en vacances.*
5. *La directrice est à Paris.*
6. *La conseillère est en réunion.*
7. *L'informaticienne était en retard.*
8. *Ma rédactrice a trouvé un nouvel emploi.*

Exercise 1-8: *C'est Qui?*

1.	*gendre*	5.	*cousins*
2.	*grand-père*	6.	*neveu*
3.	*belle-soeur*	7.	*arrière-grand-mère*
4.	*tante*	8.	*beau-père*

Exercise 1-9: Mix and Match

1.	d	4.	c
2.	e	5.	a
3.	b		

Exercise 1-10: More Than One

1.	*les chevaux*	5.	*les manteaux*
2.	*les voix*	6.	*les fourchettes*
3.	*les neveux*	7.	*les hommes*
4.	*les tasses*	8.	*les montagnes*

Exercise 1-11: Going to a Masculine or Feminine Country?

1.	*la*	6.	*la*
2.	*le*	7.	*le*
3.	*la*	8.	*les*
4.	*la*	9.	*la*
5.	*le*	10.	*la*

Exercise 1-12: Let's Travel the World!

1. *L'Italie est très agréable au printemps.*
2. *Lui, il préfère l'Espagne. Elle, elle préfère la Grèce.*
3. *La Normandie est célèbre pour ses fromages.*
4. *Les Pays-Bas exportent beaucoup de tulipes.*
5. *La Chine a signé un accord avec la Russie.*
6. *La Californie a de belles plages.*
7. *Le Mexique ou le Vietnam pour les vacances? Qui sait?*
8. *Le Mali a beaucoup de conteurs.*
9. *L'agent nous a conseillé l'Inde pour nos vacances d'hiver.*
10. *J'aime beaucoup l'Irlande mais j'adore le Maroc.*

Exercise 1-13: Can You Guess?

1. sponge
2. student
3. stranger

Exercise 1-14: What Does It Really Mean?

1. Montreal has many bookstores.
2. I'll wait ten minutes maximum.
3. We spent a nice day with the family.
4. She is presently in China.
5. Your friends are nice.
6. His boss is very friendly.
7. They have five weeks of vacation every year.
8. She lost the game. She is really disappointed.

Exercise 1-15: Let's Find the Clue to the Puzzle!

1. *La reine a cent chiens.*
2. *L'eau de la mer est très salée.*
3. *La maire de Toulouse est mère de quatre enfants.*
4. *Une fois, j'ai mangé du foie gras.*
5. *Cette photo est prise en haut de la montagne.*
6. *La voile du bateau est bleue.*
7. *Elle a tant de choses à faire!*
8. *Je n'ai pas le temps d'y aller.*
9. *Ces moules marinières sont délicieuses.*
10. *La reine sort sans son chien.*

Exercise 1-16: Matching Game

1.	d	4.	b
2.	a	5.	c
3.	e		

Exercise 1-17: What Makes Sense?

1.	e	4.	c
2.	a	5.	d
3.	b		

Exercise 1-18: Let's Recap!

1.	*une*	6.	*une*
2.	*une*	7.	*une*
3.	*des*	8.	*un*
4.	*un*	9.	*des*
5.	*un*	10.	*une*

Exercise 1-19: Eavesdropping

1. *Les hôtels en Italie sont magnifiques.*
2. *Il y a trois ou quatre chats dans le jardin.*
3. *Nous avons rencontré un couple sympathique.*
4. *Oui, cette photo est prise sur le Grand Canal.*
5. *Il est dentiste et elle est avocate.*
6. *Ils ont deux enfants. Un fils et une fille.*
7. *La fille étudie la musique.*
8. *Le fils étudie la philosophie.*
9. *Oui, des vacances magnifiques!*
10. *Les prochaines vacances? En Australie ou en Argentine.*

Part 2: Pronouns

Exercise 2-1: Is It You?

1. *Elle*
2. *Nous*
3. *Ils*
4. *Il*
5. *Elles*

Exercise 2-2: *On*

1. *On voudrait réussir dans la vie.*
2. *On va à la plage aujourd'hui?*
3. *On parle allemand ici.*
4. *En France, on boit du bon vin.*
5. *Mon frère et moi, on mange toujours dans ce restaurant.*
6. *Alors, on reste à la maison ce soir?*
7. *On ne sait jamais.*
8. *On va être en retard!*
9. *On n'accepte pas les euros ici.*
10. *À Paris, on prend le métro.*

Exercise 2-3: Oral Practice

1. *Non, nous ne l'invitons pas.*
2. *Non, je ne les comprends pas du tout.*
3. *Oui, je le fais livrer.*
4. *Oui, je les appelle ce soir.*
5. *Oui, il les cherche toujours.*
6. *Oui, je les connais.*
7. *Oui, elle les invite souvent.*
8. *Non, je ne les lis pas en français.*
9. *Oui, je la prépare avec de la sauce.*
10. *Non, elle ne l'écrit pas à la main.*

Exercise 2-4: You Know the Answer—You Know It!

1. *Elle les a achetées.*
2. *Nous l'avons consulté.*
3. *Les spectateurs les ont applaudis.*
4. *Je l'ai oublié.*
5. *Il l'ignore.*
6. *Elle le vend.*
7. *Il les accepte.*
8. *Nous les lisons tous.*
9. *Elle l'a trouvée sans difficulté.*
10. *Tu la comprends?*

Exercise 2-5: Here It Is!

1. *Elle me connaît.*
2. *Le journaliste les appelle.*
3. *Vous l'invitez.*
4. *Nous le voyons.*
5. *Elle nous comprend.*
6. *Apportez-les!*
7. *Il va le vendre.*
8. *Ne l'achetez pas!*
9. *Je dois le voir.*
10. *La connaît-il?*

Exercise 2-6: Take the Indirect Route

1. *Le grand-père leur a lu un conte.*
2. *Elle lui a fait un cadeau.*
3. *Je lui ferai parvenir le paquet dès que possible.*
4. *Il lui enverra des fleurs.*
5. *Ce restaurant lui appartient.*
6. *Est-ce que vous lui avez parlé?*
7. *Racontez-lui l'histoire ce soir.*
8. *Ne leur dîtes rien.*

9. *Elle leur annoncera sa décision la semaine prochaine.*
10. *Je lui donnerai le scénario demain matin.*

Exercise 2-7: I Am Talking to You!

1. *Apportez-lui une tasse de café!*
2. *Ne m'appelez pas avant 10 heures!*
3. *Envoyez-nous des nouvelles!*
4. *Je lui raconterai une histoire.*
5. *Ils vous donneront une réponse la semaine prochaine.*
6. *Il ne m'a pas rendu les clés.*
7. *Cette maison leur appartient.*
8. *Vous ne me parlez pas.*
9. *Elle nous a dit un mensonge.*
10. *Nous vous prêterons notre appartement pour le week-end.*

Exercise 2-8: *Y* Now?

1. *Nous nous y habituons.*
2. *Ils devraient y prêter attention.*
3. *Elle s'y intéresse.*
4. *Je m'y abonne.*
5. *Il y tient.*
6. *Nous n'y croyons pas.*
7. *Tu n'y penses jamais.*
8. *Ils n'y obéissent pas.*
9. *J'y réfléchirai.*
10. *Pourquoi n'y a-t-elle jamais répondu?*

Exercise 2-9: *En* Use

1. *Il en a parlé.*
2. *J'en ai envie.*
3. *Vous en avez besoin.*
4. *Elle s'en est approchée très lentement.*
5. *Nous nous en chargerons.*
6. *Tu t'en sers?*
7. *Il en a peur.*
8. *Je ne m'en souviens pas.*
9. *Nous nous en sommes occupés.*
10. *Elle ne pourra jamais s'en débarrasser.*

Exercise 2-10: Perfect Match

1. e
2. d

3. a
4. c
5. b

Exercise 2-11: Say It Loud, Say It Clear

1. *Oui, je les lui ai donnés.*
2. *Je te la prête, bien sûr.*
3. *Non, elle ne nous les a pas envoyées.*
4. *Oui, il nous les a racontées.*
5. *Oui, je les lui ai laissées.*
6. *Oui, elle me les a montrés.*

Exercise 2-12: Multiple Pronouns

1. *Ne lui en parlez pas!*
2. *Je lui en ai emprunté.*
3. *Vous devriez les lui envoyer.*
4. *Patrick la lui a racontée.*
5. *Le compositeur la lui a envoyée.*
6. *Le professeur le leur a donné.*
7. *Elle la lui a demandée.*
8. *Ils le leur vendront.*
9. *Le médecin le lui a prescrit.*
10. *Nous le leur recommandons.*

Exercise 2-13: In Your Own Words

1. *Nous y pensons.*
2. *Tu en as besoin.*
3. *Je m'en suis occupé(e).*
4. *Ils te l'ont donné.*
5. *Nous le (la) leur avons envoyé.*
6. *Nous leur en avons donné.*
7. *Nous en avons parlé.*
8. *Tu ne t'y intéresses pas.*
9. *Ils nous en ont emprunté.*
10. *Elle ne s'en sert jamais.*

Exercise 2-14: Oral Practice

Answers will vary. Possible
answers are shown below.

1. *Oui, nous venons avec vous.*
2. *Non, je ne vais jamais au cinéma avec elle!*
3. *Moi, je ne lis que des romans policiers.*
4. *Non, je pense que c'est lui qui est plus âgé.*
5. *Je ne sais pas. Elle n'est pas à moi.*

6. *Non, lui, il ne sait pas cuisiner!*
7. *Non, je préfère jouer avec toi.*
8. *Non, maintenant elle n'écrit que pour elle-même.*

Exercise 2-15: Say It Yourself!

1. *Il pense à elle.*
2. *Je déteste l'hiver!*
3. *Tu ne peux pas prendre cette décision sans moi.*
4. *Elle est plus grande que toi.*
5. *Nous le faisons nous-mêmes.*
6. *Il travaille pour eux.*
7. *Tu l'as dit toi-même.*
8. *Elle ira en France avec nous.*
9. *Je n'ai pas peur de lui.*
10. *À qui est cette voiture?*

Exercise 2-16: Oral Practice

1. *C'est Patrick qui téléphone.*
2. *Qui est là?*
3. *Invite qui tu veux!*
4. *Je connais l'artiste qui parle.*
5. *Qui commence? Toi ou moi?*
6. *C'est vous qui avez gagné le prix.*
7. *Je ne sais pas qui a gagné le match.*
8. *Elle ne sais pas qui il est.*
9. *Qui a de la famille au Canada?*
10. *Il a une tante qui habite à Toronto.*

Exercise 2-17: Who Is Who? What Is What?

1. *qu'*   6. *que*
2. *que*   7. *que*
3. *qui*   8. *que*
4. *qu'*   9. *que*
5. *qui*   10. *qu'*

Exercise 2-18: Oral Practice

1. *auquel*   6. *qui*
2. *qui*   7. *laquelle*
3. *lequel*   8. *auquel*
4. *lesquels* 9. *où*
5. *où*   10. *laquelle*

Exercise 2-19: Do It with *Dont*

1. *Voici la robe dont elle a envie.*
2. *Voici le film dont vous parlez.*

3. *Voici les erreurs dont j'ai peur.*
4. *Voici les idées dont ils se souviennent.*
5. *Voici le travail dont nous sommes fiers.*
6. *Voici les outils dont tu te sers.*
7. *Voici les frontières dont ils s'approchent.*
8. *Voici les mensonges dont il a honte.*
9. *Voici les exploits dont elle se vante.*
10. *Voici le danger dont nous nous méfions.*

Exercise 2-20: In Your Own Words

1. *Ce à quoi je m'intéresse, c'est à la littérature.*
2. *Ce dont tu as besoin, c'est d'un ordinateur.*
3. *Ce qu'il comprend, c'est la situation.*
4. *Ce dont vous vous souvenez, c'est de la fin du film.*
5. *Ce dont elle parle, c'est fascinant.*
6. *Ce que nous détestons, c'est le désordre.*
7. *Ce dont ils se plaignent, c'est de la pollution.*
8. *Ce à quoi vous vous attendez, c'est à des problèmes.*
9. *Ce qu'il décrit, c'est un cauchemar.*
10. *Ce dont je me méfie, c'est des conseils.*

Part 3: The Present Tense

Exercise 3-1: Translation Exercise

1. we watch
2. you visit
3. he sings
4. I give
5. she wins
6. you accept
7. they accept
8. you love
9. you eat
10. I live

Exercise 3-2: The Right Form

1. *Nous apportons des fleurs à l'hôtesse.*
2. *Elle aime voyager avec ses amis.*
3. *Je commande une bouteille de vin.*
4. *Vous regardez un bon film à la télévision.*
5. *Ils déjeunent à la terrasse.*
6. *Tu étudies l'italien.*
7. *Je cherche mes clés.*
8. *Elle porte un chapeau noir.*
9. *Vous gagnez beaucoup d'argent.*
10. *Tu travailles trop.*

Exercise 3-3: Spelling, Anyone?

1. *Nous encourageons les joueurs de cette équipe.*
2. *Nous avançons lentement dans la forêt.*
3. *Nous plaçons les invités autour de la table.*
4. *Nous partageons un appartement à Paris.*
5. *Nous prononçons les mots correctement.*
6. *Nous corrigeons les fautes dans le texte.*
7. *Nous effaçons le tableau.*
8. *Nous renonçons au projet.*
9. *Nous mélangeons les souvenirs de notre voyage.*
10. *Nous nageons dans la Méditerranée.*

Exercise 3-4: Accent or No Accent?

1. *Il lève la main pour poser une question.*
2. *Je n'exagère pas quand je dis qu'il est milliardaire.*
3. *Je lui répète toujours la même chose.*
4. *Nous préférons passer nos vacances en Bretagne.*
5. *Elle considère Léa comme sa soeur.*
6. *Ils emmènent leur nièce à l'opéra.*
7. *Comment est-ce que tu épelles ton nom?*
8. *Où est-ce que tu achètes tes fruits et légumes?*
9. *Elle renouvelle ses papiers d'identité tous les cinq ans.*
10. *Tu lui rappelles d'apporter sa raquette de tennis.*

Exercise 3-5: In French!

1. *Il n'habite pas à La Rochelle.*
2. *Elle ne cherche rien.*
3. *Est-ce qu'elle parle chinois?*
4. *Comment est-ce qu'il épelle son nom?*
5. *Ils ne vont jamais à Paris.*
6. *Elle n'aime plus Fabien.*
7. *Je ne mange ni fromage ni pain.*
8. *Nous vous encourageons.*
9. *Elle n'aime pas cette ville.*
10. *Est-ce qu'elle étudie à Berlin?*

Exercise 3-6: Meet My Friends!

1. *Marie et Lucas sont mes amis.*
2. *Ils sont artistes.*
3. *Marie est peintre et Lucas est musicien.*
4. *Ils ont trente ans.*
5. *Ils sont vraiment charmants.*
6. *Ils ont beaucoup de succès.*

7. *Ils ont de la chance d'avoir un atelier à Paris.*
8. *Marie préfère la ville.*
9. *Lucas préfère la campagne.*
10. *Qui a raison? Qui a tort?*

Exercise 3-7: Sentence Scramble

1. e
2. a
3. d
4. b
5. c

Exercise 3-8: Getting It Right

1. *vend*
2. *attendent*
3. *prenons*
4. *descend*
5. *apprenez*
6. *répond*
7. *prends*
8. *surprend*
9. *perd*
10. *entends*

Exercise 3-9: Which -ir Is It?

1. *J'offre des chocolats à ma soeur.*
2. *Elle cueille des roses dans le jardin.*
3. *Elle souffre de rhumatismes.*
4. *Ses étudiants réussissent toujours aux examens.*
5. *Je te sers un café?*
6. *Ils remplissent les verres de vin.*
7. *Tu dors bien?*
8. *Ils investissent dans une nouvelle affaire.*
9. *Je meurs de faim!*
10. *Ils applaudissent les comédiens.*

Exercise 3-10: Conjugating -oir Verbs

1. *Vous voyez souvent Julien?*
2. *Ils veulent une plus grande maison.*
3. *Nous prévoyons un voyage en Inde.*
4. *Tu reçois beaucoup de courrier?*
5. *Je peux vous envoyer de la documentation.*
6. *L'avion doit arriver à vingt heures.*
7. *Tu veux y aller?*
8. *Il pleut à Paris aujourd'hui.*
9. *Il nous doit mille euros.*
10. *Vous ne devez pas vous inquiéter.*

Exercise 3-11: Connect the Dots

1. e
2. c
3. a
4. b
5. d

Exercise 3-12: What Do I Know?

1. *Il ne connaît pas la Normandie.*
2. *Je ne sais pas à quelle heure ouvre le supermarché.*
3. *Nous ne savons pas parler anglais.*
4. *Il ne connaît pas les parents de Claude?*
5. *Il ne sait pas cette chanson.*
6. *Nous ne connaissons pas le musée du Louvre.*
7. *Il ne sait pas comment y aller.*
8. *Je ne sais pas pourquoi il est en Chine.*
9. *Il ne sait pas tout.*
10. *Elle ne sait pas faire la cuisine.*

Exercise 3-13: Which One Is Right?

1. *sait*
2. *connaît*
3. *sais*
4. *savent*
5. *connaissons*
6. *sait*
7. *connais*
8. *sais*
9. *connaissez*
10. *sait*

Exercise 3-14: What's Your Pronominal Type?

1. reflexive
2. reciprocal
3. reflexive
4. subjective
5. passive
6. reciprocal
7. passive
8. subjective
9. reciprocal
10. passive

Exercise 3-15: Reflexive, Reciprocal, Subjective, or Passive?

1. b
2. d
3. a
4. e
5. c

Exercise 3-16: In Progress!

1. *Je suis en train de lire un roman policier.*
2. *Ils sont en train de manger un couscous.*
3. *Elle est en train de regarder un film de science-fiction.*
4. *Il est en train de chanter un aria de Bellini.*
5. *Elle est en train de boire un thé au citron.*
6. *Je suis en train d'écrire une lettre de recommandation.*
7. *Je suis en train de cueillir des framboises.*
8. *Je suis en train de chercher mes lunettes.*

9. *Elle est en train d'envoyer des cartes postales.*
10. *Je suis en train de corriger les devoirs des étudiants.*

Exercise 3-17: Practicing with *–eindre* and *–aindre* Verbs

1. *Tu crains le froid.*
2. *Elle se plaint sans cesse.*
3. *Ils peignent la façade de l'édifice.*
4. *Je plains le pauvre homme sans un sou.*
5. *Cela enfreint le règlement.*
6. *Il atteint toujours le sommet.*
7. *Qu'est-ce que tu peins?*
8. *Elle éteint la lumière avant de sortir.*
9. *Il feint l'enthousiasme.*
10. *Les circonstances le contraignent à accepter leur offre.*

Exercise 3-18: Conjugate the Verbs

1. *je regarde*   *nous regardons*
   tu regardes   *vous regardez*
   il/elle regarde   *ils/elles regardent*
2. *je commence*   *nous commençons*
   tu commences   *vous commencez*
   il/elle commence   *ils/elles commencent*
3. *je sers*   *nous servons*
   tu sers   *vous servez*
   il/elle sert   *ils/elles servent*
4. *je dois*   *nous devons*
   tu dois   *vous devez*
   il/elle peint   *ils/elles doivent*
5. *je peins*   *nous peignons*
   tu peins   *vous peignez*
   vous peignez   *ils/elles peignent*
6. *j'apprends*   *nous apprenons*
   tu apprends   *vous apprenez*
   il/elle apprend   *ils/elles apprennent*
7. *je sors*   *nous sortons*
   tu sors   *vous sortez*
   il/elle nage   *ils/elles sortent*
8. *je nage*   *nous nageons*
   tu nages   *vous nagez*
   vous nagez   *ils/elles nagent*
9. *j'attends*   *nous attendons*
   tu attends   *vous attendez*
   il/elle attend   *ils/elles attendent*

10. *je reçois*   *nous recevons*
    tu reçois   *vous recevez*
    il/elle reçoit   *ils/elles reçoivent*

Exercise 3-19: Make Your Own Sentences

1. *Ils habitent dans un grand appartement à Paris.*
2. *Elle se souvient de son premier voyage en Europe.*
3. *Il ne connaît personne à Nantes.*
4. *Nous sommes français.*
5. *Elle préfère les roses.*
6. *Il a faim.*
7. *Ils emmènent leur nièce au théâtre une fois par an.*
8. *J'attends l'autobus.*
9. *Sait-il nager?*
10. *Ils investissent en Inde.*

Exercise 3-20: To Have or to Be?

1. *Oui, j'ai un jardin.*
2. *Oui, il est français.*
3. *Oui, elle est contente de son travail.*
4. *Oui, j'ai besoin d'un nouvel ordinateur.*
5. *Oui, il a un dictionnaire bilingue.*
6. *Oui, ils ont envie de déménager.*
7. *Oui, je suis libre ce week-end.*
8. *Oui, j'ai froid.*
9. *Oui, j'ai de la famille au Canada.*
10. *Oui, il a quarante ans.*

Exercise 3-21: Make It Work

1. e   4. a
2. c   5. d
3. b

Part 4: The Past

Exercise 4-2: Who Did It?

1. *Il*   6. *Ils*
2. *Nous*   7. *Il*
3. *Tu*   8. *Elle*
4. *Ils*   9. *Elle*
5. *J'*   10. *Tu*

Exercise 4-3: And What Did They Do?

1. *a perdu*
2. *a applaudi*
3. *avons marché*
4. *a fini*
5. *ont attendu*
6. *a menti*
7. *a trouvé*
8. *avez grandi*
9. *avons mangé*
10. *a vendu*

Exercise 4-4: To Be Noted

1. *est monté*
2. *sommes rentrés*
3. *est tombée*
4. *est descendu*
5. *sont revenues*
6. *est partie*
7. *sont allés*
8. *est allée*
9. *est devenu*
10. *suis né(e)*

Exercise 4-5: Complete Conjugations

1. *je donnais* — *nous donnions*
   tu donnais — *vous donniez*
   il/elle donnait — *ils/elles donnaient*
2. *je finissais* — *nous finissions*
   tu finissais — *vous finissiez*
   il/elle finissait — *ils/elles finissaient*
3. *je perdais* — *nous perdion*
   tu perdais — *vous perdiez*
   il/elle perdait — *ils/elles perdaient*
4. *je mangeais* — *nous mangions*
   tu mangeais — *vous mangiez*
   il/elle mangeait — *ils/elles mangeaient*
5. *je commençais* — *nous commencions*
   tu commençais — *vous commenciez*
   il/elle commençait — *ils/elles commençaient*
6. *j'étais* — *nous étions*
   tu étais — *vous étiez*
   il/elle était — *ils/elles étaient*

Exercise 4-6: The Perfect Form of the Imperfect Tense

1. *pleuvait*
2. *étions*
3. *faisait*
4. *pleurait*
5. *était*
6. *avait*
7. *faisait*
8. *travaillais*
9. *habitions*
10. *marchait*

Exercise 4-7: Everyone Is Imperfect!

1. *savais*
2. *donnions*
3. *grandissiez*
4. *étaient*
5. *grandissiez*
6. *étaient*
7. *mangeais*
8. *avais*
9. *choisissiez*
10. *allais*

Exercise 4-8: Perfecting Your Imperfect

1. *Les danseurs étaient magnifiques.*
2. *Tous les jours, le petit garçon allait à l'école.*
3. *Elle prenait un bain quand le téléphone a sonné.*
4. *Nous ne connaissions pas sa famille.*
5. *Son pére était écrivain à vingt-cinq ans.*
6. *Sa grand-mère avait deux chats.*
7. *Elle lisait lorsque sa soeur est arrivée.*
8. *Ils adoraient écouter le jazz.*
9. *Je ignorais ses problèmes.*
10. *Il faisait beau à la plage.*

Exercise 4-9: The Power of Suggestion

1. *Si on faisait un gâteau?*
2. *Si on prenait le train?*
3. *Si on achetait des billets pour le concert?*
4. *Si on invitait les Dumas à dîner?*
5. *Si on voyageait en Inde?*

Exercise 4-10: Past Subtleties

1. *Sylvie lisait quand son frère a téléphoné.*
2. *Vous mangiez quand on a frappé à la porte.*
3. *Nous nous promenions quand il a commencé à pleuvoir.*
4. *Il faisait la lessive quand son copain est arrivé.*
5. *Nous dansions quand la musique s'est arrêtée.*

Exercise 4-11: The *Passé Composé*

1. e
2. a
3. d
4. b
5. c

Exercise 4-12: Past and Perfect

1. *avions donné*
2. *s'étaient amusées*
3. *étais sorti(e)*
4. *avais chanté*
5. *avait menti*

Exercise 4-13: All Done, All Finished!

1. *avait loué*
2. *avait appris*
3. *m'étais arrêté(e)*
4. *avions acheté, avait annulé*
5. *avaient commencé*
6. *s'était habituée*
7. *avaient parlé, s'étaient recontrés*
8. *avions refait*
9. *avait commandé*
10. *avait oublié*

Exercise 4-14: Back to the Future

1. *aura fini*
2. *auront signé*
3. *aurai réuni*
4. *aura trouvé*
5. *aurai reçu*
6. *aurai trouvé*
7. *aura obtenu*
8. *sera arrivée*
9. *aurons examiné*
10. *aura lu*
11. *aurez lu*
12. *aurai trouvé*

Exercise 4-15: Perfect Future Ahead

1. *j'aurai fini*
2. *aura gagné*
3. *auront terminé*
4. *aurons résolu*
5. *se seront endormis*

Exercise 4-16: When Is It the Right Time?

1. *demain, demain matin*
2. *la semaine prochaine, la semaine prochaine*
3. *aujourd'hui, aujourd'hui*
4. *tous les jours, un jour sur deux*
5. *tard, tôt*
6. *souvent, rarement*
7. *quelquefois, jamais*
8. *ces jours-ci, plus que jamais*

Exercise 4-17: Time to Change

1. *Nous voyagions souvent en France.*
2. *On dînait tôt chaque jour.*
3. *Ils sortaient rarement le soir.*
4. *Elles écrivaient des lettres de temps en temps.*
5. *Ils lisaient parfois des journaux étrangers.*

Exercise 4-18: Time to Say It Yourself

1. *Hier, c'était le premier jour de l'hiver.*
2. *Elle téléphone rarement.*
3. *Je n'étais jamais à l'heure.*
4. *Ils sont partis la semaine dernière.*
5. *Son anniversaire est le mois prochain.*

Exercise 4-19: Animal Life

Adjectives: *heureux, beau, jeune, vieux, petit, timide*
Adverbs: *ici, partout, là-haut, sur le toit devant la maison, ça et là, près de la fontaine, dessous, ailleurs, au-dessus des nuages*

Exercise 4-20: Adverbs

1. *Il voit des erreurs partout.*
2. *Hier, nous avons dîné dehors.*
3. *J'habitais ici mais je travaillais ailleurs.*
4. *Elle a mis sa main dessus.*
5. *Si on allait à la plage? Ce n'est pas trop loin.*
6. *Il est devant toi.*
7. *Il est derrière nous.*
8. *Ce n'est pas loin.*
9. *Il y a de la poussière ça et là.*
10. *Elle doit être quelque part.*

Exercise 4-21: There Are Many Ways to Express Yourself

1. *Il y a un problème avec le train ce matin.*
2. *Il y a une heure que j'attends.*
3. *Elle est allée à Paris il y a cinq ans.*
4. *Il y a cinq ans que nous habitons à New York.*
5. *Il est parti il y a deux heures.*

Part 5: Future, Conditional, and Idiomatic Expressions

Exercise 5-1: Upcoming Events

1. *J'irai au musée.*
2. *Nous arriverons en retard.*
3. *Elle lira votre livre.*
4. *Vous apprendrez le chinois.*
5. *Ils dîneront chez leurs parents.*
6. *Nous partirons en vacances.*
7. *Caroline travaillera le week-end.*
8. *Tu prendras le métro.*
9. *Robert fera du ski en hiver.*

Exercise 5-2: Find the Mistake!

1. *Elle viendra à la réunion demain.*
2. *Nous prendrons le train à midi.*
3. *Savez-vous qu'elle obtiendra son diplôme en juin?*
4. *Je pense qu'il ira à Nouméa.*
5. *Il est évident qu'elle aura du succès.*
6. *Finira-t-il le projet avant septembre?*
7. *Je ferai un stage de six mois.*
8. *Vous nous tiendrez au courant.*
9. *Vous croyez que vous pourrez assister à la conférence?*
10. *Tu iras à la plage même s'il pleut?*

Exercise 5-3: Future x 2

1. *commencera, sera*
2. *prendrons, voyagerons*
3. *achèterai, irai*
4. *sera, deviendra*
5. *arriveras, expliquerai*
6. *prendrons, aurons*
7. *apprendra, habitera*
8. *jouerai, serai*
9. *finirez, partirez*
10. *fermera, commencera*

Exercise 5-4: The Future Is Perfect

1. *aura étudié*
2. *aurai fini*
3. *aurons visité*
4. *auront joué*
5. *aura développé*
6. *aurez écrit*
7. *nous serons reposés*
8. *aura complété*
9. *sera mort*
10. *n'aura jamais vu*

Exercise 5-5: In the Future

1. *ferons, aurons gagné*
2. *applaudira, aura terminé*
3. *me sentirai mieux, se sera amélioré*
4. *regarderont, se seront endormis*
5. *enverras, auras reçu*

Exercise 5-6: Will You Translate This?

1. *Nous irons au cinéma.*
2. *Il aura besoin de vendre sa voiture.*
3. *Je suivrai un cours de littérature.*
4. *Elle visitera la Bretagne quand elle sera en France.*
5. *Ils iront en Espagne l'été prochain.*
6. *Nous marcherons le long de la plage.*
7. *Il étudiera l'italien quand il sera à Rome.*
8. *Je verrai l'exposition Matisse quand je serai à Paris.*
9. *Ils voyageront en Asie quand ils auront le temps.*
10. *Elle deviendra avocate.*

Exercise 5-7: Would You Please . . .

1. *irais*
2. *comprendrait*
3. *liriez*
4. *aurions*
5. *chanterait*
6. *vendrais*
7. *seraient*
8. *anticiperiez*
9. *défendraient*
10. *saurions*

Exercise 5-8: Nothing but Conditions!

1. *Si nous avions plus de temps, nous aimerions bien voyager en hiver.*
2. *Si elle avait un autre enfant, elle devrait travailler à mi-temps*
3. *Si je perdais mon travail, je devrais vendre ma voiture.*
4. *Si vous vendiez votre appartement, vous pourriez acheter cette maison.*
5. *Si je pouvais, je la mettrais à la porte.*
6. *Si vous les contactiez, ils seraient ravis.*
7. *Si son ordinateur tombait en panne, il piquerait une crise.*
8. *Si j'allais chez elle, je lui apporterais des fleurs.*
9. *Si elle se présentait aux élections, tu la soutiendrais?*
10. *Si elle pouvait trouver des associés, Sophie ouvrirait une pâtisserie.*

Exercise 5-9: Make It Conditional

1. *Irais-tu en Mongolie?*
2. *Passerait-il chez toi?*
3. *Changerais-tu l'heure de ton départ?*
4. *Aimerais-tu venir avec nous?*
5. *Refuserait-il de le voir?*
6. *Nourrirais-tu mon chien?*
7. *Predrait-il un vol plus tard?*
8. *Suivrais-tu un cours de danse avec moi?*
9. *Discuterions-nous ce projet au printemps?*
10. *Accepteraient-ils notre offre?*

Exercise 5-10: It's All Conditional

1. *seraient, venions*
2. *irais, faisait*
3. *prendrait, pouvait*
4. *emmènerions, venait*
5. *aurait, étaient*
6. *étudierait, était*
7. *achèterais, pleuvait*
8. *donnerais, avait*
9. *serions, invitais*
10. *viendrais, demandais*

Exercise 5-11: What If?

1. *avais, travaillerais*
2. *attendait, obtiendrait*
3. *plantais, aurais*
4. *vendais, pourrais*
5. *pouvions, partirions*
6. *invitiez, serions*

Exercise 5-12: Demanding Conditions

1. *Nous irions à Paris si nous avions plus de temps.*
2. *Elle achèterait cette robe si elle était moins chère.*
3. *Je serais reconnaissant(e) si vous m'accompagniez à la gare.*
4. *Il écrirait une lettre si vous en aviez besoin.*
5. *Le premier ministre serait en Inde aujourd'hui.*

Exercise 5-13: I Would Have Said It!

1. *aurais fait*
2. *n'aurais pas attrapé*
3. *aurait gagné*
4. *aurait été*
5. *ne seriez pas tombé*
6. *n'aurait pas pu*
7. *n'aurais pas pu*
8. *aurait aimé*
9. *aurions accepté*
10. *aurais été*

Exercise 5-14: Past Conditional and Pluperfect

1. *serions allés, avions pu*
2. *aurait visité, avait eu*
3. *auraient vu, avait été*
4. *aurais invité, n'avait pas travaillé*
5. *aurait écrit, avait trouvé*
6. *aurait vendu, avaient décidé*
7. *seriez arrivé(e)(s), était tombée*

Exercise 5-15: Pluperfect and Conditional

1. *avait fini, aurait pu*
2. *avais mis, n'aurais pas eu*
3. *avait pu, aurait été*
4. *n'avait pas guillotiné, aurait pris*
5. *avions étudié, aurions fait*

Exercise 5-16: Conditional Past and Present

1. *Le chat aurait mangé s'il avait eu faim.*
2. *J'aurais assisté au concert si j'avais été en ville.*
3. *Nous aurions joué au tennis s'il n'avait pas plu.*
4. *Il vous aurait envoyé un message s'il n'avait pas été si occupé.*
5. *Tu lui aurais expliqué la décision s'il t'avait contacté.*

Exercise 5-17: Our Sources Tell Us . . .

1. *Le président serait allé en Chine la semaine dernière.*
2. *La victime aurait donné une description complète à la police.*
3. *La tempête de neige aurait tué plusieurs personnes dans les Alpes.*
4. *Le directeur aurait démissionné.*
5. *L'incendie aurait détruit des douzaines de maisons.*
6. *Le chômage augmenterait l'année prochaine.*
7. *Le président aurait signé l'accord.*
8. *De nombreuses espèces seraient en danger à cause du réchauffement global.*
9. *Un employé de banque aurait volé l'argent.*
10. *L'écrivain aurait refusé de signer le contrat.*

Exercise 5-18: Just in Case

1. c
2. e
3. a
4. b
5. d

Exercise 5-19: I Would if I Could

1. *Pourrais-tu m'aider?*
2. *Il n'aurait pas dû te raconter la fin du film.*
3. *Voudriez-vous venir plus tard?*
4. *Nous irions à Rome si nous avions le temps.*
5. *Je n'aurais pas dû manger tant de chocolat!*

Exercise 5-20: Julie's Sunday

Answers will vary.

Summary: *Julie a décidé de faire une promenade dans le parc avec Hugo.*

Exercise 5-21: Make a Match

1. d
2. e
3. b
4. a
5. c

Exercise 5-22: How Do You Do . . .

Answers will vary. Possible answers are shown below.

1. *Non, je fais dessiner les plans par un architecte.*
2. *Non, ils font faire la cuisine par un chef.*
3. *Non, elle fait faire ses vêtements par une couturière.*
4. *Non, je fais peindre les chambres par un peintre professionnel.*
5. *Non, je fais répondre aux messages par mon secrétaire.*

Exercise 5-23: Whodunit

1. *Vous faites écrire la lettre.*
2. *Je fais faire la cuisine.*
3. *Il fait réparer la voiture.*
4. *Tu fais envoyer le message.*
5. *Nous faisons préparer le dîner.*
6. *Vous faites lire le dossier.*
7. *Il fait investir sa fortune.*
8. *Vous faites remplacer l'employé malade.*
9. *Le professeur fait corriger les examens des étudiants.*
10. *Je fais chanter la chanson.*

Exercise 5-24: What's It All About?

1. *Dans ce roman, il s'agit d'un artiste.*
2. *Dans ce film, il s'agit de gangsters à Chicago.*
3. *Dans ce livre, il s'agit de politique.*
4. *Dans ce film, il s'agit d'amour.*

Part 6: Adjectives and Adverbs

Exercise 6-1: Which Adjective?

1. *américain*
2. *bruyante*
3. *gentille*
4. *grand*

5. *violette*
6. *bleue*
7. *belle*
8. *fatigué*
9. *fou*
10. *longue*

Exercise 6-2: Masculine to Feminine

1. *Élodie est russe.*
2. *Élodie est élégante.*
3. *Élodie est drôle.*
4. *Élodie est belle.*
5. *Élodie est frileuse.*
6. *Élodie est capricieuse.*
7. *Élodie est bavarde.*
8. *Élodie est petite.*
9. *Élodie est amusante.*
10. *Élodie est amoureuse.*

Exercise 6-3: Let's Figure Out the Adjectives!

1. *jolie* (feminine singular)
   rond (masculine singular)
2. *grande* (feminine singular)
   nouvel (masculine singular)
3. *vide* (feminine singular)
4. *nouvelle* (feminine singular)
   pleine (feminine singular)
   belles (feminine plural)
5. *petit* (masculine singular)
   délicieux (masculine singular)
6. *vieille* (feminine singular)
   américaine (feminine singular)
   charmante (feminine singular)
7. *longue* (feminine singular)
   tumultueuse (feminine singular)
   passionnante (feminine singular)
8. *française* (feminine singular)
   entier (masculine singular)
9. *annuelle* (feminine singular)
   ovale (masculine singular)
10. *belle* (feminine singular)
    petite (feminine singular)

Exercise 6-4: Where to Place It?

1. *un beau spectacle*
2. *une vieille ferme*
3. *des yeux bleus*
4. *l'art moderne*
5. *un grand appartement*
6. *la cuisine française*

7. *une grande distance*
8. *un bon prix*
9. *un pull chaud*
10. *un gros chat*

Exercise 6-5: Beginning to End

1. b
2. c
3. d
4. a
5. e

Exercise 6-6: What's the Order?

1. *Pierre est plus sportif que Luc.*
2. *Carole est aussi grande que sa mère.*
3. *Manuel est plus gentil que Vincent.*
4. *Ce livre-ci est moins intéressant que ce livre-là.*
5. *L'hiver à Paris est moins froid que l'hiver à New York.*
6. *Le cinéma est plus intéressant que la télévision.*
7. *Le chocolat est moins amer que le café.*
8. *Martine est aussi compétente que Marianne.*
9. *Le poisson est meilleur que la viande.*
10. *Ma belle-mère est aussi généreuse que ta belle-mère.*

Exercise 6-7: Practicing Comparisons

1. The countryside is quieter than the city.
2. My Internet connection is faster than yours.
3. Isabelle is as generous as Bertrand.
4. Your idea is better than Sara's.
5. I did not have the least problem.
6. His (her) new apartment is smaller than his/her former house.
7. The daughter is as tall as the mother.
8. I don't have the least desire to go with you.
9. This poor Denis is not happier than Dominique.
10. Philippe is not more courageous than Jean.

Exercise 6-8: Can You Guess?

1. *Je n'en ai pas la moindre idée.*
2. *C'est la pire chose que j'aie jamais entendue.*
3. *C'est un des pays les plus pauvres du monde.*
4. *C'est le meilleur spectacle que j'aie jamais vu.*
5. *Mon oncle est l'homme le plus drôle de la famille.*

6. *C'est son meilleur film.*
7. *Mon frère est la personne la plus gentille du monde.*
8. *Kéda est le meilleur cuisinier que j'aie jamais connu.*
9. *C'était l'homme le plus riche de la ville.*
10. *Angélique est la moins talentueuse de votre groupe.*

Exercise 6-9: It Comes in All Colors

1. *gris*
2. *bleu clair*
3. *jaunes*
4. *verte*
5. *marron*
6. *rouges*
7. *orange*
8. *noire*
9. *blanc*
10. *rose bonbon*

Exercise 6-10: What Color?

1. c
2. d
3. e
4. a
5. b

Exercise 6-11: Today, Tomorrow, or Another Time

Summary: *Grégoire se demande qui va l'accompagner chez Marie le week-end prochain.*

Exercise 6-12: What's the Adverb?

1. *de temps en temps*
2. *à l'heure*
3. *souvent*
4. *tous les jours*
5. *quelquefois*
6. *Hier*
7. *dans deux jours*
8. *un jour sur deux*
9. *l'année dernière*
10. *En ce moment*

Exercise 6-13: All Manners!

1. *Il est plutôt stupide.*
2. *Est-ce qu'il l'a fait exprès?*
3. *Pourquoi les traites-tu ainsi?*
4. *Pouvez-vous m'aider? / Volontiers.*
5. *Il s'est mal comporté.*

Exercise 6-14: A Lot of Translation Practice

1. *Il mange trop peu.*
2. *Elle sourit beaucoup.*
3. *Vous parlez trop.*
4. *Elle ne lit pas assez.*
5. *Je vous remercie beaucoup.*

6. *Vous travaillez déjà assez.*
7. *Ne vous inquiétez pas trop.*
8. *Elle marche beaucoup.*
9. *Il dort trop peu.*
10. *Elle rit beaucoup.*

Exercise 6-15: Past Events

1. *Frédéric a trop dépensé.*
2. *Marine a assez travaillé.*
3. *Pascal a mal réagi.*
4. *Valérie a souvent voyagé en Asie.*
5. *Nous avons beaucoup ri.*
6. *Christine m'a rarement appelé.*
7. *Samuel ne s'est pas assez amusé en vacances.*
8. *Tu as bien parlé.*
9. *Éric n'a pas souvent séjourné à Paris.*
10. *Isabelle a assez dormi.*

Exercise 6-16: Translation Time

1. *Il a de belles dents blanches.*
2. *Martine est toujours gentille et de bonne humeur.*
3. *Il joue avec un gros ballon orange.*
4. *Elisa est une jolie petite fille.*
5. *Cette pauvre Juliette est tout le temps malade.*
6. *Mon frère cadet a une nouvelle petite amie.*
7. *Demain, nous partons pour Amsterdam.*
8. *L'année dernière, j'étais le meilleur élève de mon école.*
9. *C'est la pire chose que j'aie jamais entendue.*
10. *J'ai acheté une grosse voiture rouge.*

Exercise 6-17: How Do You Say It?

1. *Tu as la nationalité américaine? Non, j'ai toujours eu la nationalité française.*
2. *Vous êtes arrivés hier? Non, nous sommes arrivés ici la semaine dernière.*
3. *Tu travailles tous les jours? Non, je travaille de temps en temps.*
4. *Élodie est grande? Oui, elle est plus grande que son mari.*
5. *Ton travail est intéressant? Non, il est plus ennuyeux que celui de l'année dernière.*
6. *Tu te sens bien aujourd'hui? Oui, je suis en meilleure forme qu'hier.*
7. *Il se marie la semaine prochaine? Oui, il se marie avec son amie italienne.*
8. *Tu pars en week-end quelquefois? Oui, je vais voir ma meilleure amie tous les mois.*
9. *Tu crois qu'elle est folle? Non, je crois qu'elle travaille trop.*
10. *C'est un long voyage? Oui, nous arriverons dans deux jours.*

Exercise 6-18: The Matching Exercise

1. b
2. a
3. d
4. e
5. c

Exercise 6-19: It's Happening Now

1. *Françoise voyage beaucoup.*
2. *Élisabeth a moins de talent que Muriel.*
3. *Pierre dessine bien.*
4. *Donne-moi la petite clé!*
5. *Martin est plus paresseux que Thierry.*
6. *Anna travaille trop.*
7. *André mange trop.*
8. *Il aime la bonne cuisine.*
9. *Noah calcule mal.*
10. *Léopold joue bien.*

Part 7: The Infinitive, the Imperative, and Objects

Exercise 7-1: What's the Pronoun?

1. *Elle l'a acceptée.*
2. *Nous devons le prendre.*
3. *Il est en train de le lire.*
4. *Tu devrais l'appeler.*
5. *Claire les aime.*
6. *Nous voulons la louer.*
7. *Prenez-la maintenant.*
8. *Ouvrez-les.*
9. *Il va la conduire.*
10. *Ne les regarde pas comme ça!*

Exercise 7-2: In the Past

1. *Oui, il les a prises.*
2. *Oui, elle l'a rangée dans sa chambre.*
3. *Non, je ne l'ai pas lu.*
4. *Oui, il l'a nourri.*
5. *Non, il ne les a pas remerciés.*

6. *Oui, je l'ai trouvée.*
7. *Non, il ne l'a pas ouverte.*
8. *Oui, je les ai écoutées.*
9. *Non, il ne l'a pas acceptée.*
10. *Oui, je les ai remises à la gardienne.*

Exercise 7-3: *Voici! Voilà!*

1. *Le voici!*
2. *Les voilà!*
3. *La voici!*
4. *Me voilà!*
5. *La voici!*
6. *Le voilà!*
7. *Nous voici!*
8. *Les voilà!*
9. *Les voici!*
10. *La voilà!*

Exercise 7-4: Indirect Objects in Action

1. *Lui as-tu raconté l'histoire?*
2. *Elle m'a donné son opinion.*
3. *Ils ne nous ont pas mentionné l'incident.*
4. *Je lui ai parlé de la réunion.*
5. *Lui as-tu rendu la vidéo?*
6. *Cette maison leur appartient.*
7. *Sa grand-mère t'a donné sa collection entière.*
8. *Lui as-tu emprunté de l'argent?*
9. *Quand me diras-tu la vérité?*
10. *Nous ne pouvons pas te payer le loyer.*

Exercise 7-5: Pronoun Switch!

1. *Elle nous a téléphoné hier.*
2. *Je leur ai appris la bonne nouvelle.*
3. *Ils vous ont donné combien de temps?*
4. *Pourquoi m'a-t-il menti?*
5. *Vas-tu nous dire la vérité?*
6. *Rapportez-moi les livres.*
7. *Commande-nous un café, s'il te plaît.*
8. *Elle t'a apporté des biscuits.*
9. *Je lui ai demandé pardon.*
10. *Elles leur ont fait un beau cadeau.*

Exercise 7-6: Question and Answer

1. c
2. e
3. b
4. a
5. d

Exercise 7-7: All about *Y*!

1. *Y as-tu pensé?*
2. *Ne m'y oblige pas!*

3. *Il y tenait beaucoup.*
4. *Prends-y garde!*
5. *Nous n'y voyons pas d'inconvénient.*
6. *Y a-t-il goûté?*
7. *Nous devons y réfléchir.*
8. *Ils ne s'y intéressent pas.*
9. *Je m'y habitue assez bien.*
10. *Elles y ont renoncé.*

Exercise 7-8: Listen Carefully!

1. *Oui, je m'en suis occupée.*
2. *Oui, vous devez vous en charger.*
3. *Oui, il en a envie.*
4. *Oui, je veux que tu en parles.*
5. *Oui, il s'en est débarrassé.*
6. *Oui, je m'en souviens.*
7. *Oui, il s'en est approché.*
8. *Oui, vous nous en avez déjà parlé.*
9. *Oui, il en a peur.*
10. *Oui, elles pourront s'en passer.*

Exercise 7-9: Is It *Y* or *En*?

1. *Elle en a parlé toute la soirée.*
2. *Je vais y réfléchir.*
3. *Il en a très envie.*
4. *Y voyez-vous un inconvénient?*
5. *Ne t'en décharge pas sur moi!*
6. *Elle en a besoin.*
7. *Y as-tu remédié?*
8. *Ils en ont la preuve.*
9. *Elle s'en est approchée.*
10. *Nous devons y obéir.*

Exercise 7-10: From Noun to Pronoun

1. c
2. e
3. d
4. b
5. a

Exercise 7-11: What Pronoun?

1. *Elle nous en a apporté.*
2. *Je ne vous en donnerai pas.*
3. *Il la leur a ouverte.*
4. *Elles le lui offriront.*
5. *Tu nous en as raconté.*
6. *Il nous l'a racontée.*

7. *Vous la leur avez vendue.*
8. *Je le lui ai dit.*
9. *Il me l'a demandé.*
10. *Ils nous l'avaient recommandé.*

Exercise 7-12: Twosome

1. *Il lui en a parlé.*
2. *Je te conseille de les lui envoyer.*
3. *Je la lui enverrai.*
4. *Il leur en a apporté.*
5. *Donne-la-lui!*
6. *Nous les leur avons racontées.*
7. *Ils la lui ont prêtée.*
8. *Les lui avez-vous rendues?*
9. *Il la lui a cédée.*
10. *Nous devrions leur en parler.*

Exercise 7-13: Listen to Me!

1. *Ne mange pas si vite!*
2. *Dépêchez-vous!*
3. *Ne fermons pas les yeux!*
4. *Va au zoo avec les enfants.*
5. *Prenez place à mes côtés!*
6. *Soyez fier de lui!*
7. *Buvez deux litres d'eau par jour!*
8. *Prends soin d'elle.*
9. *Réconcilions-nous!*
10. *Sache que je serai toujours là!*

Exercise 7-14: It's Imperative

1. c
2. d
3. a
4. e
5. b

Exercise 7-15: Using Infinitives

1. *Ne pas entrer.*
2. *Ils étaient appuyés contre le mur à écouter de la musique.*
3. *Elle m'a demandé de retourner à ma place.*
4. *J'étais assis à examiner son tableau.*
5. *Ajouter de l'ail et mélanger.*
6. *Quoi dire?*
7. *Partir avant sept heures serait une bonne idée.*
8. *J'ai vu l'homme monter l'escalier.*
9. *Tu passes ta vie à travailler.*

10. *Elle est accroupie au milieu de la pièce à faire du yoga.*

Exercise 7-16: What's the Deal?

1. *Elle a passé ses vacances à se reposer.*
2. *Henri a passé son temps à réparer sa voiture.*
3. *Ma tante a passé son temps à faire des courses.*
4. *Il a passé ses soirées à jouer au ping-pong.*
5. *Tu as passé ta vie à rêver.*

Exercise 7-17: Still Infinitive!

1. *Tu es gentille d'être venue jusqu'ici.*
2. *Il s'excuse d'être parti avant la fin.*
3. *Elle nous remercie d'avoir pensé à elle.*
4. *Corinne regrette de ne pas avoir eu de magnétoscope chez elle.*
5. *Laure espère ne pas avoir raté son examen.*
6. *Jean-Louis souhaite avoir récupéré son canapé avant le mois prochain.*
7. *Pascale nous remercie d'avoir gardé son chat en son absence.*
8. *Quel dommage d'avoir quitté ce quartier!*
9. *Pardonnez-nous d'avoir été en retard.*
10. *Jure-moi d'avoir tout fait comme je te l'ai demandé.*

Exercise 7-18: Time Will Tell

1. *Il a ouvert la porte après avoir entendu la sonnette.*
2. *Le boulanger fait cuire le pain après avoir ouvert la boulangerie.*
3. *Je suis partie après lui avoir dit que je l'aimais.*
4. *Elles riaient après avoir découvert la surprise.*
5. *Après avoir mangé, fais une petite sieste.*
6. *Viens me chercher après être allé au supermarché.*
7. *Elle prépare le dessert après avoir servi le plat principal.*
8. *Vous dînerez après être allé au cinéma.*
9. *Il peint après avoir collé les morceaux de textile sur la toile.*
10. *Elle se douche après avoir pris son petit-déjeuner.*

Exercise 7-19: All in Order!

1. *Clara nous demande une explication.*
2. *Je vais en apporter ce soir.*
3. *Ma tante m'invite pour le réveillon de Noël.*
4. *L'enfant leur a tiré la langue.*
5. *Donne-le-nous!*
6. *Ne les regarde pas!*
7. *Tu les as envoyés à tes parents?*
8. *Marion veut les lui rendre.*
9. *Elle y pense beaucoup.*
10. *Boris ne s'en est pas excusé.*

Exercise 7-20: Which One Is It?

1. *Vas-tu t'en plaindre?*
2. *Ne les mange pas!*
3. *Il va y réfléchir.*
4. *Il lui apporte un gros gâteau.*
5. *En avez-vous peur?*
6. *Y a-t-elle pensé?*
7. *A-t-elle pensé à lui?*
8. *N'en rêvez pas trop!*
9. *Pense à elle!*
10. *Elle le lui a envoyé.*

Exercise 7-21: Mixing It Up

1.	c	4.	b
2.	a	5.	d
3.	e		

Exercise 7-22: Translate These Sentences!

1. *Tirez les rideaux avant d'aller au lit!*
2. *N'oubliez pas de lui envoyer un courriel avant de partir!*
3. *Après avoir entendu les nouvelles, il a fondu en larmes.*
4. *C'est gentil de votre part de m'appeler.*
5. *Y avez-vous pensé suffisamment avant de leur poser la question?*
6. *Pouvez-vous acheter du pain avant de rentrer à la maison?*
7. *Promettez-moi de ne pas ouvrir cette lettre avant de monter dans l'avion.*
8. *S'habille-t-elle avant de se maquiller?*
9. *Je n'accepte pas d'être traité ainsi.*
10. *Elle devrait négocier avant de signer le contrat.*

Exercise 7-23: Let's Go to Avignon!

1. *As-tu pensé à réserver les billets pour aller en Avignon cet été?*
2. *Oui, les voici! Je les ai réservés avant-hier et on nous les a envoyés par la poste aujourd'hui.*
3. *As-tu aussi consulté le programme du festival de théâtre?*
4. *Oui, je l'ai consulté et j'ai trouvé des pièces qui devraient te plaire.*
5. *Dépêchons-nous de réserver alors. Ne perdons pas de temps!*
6. *Je suis justement en train de le faire. Laisse-moi me concentrer!*
7. *C'est vraiment gentil de t'en occuper. Merci.*
8. *De rien, cela fait des semaines que j'y pense.*
9. *Pour te remercier, je t'invite au restaurant.*
10. *D'accord, mais avant d'y aller, repassons à la maison.*

Part 8: The Subjunctive

Exercise 8-1: Present Subjunctive Practice

1.	*disions*	6.	*répondiez*
2.	*chante*	7.	*mette*
3.	*prenne*	8.	*finisses*
4.	*voie*	9.	*compreniez*
5.	*croyiez*	10.	*choisisse*

Exercise 8-2: In the Mood?

1.	S	5.	S
2.	I	6.	I
3.	S	7.	I
4.	S	8.	S

Exercise 8-3: Let's Talk Subjunctive!

1.	*prenne*	5.	*puisse*
2.	*sache*	6.	*n'assistiez pas*
3.	*soit*	7.	*vienne*
4.	*ait*	8.	*prépariez*

Exercise 8-4: Yes It Is!

1.	*soit*	6.	*ayez*
2.	*veuille*	7.	*ne réponde pas*
3.	*ait*	8.	*fasse*
4.	*soit*	9.	*ailles*
5.	*puisse*	10.	*parliez*

Exercise 8-5: Superlative!

1. *connaisse*
2. *possédiez*
3. *ait*
4. *soit*
5. *connaissions*
6. *fassions*
7. *sache*
8. *aille*
9. *fréquentions*
10. *ait*

Exercise 8-6: Spell It Out!

1. *Il lui explique jusqu'à ce qu'il comprenne.*
2. *Je me promène dans le parc quoiqu'il fasse froid.*
3. *Fais une réservation avant qu'il ne soit trop tard.*
4. *Elle a acheté une maison sans que personne ne le sache.*
5. *Prends ton parapluie de peur qu'il pleuve.*
6. *Je les contacte à moins que tu ne sois pas d'accord.*
7. *J'accepte ce cadeau à condition que vous acceptiez le mien.*
8. *Il travaille tard bien qu'il soit fatigué.*
9. *Nous faisons des économies afin que tu ailles à l'université.*
10. *Achète la voiture avant que le prix augmente.*

Exercise 8-7: What Do You Think?

1. e
2. a
3. d
4. c
5. b

Exercise 8-8: Let's Hope!

1. *Pourvu qu'il ne pleuve pas demain!*
2. *Pourvu que le magasin soit ouvert!*
3. *Pourvu qu'ils n'arrivent pas avant nous!*
4. *Pourvu que vous puissiez acheter cette maison!*
5. *Pourvu qu'il vienne seul!*
6. *Pourvu qu'ils soient heureux!*
7. *Pourvu que vous ayez raison!*
8. *Pourvu qu'ils soient à l'heure!*
9. *Pourvu qu'il puisse assister à la réunion!*
10. *Pourvu qu'elle aille à Paris cet été!*

Exercise 8-9: It All Happened!

1. *subjonctif passé*
2. *subjonctif passé*
3. *subjonctif présent*
4. *subjonctif passé*
5. *subjonctif présent*
6. *subjonctif passé*
7. *subjonctif présent*
8. *subjonctif passé*
9. *subjonctif passé*
10. *subjonctif présent*

Exercise 8-10: It's All Behind Us!

1. *Je suis contente que tu aies pu venir.*
2. *J'ai peur qu'elle n'ait pas pris la bonne décision.*
3. *Il ne pense pas que tu aies fait assez d'effort.*
4. *Nous sommes désolés que tu n'aies pas accepté cette offre.*
5. *C'est la seule recette qu'il ait su faire.*
6. *Il est incroyable qu'il ait dit des choses pareilles.*
7. *Je doute qu'il ait envoyé son C.V.*
8. *Tu es surpris qu'il n'ait rien dit.*
9. *Je ne crois pas qu'ils aient compris le problème.*
10. *Il est naturel qu'elle soit allée chez sa grand-mère.*

Exercise 8-11: Find the Ending, Wherever It Is

1. e
2. a
3. d
4. b
5. c

Exercise 8-12: *Present* Participles

1. *protégeant*
2. *apprenant*
3. *sachant*
4. *lisant*
5. *se promenant*
6. *influençant*
7. *voyant*
8. *fascinant*
9. *Étant*
10. *choisissant*

Exercise 8-13: Make a Sentence

1. b
2. e
3. d
4. c
5. a

Exercise 8-14: While Doing This . . .

1. *traversant*
2. *voyageant*
3. *faisant*
4. *revenant*
5. *sortant*
6. *patinant*
7. *écrivant*
8. *arrivant*
9. *acceptant*
10. *Étant*

Exercise 8-15: Listening Comprehension

1. *gérondif*
2. *gérondif*
3. *gérondif*
4. *participe présent*
5. *gérondif*
6. *adjectif*
7. *participe présent*
8. *adjectif*
9. *participe présent*
10. *gérondif*

Exercise 8-16: Something Is Being Done!

1. *La lettre est écrite par le secrétaire.*
2. *Quinze employés seront engagés en septembre.*
3. *Ce contrat a été signé ce matin.*
4. *Ce verbe est suivi du subjonctif.*
5. *Ces fleurs ont été plantées en mars.*
6. *Aucune solution n'a été trouvée.*
7. *Ce vin blanc se mange avec le poisson.*
8. *Le chien est attaqué par le chat.*
9. *Le verre est rempli par le serveur.*
10. *Il s'est fait conduire par son chauffeur.*

Exercise 8-17: Let's Be Passive!

1. *Le château est en train d'être construit par le roi.*
2. *Son tableau sera vendu samedi.*
3. *Ce vin se boit frais.*
4. *Un nouvel ordinateur est en train d'être installé.*
5. *Le dîner sera servi sur la terrasse.*

Exercise 8-18: Setting the Mood

1. S		6.	S
2. I		7.	S
3. I		8.	I
4. S		9.	S
5. S		10.	I

Exercise 8-19: What's the Deal?

1. *ne puissiez pas*		6.	*est*
2. *apprennes*		7.	*soit*
3. *aimiez*		8.	*est*
4. *devienne*		9.	*réussissiez*
5. *aille*		10.	*a*

Exercise 8-20: All Impersonals Are Not Equal

1. *reçoives*		5.	*soient*
2. *dit*		6.	*trouviez*
3. *ne puissent pas*		7.	*sois*
4. *fassiez*		8.	*sache*
		9.	*hésitiez*

Exercise 8-21: How to Say?

1. *Je serai dans le parc à moins qu'il ne pleuve.*
2. *Je vous enverrai son livre pour que vous puissiez le lire avant la réunion.*
3. *Jean peut l'appeler avant que vous arriviez.*
4. *Je doute qu'elle sache comment le contacter.*
5. *Il faut que vous fassiez la cuisine pour nous.*
6. *Quoi que vous prépariez, je le mangerai.*
7. *Bien qu'il ne soit pas riche, il est très généreux.*
8. *Où que vous soyez, j'y serai.*
9. *Quelles que soient ses opinions, ils voteront pour lui.*

Exercise 8-22: Talking About the Past

1. *n'ait pas téléphoné*		5.	*aient eu*
2. *aient vendu*		6.	*n'ait rien dit*
3. *soient arrivés*		7.	*ait visité*
4. *ayez laissé tomber*		8.	*ait perdu*

Exercise 8-23: This Is the Way It Goes

1. *Cette viande se sert avec du vin rouge.*
2. *Ils se sont rencontrés en voyageant en bateau.*
3. *Ayant appris l'italien, il a décidé d'apprendre le français.*
4. *Elle a trouvé la réponse en surfant sur Internet.*
5. *Ce vin rouge se sert frais.*
6. *Ce verbe est suivi de l'indicatif.*
7. *Il s'est fait couper les cheveux à Paris.*
8. *Le roi construit un nouveau château.*
9. *Ici, on parle chinois.*
10. *Ça ne se répète pas.*

Part 9: Prepositions

Exercise 9-1: What's the Preposition?

1. *au*		6.	*au*
2. *en*		7.	*en*
3. *aux*		8.	*au*
4. *en*		9.	*à*
5. *au*		10.	*en*

Exercise 9-2: Where Are They All Going?

1. *Je voyagerai en Grèce.*
2. *Ils sont allés à Strasbourg.*
3. *Nous allons envoyer notre fils en Irlande.*
4. *Tu iras au Luxembourg?*
5. *Elle fera du ski au Colorado.*
6. *L'agent de voyages leur a conseillé d'aller en Inde.*
7. *Son nouvel emploi sera en Chine.*

8. *Ils passeront leurs vacances en Turquie.*
9. *Je voudrais aller au Mexique.*
10. *Nous sommes invités à un mariage en Hongrie.*

Exercise 9-3: Where Are They Working?

1. *Marc travaille à Paris, en France.*
2. *Jérôme travaille à Boston, aux États-Unis.*
3. *Pedro travaille à Buenos Aires, en Argentine.*
4. *Aziz travaille à Carthage, en Tunisie.*
5. *Maria travaille à Porto, au Portugal.*
6. *Chloé travaille à Amsterdam, en Hollande.*
7. *Aruna travaille à Bangkok, en Thaïlande.*
8. *Fatiha travaille à Casablanca, au Maroc.*
9. *Nora travaille à Shangai, en Chine.*
10. *Pierre travaille à Ottawa, au Canada.*

Exercise 9-4: What Are They Saying?

1. *Caroline va s'installer à Tokyo.*
2. *Nous passerons les vacances à Tahiti.*
3. *Elle cherche un appartement à Paris.*
4. *La conférence aura lieu en Australie.*
5. *Il a accepté un poste en Pologne.*
6. *Ils ont habité à La Rochelle pendant cinq ans.*
7. *Pourquoi est-elle au Venezuela en ce moment?*
8. *Ils vont ouvrir un magasin à Lyon.*
9. *Son cousin est en mission au Sénégal.*
10. *Quand serez-vous à Moscou?*

Exercise 9-5: Where Are They From?

1. *Il est originaire de Belgique.*
2. *Cette sculpture provient du Mali.*
3. *Elle est revenue de Jordanie hier soir.*
4. *Cette sculpture vient du Vietnam.*
5. *Ça vient du Colorado.*
6. *Rapporte-moi un souvenir d'Argentine.*
7. *Ils rentrent tout juste de Chine.*
8. *Qu'est-ce que tu as rapporté de Turquie?*
9. *Elle est originaire du Japon.*
10. *Cette horloge vient de Suède.*

Exercise 9-6: Elizabeth's Crazy Vacation

1. *Elizabeth va en Argentine.*
2. *Elle veut apprendre à danser le tango.*
3. *Non, sa mère n'approuve pas ce voyage.*

4. *Non, Elizabeth ne parle pas espagnol.*
5. *La soeur d'Elizabeth pense qu'elle a un petit ami argentin.*

Exercise 9-7: *Traductions*

1. *Elle est venue avec moi.*
2. *Le chat se cache sous le buffet.*
3. *D'après moi, vous avez tort.*
4. *Hélène s'appuie contre le mur.*
5. *Il est venu sans sa femme.*
6. *Elle est allée faire une promenade malgré la neige.*
7. *Vu les circonstances, je pense que vous avez fait le bon choix.*
8. *Vous pouvez rester chez moi.*
9. *Attendez-moi devant la gare.*
10. *Ils ont tout payé sauf le taxi.*

Exercise 9-8: A Tea Cup or a Cup of Tea?

1. *À Las Vegas, nous avons passé des heures devant les machines à sous.*
2. *Tu veux un bol de potage?*
3. *Va chercher des verres à limonade dans le buffet!*
4. *Elle a ouvert une boîte de cassoulet.*
5. *Nous avons bu une bouteille d'eau.*
6. *Nous venons d'acheter une machine à sécher le linge.*
7. *Regarde le vieux moulin à vent!*
8. *Je prendrai une assiette de crudités.*
9. *Il refuse d'utiliser sa vieille machine à écrire.*
10. *Ils apportent un panier de fruits.*

Exercise 9-9: Identify the Correct Preposition

1. *Elle a dormi chez son oncle et sa tante.*
2. *Le supermarché est ouvert six jours sur sept.*
3. *Apporte-moi des pinces à cheveux.*
4. *Hier, nous avons diné chez Juliette.*
5. *Elle a apporté une bouteille de champagne.*
6. *Je n'ai plus rien sur mon compte en banque.*
7. *Il est parti avec tous mes dossiers.*
8. *Il y a quelque chose d'étrange chez ce garçon.*
9. *Tu n'as pas de machine à laver la vaisselle?*
10. *Elle lui a offert un bouquet de fleurs.*

Exercise 9-10: Let's Get Reconciled with Prepositions!

1. *La fille aux cheveux roux est ma nièce.*
2. *Ici, les magasins sont-ils ouverts le dimanche?*
3. *Mon salon mesure dix mètres sur cinq.*
4. *À votre gauche se trouve la Tour Eiffel.*
5. *La femme au pull jaune nous regarde.*
6. *Julien travaille au troisième étage.*
7. *Ma chambre donne sur la rue.*
8. *Qu'est-ce qui ne va pas chez lui?*
9. *Leur nouvelle maison donne sur l'océan.*
10. *Vous pouvez m'appeler 24 heures sur 24.*

Exercise 9-11: *En* or *Dans?*

1. *Ils sont partis vivre en Afrique.*
2. *Tu es venu en avion?*
3. *Marianne a préparé le repas en une demi-heure.*
4. *Ils sont montés dans l'avion avec deux heures de retard*
5. *Notre train part dans quinze minutes.*
6. *Montez dans le train tout de suite!*
7. *Dans la France de Louis XIV, le peuple était asservi.*
8. *Je préférerais y aller en voiture.*
9. *Dans le Paris des années folles, les gens s'amusaient beaucoup.*
10. *Elle a envie de vivre en Amérique du Nord.*

Exercise 9-12: *À* or *En?*

1. *Pierre va au travail en vélo tous les jours.*
2. *Vincent van Gogh est mort en 1890 à Auvers-sur-Oise.*
3. *Mon vol arrive à midi et demi.*
4. *Ils ont décidé d'aller à Chartres en vélo.*
5. *En hiver, j'aime rester chez moi.*
6. *Les invités sont arrivés à minuit.*
7. *Les roses s'épanouissent au printemps.*
8. *Pouvez-vous aller au travail en voiture?*
9. *Elle est allée au zoo à pied.*
10. *Julie a commencé à travailler ici en 2002.*

Exercise 9-13: Which Preposition to Choose?

1. *George vit toujours chez sa mère.*
2. *Je vais à Madrid par le train de nuit.*
3. *Floriane nous rendra visite au printemps.*

4. *On dit que Christophe Colomb a découvert l'Amérique en 1492.*
5. *Appelle-moi à midi.*
6. *Ne me regarde pas de cet air-là!*
7. *J'irai toute seule, sans toi.*
8. *Chez Mozart, j'aime tout.*
9. *Le salon fait six mètres sur quatre.*
10. *Je te rappelle dans dix jours.*

Exercise 9-14: Putting Your Knowledge to the Test

1. *Selon la météo, le temps sera ensoleillé tout le week-end.*
2. *Malgré votre avis, je vais aller à cette réunion.*
3. *Renée vit loin de la ville.*
4. *Il a acheté une maison au bord d'un lac.*
5. *Tu peux m'appeler au milieu de la nuit, s'il le faut.*
6. *À part toi, je ne connais personne ici.*
7. *Je n'ai pas écrit faute de temps.*
8. *Au lieu de regarder les gens s'amuser dans l'eau, pourquoi n'y vas-tu pas toi-même?*
9. *Barbara fume à l'insu de ses parents.*
10. *Grâce à mon amie Roselyne, j'ai trouvé un nouvel appartement très rapidement.*

Exercise 9-15: Which Is Correct?

1. *Jérôme a dû partir plus tôt en raison du mauvais temps.*
2. *Natacha s'est assise à côté de Laurent.*
3. *Nous avons skié dans la forêt.*
4. *Ma tante possède une maison au bord de la mer.*
5. *Au lieu de le réprimander tout le temps, tu ferais mieux d'essayer de comprendre pourquoi ton fils agit ainsi.*
6. *D'après les dernières nouvelles, il y aurait des survivants à la catastrophe aérienne.*
7. *Au lieu de prendre la voiture, je préfère y aller en train.*
8. *C'est au cours du discours du président que nous avons appris qu'il avait été promu.*
9. *Elle n'a rien dit à Pierre de peur de le décevoir.*
10. *Philippe habite une ferme au milieu des champs de blé.*

Exercise 9-16: What Do You Hear?

1. The teacher is in a position to give advice to his/her students.
2. She lost the game because she hurt herself.
3. He put the tablecloth on the bare ground.
4. Your brother is in a position to help you.
5. Cara is extremely touchy.
6. He cancelled the picnic because of the rain.
7. In comparison with him, your life is easy.
8. I discovered this book thanks to a friend.
9. Jeanne drinks milk directly from the bottle.
10. Don't put your muddy boots right on the rug!

Exercise 9-17: Practice with Preposition À

1. *Vous devriez apprendre à conduire.*
2. *Henri a réussi à obtenir l'emploi.*
3. *Jocelyn est impatiente de faire votre connaissance.*
4. *Faites attention au prix!*
5. *Il a essayé de vous appeler toute la journée.*
6. *Ne vous attendez pas à me voir à la soirée!*
7. *Je m'habitue à Marc, mon nouveau collègue.*
8. *Je tiens à vous parler.*
9. *Janine s'est intéressée à la philosophie quand elle avait seize ans.*
10. *Tout le monde aspire à un meilleur monde.*

Exercise 9-18: À or *De*?

1. *Le policier nous a conseillé de prendre une autre route.*
2. *Laurent ne parvient pas à joindre Sophie par téléphone.*
3. *Ma tante s'attend à nous voir arriver vers 15 heures.*
4. *Ne commence pas à m'énerver!*
5. *Mon ami m'a promis de m'écrire dès son arrivée à Bali.*
6. *Les parents interdisent à leurs enfants de regarder la télévision le week-end.*
7. *Il s'est amusé à changer les noms sur les boîtes aux lettres.*
8. *Tu devrais faire attention à ne pas trop manger.*
9. *Elle soupçonne son petit frère de faire des bêtises dans son dos.*
10. *J'hésite à appeler ma grand-mère si tôt.*

Exercise 9-19: No Guessing with the Preposition!

1. *Continue à étudier!*
2. *Il devrait apprendre à chanter.*
3. *Il m'a proposé de venir avec lui à la campagne.*
4. *Je te conseille de cesser de fumer.*
5. *Le propriétaire a refusé de signer le contrat de vente.*
6. *Nicolas envisage de faire le tour du monde pendant un an.*
7. *J'ai envie d'aller à la piscine.*
8. *Les responsables ont été accusés de laisser la situation empirer.*
9. *Son père l'a aidé à déménager ses affaires.*
10. *Je t'invite à te joindre à nous.*

Exercise 9-20: Before or After?

1. *Elle a éclaté de rire après avoir fini de nous raconter son histoire.*
2. *Grégoire a avalé un sandwich après avoir pris la route.*
3. *Lucie a pris un bain après être allée à la soirée.*
4. *Fabienne est venue me parler après avoir pris sa décision.*
5. *Arnaud est tombé malade juste après être parti en vacances.*
6. *Patricia a prévenu le gardien de la fuite d'eau après avoir appelé le plombier.*
7. *Les touristes lisent le guide après être arrivés à destination.*
8. *Le peintre prépare ses couleurs après avoir commencé un nouveau tableau.*
9. *Le président annonce une augmentation de salaire après avoir acheté une autre voiture.*
10. *Elle dit bonjour après avoir commencé son discours.*

Exercise 9-21: Where Have the Prepositions Gone?

Marie tient à sa mère. Comme elle, elle rêve d'un meilleur monde. Elle vient de finir ses études. Elle a décidé de faire un tour du monde. Elle a parlé au président d'une association humanitaire. Elle lui a demandé d'être volontaire dans cette association. Marie croit à la bonté humaine. Elle tient à ne pas rester dans l'inaction. Marie ne manque pas de courage. Elle n'a pas fini de nous étonner!

Exercise 9-22: Putting Prepositions to Work

1. *Patricia passe ses vacances à la campagne.*
2. *Tu m'as manqué.*
3. *Jean-Louis tient à son neveu Patrick.*
4. *Fabiola croit à la réincarnation.*
5. *Je tiens à aller à ce dîner.*
6. *Tu devrais leur parler.*
7. *Veux-tu jouer aux échecs ce soir?*
8. *Arrête de parler tout le temps de ton travail!*
9. *Tu tiens de ta soeur.*
10. *Ils pensent l'avoir vue dans la rue.*

Exercise 9-23: Beginning and End

1. b
2. d
3. e
4. a
5. c

Exercise 9-24: Pick the Right Preposition?

1. *Elle porte son gilet à même la peau car il fait trop chaud.*
2. *Quitte à être en retard, je vais rester jusqu'à la fin de la séance.*
3. *Ce plat manque vraiment d'épices.*
4. *Je ne t'ai pas appelé de peur de te réveiller, je croyais que tu dormais.*
5. *La police a relâché le suspect faute de preuves.*
6. *Il a agi à l'insu de tout le monde, sans rien dire à personne.*
7. *Elle n'en peut plus, elle est au bord de la crise de nerfs.*
8. *Merci Olivier, grâce à toi, j'ai retrouvé le moral.*
9. *Denise est partie pour Paris, elle avait besoin de prendre l'air.*
10. *Elle tient à l'armoire de la grand-mère. Elle ne te la donnera jamais.*

Exercise 9-25: Intruder Alert

1. *Aidez-le à trouver du travail.*
2. *Jean envisage d'acheter un nouvel appartement.*
3. *Les pompiers ont cherché à entrer dans la maison en feu.*
4. *J'ai oublié de mettre le réveil.*
5. *Kim hésite à partir maintenant en vacances.*
6. *Le professeur s'est efforcé de ne pas mettre trop de mauvaises notes.*
7. *Je t'invite à lire ce livre passionnant.*
8. *La voisine m'a remercié de lui avoir apporté des biscuits.*
9. *Fais attention à ne pas prendre trop de coups de soleil!*
10. *Ils soupçonnent le gardien d'être le voleur.*

Part 10: The Final Exam

Exercise 10-1: To Be Noted

1. *Je mange rarement des légumes crus.*
2. *Ils ont souvent fait semblant de ne pas me voir.*
3. *Il prétend toujours m'aimer.*
4. *Nous avons habité cette maison pendant des années.*
5. *Je veux bien répondre à sa question.*
6. *Il s'est déjà trompé.*
7. *Il semble très heureux en province.*
8. *Elle n'a jamais avoué son amour pour lui.*
9. *Je profite du beau temps pour faire du vélo.*
10. *Il a reconnu ses erreurs.*

Exercise 10-2: What About?

1. *Si on partait en Asie?*
2. *Si on invitait Valérie à déjeuner?*
3. *Si on achetait un appartement?*
4. *Si on se mariait?*
5. *Si on créait une entreprise?*
6. *Si on vendait la maison?*
7. *Si on allait à l'opéra?*
8. *Si on allait faire une promenade?*
9. *Si on fermait les volets?*
10. *Si on fêtait ma promotion?*

Exercise 10-3: Who Is in Charge?

1. *il*
2. *nous*
3. *tu*
4. *ils*
5. *j'*
6. *ils*
7. *il*
8. *elle*
9. *elle*
10. *tu*

Exercise 10-4: Get Tense

1. *Ils ont donné de la nourriture aux animaux.*
2. *Nous regarderons l'émission à la télévision vendredi soir.*

3. *Tu parlais de prendre des vacances la semaine prochaine?*
4. *Elles correspondent depuis plusieurs années.*
5. *Vous comprendrez plus tard ce que je vous dis.*
6. *Elle étudie la philosophie à la Sorbonne.*
7. *Il contredit sans arrêt mes arguments.*
8. *Nous imaginions une grande maison avec un jardin.*
9. *J'ai dit à Tim de passer nous voir.*
10. *Il aura fini sa thèse dans un an.*

Exercise 10-5: Perfecting Your Imperfect

1. *Les acteurs étaient vraiment très bons.*
2. *Tous les matins, Martha allait faire le marché.*
3. *Le conducteur s'énervait au volant.*
4. *L'arbre faisait de l'ombre dans le jardin.*
5. *Ma grand-mère préparait mon goûter tous les jours après l'école.*
6. *Le conservateur de musée connaissait très bien sa collection.*
7. *La promenade quotidienne durait des heures.*
8. *La gardienne interdisait aux enfants de jouer dans la cour de l'immeuble.*
9. *Valentin offrait des fleurs à sa mère toutes les semaines.*
10. *La neige ne faisait que tomber.*

Exercise 10-6: Past Subtleties

1. *Julien cuisinait quand Vincent est tombé dans les escaliers.*
2. *Nous faisions les courses quand il a téléphoné.*
3. *Les touristes prenaient des photos quand il s'est mis à neiger.*
4. *Patrick était en réunion quand sa secrétaire est rentrée dans son bureau.*
5. *Les comédiens se préparaient dans leur loge quand le directeur du théâtre a décidé d'annuler le spectacle.*
6. *Boris chantait quand Madeleine est entrée sur scène.*
7. *Le bus était à l'arrêt quand le piéton est tombé du trottoir.*
8. *Je regardais les livres en vitrine quand le libraire m'a proposé ses conseils.*
9. *Tout le monde dormait quand la tempête s'est abattue sur le village.*

10. *Je m'ennuyais dans mon travail lorsque j'ai reçu une nouvelle proposition d'emploi.*

Exercise 10-7: Perfect Future Ahead

1. *Elle se mariera quand elle aura trouvé quelqu'un qui lui plaît vraiment.*
2. *Je partirai en vacances quand j'aurai économisé assez d'argent.*
3. *Le plombier changera le tuyau quand il en aura trouvé un autre pour le remplacer.*
4. *Anna se sentira mieux quand elle aura pris une décision.*
5. *Mon fils s'installera à Paris quand il aura trouvé un travail.*
6. *Valentin demandera Ariane en mariage quand elle sera rentrée de voyage.*
7. *Il sera de bonne humeur quand il aura assez dormi.*
8. *Mon appartement sera moins bruyant quand on y aura installé des doubles vitrages.*
9. *Ma colocataire ne sera pas contente quand elle aura vu que sa télévision ne marche plus.*
10. *Nous rendrons visite à tes parents dès que nous aurons terminé les travaux dans la maison.*

Exercise 10-8: The Right Time and the Right Place

1. *Demain, je dois aller travailler tôt.*
2. *J'habite ici depuis que je suis né.*
3. *Il rentre toujours tard.*
4. *Sa maison est là-bas.*
5. *J'ai besoin de passer quelques jours au bord de la mer.*
6. *Elle habite loin mais elle sera ici en moins d'une heure.*
7. *Les enfants jouent dehors.*
8. *Ils travaillent en ville mais ils habitent à des heures d'ici.*
9. *Regardez sous le lit pour voir si le chat y est.*
10. *Je suis allé à la nouvelle boulangerie avant-hier.*

Exercise 10-9: It's All Conditional!

1. *Elle serait en colère si tu la réveillais.*
   Elle aurait été en colère si tu l'avais réveillée.
2. *Je prendrais ma décision tout de suite si j'avais tous les éléments en main.*

J'aurais pris ma décision tout de suite si j'avais eu tous les éléments en main.

3. *Les enfants dormiraient plus longtemps s'il y avait moins de bruit dans la chambre.*
   Les enfants auraient dormi plus longtemps s'il y avait eu moins de bruit dans la chambre.
4. *Les éditeurs publieraient plus de livres d'art si le public en achetait plus.*
   Les éditeurs auraient publié plus de livres d'art si le public en avait acheté plus.
5. *Les musiciens joueraient plus fort si le patron de la salle de concert le leur autorisait.*
   Les musiciens auraient joué plus fort si le patron de la salle le leur avait autorisé.
6. *Mon frère sortirait tous les soirs si ma mère le laissait faire.*
   Mon frère serait sorti tous les soirs si ma mère l'avait laissé faire.
7. *Cette plante verte s'épanouirait si elle la laissait au soleil.*
   Cette plante verte se serait épanouie si elle l'avait laisée au soleil.
8. *Il lui téléphonerait s'il était sûr de ne pas la déranger.*
   Il lui aurait téléphoné s'il avait été sûr de ne pas la déranger.
9. *Je viendrais à Barcelone ce week-end si je trouvais un billet d'avion bon marché.*
   Je serais venu à Barcelone ce week-end si j'avais trouvé un billet d'avion bon marché.
10. *Accepterais-tu de venir nous présenter ton travail si nous te payions les frais de déplacement?*
    Aurais-tu accepté de venir nous présenter ton travail si nous t'avions payé les frais de déplacement?

Exercise 10-10: News Stories

1. *Le maire aurait refusé de serrer la main du président.*
2. *Le gagnant aurait donné tout l'argent à une église.*
3. *Cinq personnes auraient été blessées.*
4. *La tornade aurait détruit deux villages.*
5. *Les désastres naturels augmenteraient dans les années à venir.*

6. *Un tableau de Van Gogh aurait été vendu un million de dollars.*
7. *Le directeur aurait signé sa démission.*
8. *Le capitaine serait responsable de l'accident.*
9. *Les étudiants auraient commencé la grève la semaine dernière.*
10. *Les musiciens auraient très bien joué.*

Exercise 10-11: Who Does It?

1. *Vous avez fait faire les courses.*
2. *J'ai fait préparer ma valise.*
3. *Elle a fait réparer la machine à laver.*
4. *Il a fait expédier le colis aux États-Unis.*
5. *Nous avons fait appeler le directeur tout de suite.*
6. *Vous avez fait apporter le repas à la chambre.*
7. *Il a fait écrire au juge d'instruction.*
8. *Ils ont fait interdire l'entrée du bâtiment.*
9. *L'artiste a fait expliquer son oeuvre au journaliste.*
10. *Le directeur du musée a fait assurer le tableau.*

Exercise 10-12: Grammar Rule and Order

1. *Valérie adore les peintres cubistes.*
2. *Boris joue à des jeux de hasard stupides.*
3. *Le directeur veut bien augmenter les salariés.*
4. *Carine voit peu sa soeur aînée.*
5. *Le musicien donne un concert gratuit.*
6. *Tu travailles trop.*
7. *La Tour Eiffel scintille tous les soirs.*
8. *Je n'aime pas la cuisine chinoise.*
9. *Ce chanteur interprète bien cette ballade.*
10. *Eléonor ne comprend pas sa petite soeur.*

Exercise 10-13: In What Order?

1. *Mes voisins du dessus sont moins bruyants que mes voisins du dessous.*
2. *Le violoniste est un meilleur musicien que le guitariste.*
3. *Paul est aussi généreux que son frère.*
4. *Cette jupe-ci est moins jolie que celle-là.*
5. *Les vacances à Marseille sont plus fatigantes que les vacances à la campagne.*
6. *Nager le crawl est beaucoup plus difficile que nager la brasse.*
7. *Aimer est plus facile qu'être aimé.*

8. *Lucas est moins gentil que son colocataire.*
9. *Ma fille est une meilleure élève que mon fils.*
10. *Je suis moins enthousiaste que toi.*

Exercise 10-14: From Time to Time . . .

1. *Je vais rarement dans ce quartier.*
2. *Demain? Bonne idée!*
3. *Quelquefois, j'ai l'impression de ne pas connaître ma ville.*
4. *Une visite guidée de la Butte aux Cailles?*
5. *Ah oui, je veux bien!*
6. *Mais c'est pour les touristes?*
7. *Les Parisiens font ces tours le week-end?*
8. *Non, c'est pas vrai? Ta cousine Danièle est guide?*
9. *Bon, c'est d'accord pour demain.*
10. *Rendez-vous à 10 heures demain matin.*

Exercise 10-15: Match the Phrase

1. c
2. e
3. b
4. a
5. d

Exercise 10-16: Let's See If We Have Our Genders Together

1. *La, bonne*
2. *La, ouverte*
3. *Les, courageux*
4. *La, peinte*
5. *L', fidèle*
6. *Les, contentes*
7. *Les, municipales*
8. *Le, lumineux*
9. *La, verte*
10. *La, fabuleuse*

Exercise 10-17: What Does It All Mean?

1. The bookstore is open every day.
2. He studies art.
3. I'll possibly come with my aunt.
4. He'll finish his thesis at the end of May.
5. Buy another sponge!
6. I met my new boss.
7. The baker is very friendly.
8. Presently I make 2000 euros a month.
9. I love this writer's short stories.
10. There are many foreign artists here.

Exercise 10-18: *Famille et Compagnie . . .*

1. *Mon grand-père était ingénieur.*
2. *Son père, mon arrière-grand-père, était militaire.*
3. *Avec sa famille, il s'est installé à Paris dans les années 1920.*
4. *Puis mon grand-père a rencontré ma grand-mère.*
5. *Mon arrière-grand-mère était institutrice.*
6. *Mes grands-parents ont eu neuf enfants.*
7. *Mes trois tantes sont enseignantes.*
8. *Mes oncles sont ingénieurs, avocats ou journalistes.*
9. *J'ai vingt-et-un cousins et cousines. Nous sommes nombreux pour les repas de famille.*
10. *Qu'est-ce que vous voulez savoir de plus?*

Exercise 10-19: Build Your Own Sentence

1. *Ce que nous envisageons, c'est la vente de notre appartement.*
2. *Ce que nous vous souhaitons, c'est une bonne nuit de sommeil.*
3. *Ce qu'il ne comprend pas, c'est comment c'est arrivé.*
4. *Ce qu'elles manigancent, c'est le renvoi de leur collègue.*
5. *Ce qu'il appréhende, c'est la réaction de sa belle-soeur.*
6. *Ce dont nous avons peur, c'est de ne pas trouver le chemin.*
7. *Ce qu'ils espèrent, c'est la fin de la guerre.*
8. *Ce que tu te demandes, c'est combien ça coûte.*
9. *Ce qu'il voit, c'est les fleurs du jardin.*
10. *Ce que je veux, c'est la vérité.*

Exercise 10-20: Who? What?

1. *que*
2. *dont*
3. *qui*
4. *auquel*
5. *qui*
6. *dont*
7. *qui*
8. *dont*
9. *qui*
10. *que*

Exercise 10-21: Multiple Pronouns

1. *Je ne lui en parlerai pas.*
2. *Il lui en a donné.*
3. *Cet hôtel en aurait besoin.*

4. *Fabienne les lui raconte.*
5. *Le peintre le lui envoie.*
6. *Le policier leur en a demandé.*
7. *Vous m'y emmènerez.*
8. *Sylvie en a besoin.*
9. *Mon père les lui a données.*
10. *Je vous le déconseille.*

Exercise 10-22: *En* or *Y*?

1. *Je les y ai rapportées.*
2. *Il n'y prête aucune attention.*
3. *Nous en aurions bien besoin.*
4. *Il s'en éloigne.*
5. *Tu devrais y renoncer.*
6. *Elle en a peur.*
7. *Elle en sont conscientes.*
8. *Nous nous y rendrons.*
9. *J'en ai envie.*
10. *Tu en seras responsable.*

Exercise 10-23: On Your Mark . . .

1. *On devrait être conscient du danger.*
2. *On n'est pas stupides!*
3. *On parle chinois ici.*
4. *On n'est jamais sûr à cent pour cent.*
5. *Ici, on accepte les dollars.*
6. *Au Canada, on est habitué à la neige.*
7. *En France, on mange beaucoup de fromage.*
8. *Elena et moi, on va en Asie en été.*
9. *On fait la sieste?*
10. *Alors, on regarde un film ce soir?*

Exercise 10-24: How Do You Say?

1. *À présent, ils sont en vacances en Europe.*
2. *Rappelle-moi de lui téléphoner après le travail.*
3. *Elle est allée à la campagne en voiture la semaine dernière.*
4. *Elle est française.*
5. *Elle n'aime pas parler en public.*
6. *La semaine dernière, j'ai vu Julie au supermarché.*
7. *J'avais l'impression que tu partirais maintenant si tu le pouvais.*
8. *Ils attendent à l'arrêt d'autobus depuis vingt minutes.*
9. *Ils parlent italien.*
10. *Nous avons faim.*

Exercise 10-25: Say It Your Way

1. *Je resterai ici jusqu'à ce que vous me demandiez de partir.*
2. *Oú que vous alliez, je vous suivrai.*
3. *Valérie vous téléphonera dès qu'elle pourra.*
4. *Elle imprimera son essai pour son professeur.*
5. *Quel est le prix de cette belle lampe?*
6. *Malgré son manque de compétence, j'aime travailler avec elle.*
7. *Au lieu de rester ici, allez à Paris!*
8. *Quoi que vous pensiez, je suis sûr qu'il a tort.*
9. *Je suis surpris qu'il ne soit pas arrivé plus tôt.*
10. *Grâce à mon oncle, j'ai trouvé un grand appartement en peu de temps.*

Exercise 10-26: Which One Is the Right Preposition?

1. *à*
2. *de*
3. *de*
4. *à*
5. *à*
6. *d'*
7. *à*
8. *d'*
9. *aux*
10. *de*

Exercise 10-27: *Balzac à sa Comtesse*

1. *Chère.*
2. *cherie*
3. *regrettée.*
4. *triste.*
5. *mon.*
6. *Chère.*
7. *adorée.*
8. *heureux*
9. *ma*
10. *autres.*

Index

SOFTWARE LICENSE AGREEMENT

YOU SHOULD CAREFULLY READ THE FOLLOWING TERMS AND CONDITIONS BEFORE USING THIS SOFTWARE PRODUCT. INSTALLING AND USING THIS PRODUCT INDICATES YOUR ACCEPTANCE OF THESE CONDITIONS. IF YOU DO NOT AGREE WITH THESE TERMS AND CONDITIONS, DO NOT INSTALL THE SOFTWARE AND RETURN THIS PACKAGE PROMPTLY FOR A FULL REFUND.

1. Grant of License
This software package is protected under United States copyright law and international treaty. You are hereby entitled to one copy of the enclosed software and are allowed by law to make one backup copy or to copy the contents of the disks onto a single hard disk and keep the originals as your backup or archival copy. United States copyright law prohibits you from making a copy of this software for use on any computer other than your own computer. United States copyright law also prohibits you from copying any written material included in this software package without first obtaining the permission of F+W Media, Inc.

2. Restrictions
You, the end-user, are hereby prohibited from the following:
You may not rent or lease the Software or make copies to rent or lease for profit or for any other purpose.
You may not disassemble or reverse compile for the purposes of reverse engineering the Software.
You may not modify or adapt the Software or documentation in whole or in part, including, but not limited to, translating or creating derivative works.

3. Transfer
You may transfer the Software to another person, provided that (a) you transfer all of the Software and documentation to the same transferee; (b) you do not retain any copies; and (c) the transferee is informed of and agrees to the terms and conditions of this Agreement.

4. Termination
This Agreement and your license to use the Software can be terminated without notice if you fail to comply with any of the provisions set forth in this Agreement. Upon termination of this Agreement, you promise to destroy all copies of the software including backup or archival copies as well as any documentation associated with the Software. All disclaimers of warranties and limitation of liability set forth in this Agreement shall survive any termination of this Agreement.

5. Limited Warranty
F+W Media, Inc. warrants that the Software will perform according to the manual and other written materials accompanying the Software for a period of 30 days from the date of receipt. F+W Media, Inc. does not accept responsibility for any malfunctioning computer hardware or any incompatibilities with existing or new computer hardware technology.

6. Customer Remedies
F+W Media, Inc.'s entire liability and your exclusive remedy shall be, at the option of F+W Media, Inc., either refund of your purchase price or repair and/or replacement of Software that does not meet this Limited Warranty. Proof of purchase shall be required. This Limited Warranty will be voided if Software failure was caused by abuse, neglect, accident or misapplication. All replacement Software will be warranted based on the remainder of the warranty or the full 30 days, whichever is shorter and will be subject to the terms of the Agreement.

7. No Other Warranties
F+W MEDIA, INC., TO THE FULLEST EXTENT OF THE LAW, DISCLAIMS ALL OTHER WARRANTIES, OTHER THAN THE LIMITED WARRANTY IN PARAGRAPH 5, EITHER EXPRESS OR IMPLIED, ASSOCIATED WITH ITS SOFTWARE, INCLUDING BUT NOT LIMITED TO IMPLIED WARRANTIES OF MERCHANTABILITY AND FITNESS FOR A PARTICULAR PURPOSE, WITH REGARD TO THE SOFTWARE AND ITS ACCOMPANYING WRITTEN MATERIALS. THIS LIMITED WARRANTY GIVES YOU SPECIFIC LEGAL RIGHTS. DEPENDING UPON WHERE THIS SOFTWARE WAS PURCHASED, YOU MAY HAVE OTHER RIGHTS.

8. Limitations on Remedies
TO THE MAXIMUM EXTENT PERMITTED BY LAW, F+W MEDIA, INC. SHALL NOT BE HELD LIABLE FOR ANY DAMAGES WHATSOEVER, INCLUDING WITHOUT LIMITATION, ANY LOSS FROM PERSONAL INJURY, LOSS OF BUSINESS PROFITS, BUSINESS INTERRUPTION, BUSINESS INFORMATION OR ANY OTHER PECUNIARY LOSS ARISING OUT OF THE USE OF THIS SOFTWARE.
This applies even if F+W Media, Inc. has been advised of the possibility of such damages. F+W Media, Inc.'s entire liability under any provision of this agreement shall be limited to the amount actually paid by you for the Software. Because some states may not allow for this type of limitation of liability, the above limitation may not apply to you.
THE WARRANTY AND REMEDIES SET FORTH ABOVE ARE EXCLUSIVE AND IN LIEU OF ALL OTHERS, ORAL OR WRITTEN, EXPRESS OR IMPLIED. No F+W Media, Inc. dealer, distributor, agent, or employee is authorized to make any modification or addition to the warranty.

9. General
This Agreement shall be governed by the laws of the United States of America and the Commonwealth of Massachusetts. If you have any questions concerning this Agreement, contact F+W Media, Inc., via Adams Media at 508-427-7100. Or write to us at: Adams Media, a division of F+W Media, Inc., 57 Littlefield Street, Avon, MA 02322.